The Concierge Class

How an unseen army of fixers is
undermining democracy
on behalf of corporations and the rich.
And what we can do about it.

Kit Sadgrove

Blackford Books

CONTENTS

1. Who runs capitalism? It isn't what you think. **4**
Who exactly are they? 5
The four categories of the Concierge Class 6
The harm caused by the Concierge Class 12
A concierge? What's that exactly? 14
The Professional Managerial class 15
Aren't corporations and the wealthy two different things? 22
Who are the Rich? 26
Do the rich matter? 30
The unsustainable rich 36
It's not just the rich. The aristocracy has an effect, too. 39
The trouble with corporations 45
But first, I have a favour to ask you. 57

2. The Magicians **58**
Why accountants aren't good at their job 58
Lawyers: in a rich man's world 74
Stocking up on the money 88
Asset managers: milking the state 99

3. The Enablers **106**
The next banking crash isn't too far away 106
Why legislation fails us 119
Heaven is a tax haven 137
How central banks support the wealthy 144
The management consultants' playbook 153
A slap on the wrist by the regulators 162
Justice - but only for some 168

4. The Pushers **184**
The media megaphone 184
Shameless marketing 194
The new influencers 199
The lobbyists who pervert democracy 202
Trade associations: the corporate pushers 216
Why politicians support the capitalists 222
The junk tanks 224
Economists are more political than you'd think 229
Pleading poverty: museums and galleries 234
How the clerics side with the rich 239

When science allies with the corporations 244
The gilded cage... 248
The sweet taste of money 252
How corruption became a fixture in sport... 255

5. The Suppliers.. 262
How architects and developers make sky high profits............................ 262
Cleaning up in the housing market 269
Private schools: how to buy privilege.. 274
Algorithms that make you angry 279
Slave labour and the recruitment agents 282
We're headed back to the Edwardian era 290

6. Conclusions 298
Why the Concierge Class needs to change 298
Can the Concierge Class be persuaded? 302
Who is the most culpable?.. 306
An Ethical Assessment... 309
Steps you can take... 312
Getting started... 313
The Ethical Blueprint 314
What did you think of the book? 316

Appendices 318
Appendix 1: The problems and their solutions....................................... 318
Appendix 2: Methods of non-violent protest and persuasion................... 322

Index 328

References 334

1. Who runs capitalism? It isn't what you think.

Most people think capitalism is run by corporations and the wealthy. But that's not true.

The truth is, capitalism is run by an invisible group of middle-class intermediaries.

That may sound like a conspiracy theory. But stay with me.

Put it this way: capitalism is a busy, complex system. All those wheels turning. All those people working. Offices. Factories. Lorries. Shops.

Someone has to make that work.

And that someone, or to be more precise, *those people*, are the Concierge Class.

Every day, that unseen army is working to advance the aims of corporations and the rich.

From accountants to trade associations, and from scientists to think tanks, the members of the Concierge Class serve their masters diligently, devising ways to help them evade taxes, change legislation, and sway public opinion.

Talking about the ultra-rich, the Guardian's George Monbiot wrote:

> "In this way, a few dozen people, assisted by thousands of concierges, can dominate our lives. The system we call democracy is a mere patina ... on the surface of oligarchic power."[1]

As they adopt the values and beliefs of the wealthy, the Concierge Class rarely stop to consider the impact of their actions.

And the result is more profit for the rich, a widening of inequality, and a weakening of democracy.

That's why I've written *The Concierge Class*, the first book to explain the inner workings of concierge capitalism. It shows how corporations and the wealthy co-opt skilled professionals into hiding their cash, pushing their agenda, and whispering in the ears of politicians.

In it, you'll get to know the people who protect and promote the aims of the rich.

Are you a member of this select group? Or one of their victims? The book's Culpability Index will let you know, and show you how to fight back.

Who exactly are they?

For most people, the term 'Concierge Class' refers to a cruise round the Caribbean.

If that's what you were looking for, you're out of luck.

No, this is an altogether different kind of book, one that looks at the millions of people who earn their living by working for corporations and the wealthy (the CAW, for short).

Specifically, it's the people who:

- Help the rich increase their wealth, for example by devising tax avoidance schemes

- Promote their ideology, perhaps by hindering legislation that might restrict their profits or freedom of action

- Provide them with goods and services, including workers.

Just to be clear, if you're working for a shipping line that happens to be owned by a Russian oligarch, that doesn't necessarily brand you as a member of the concierge class. It depends on the kind of work you're doing.

We aren't talking about someone who picks stock in an Amazon warehouse, works in a shoe shop, or arranges rich people's travel. Similarly, writing code for Google doesn't make you a bad person - unless, of course, your code is designed to unfairly lock out Google's competitors.

Equally, the Concierge Class isn't just about the high paid lawyers and city accountants. As we'll see, many lower-ranking people are members, too.

Later in the book, I unveil the Culpability Index, which measures the degree of blame attached to you, me or anyone else.

The four categories of the Concierge Class

The Concierge Class consists of four categories. They're the Magicians, the

Fixers, the Pushers, and the Suppliers. Let's have a quick review of who they are and what they do.

1. The Magicians

The Magicians operate at the very start of the process.

Concierge Class magicians can make money appear and disappear.

They can transport revenues across thousands of miles, so that sales made in Britain seem to have happened in Luxembourg.

They create imaginary costs when a tax loss needs to be made.

They bestow immunity on white-collar criminals.

And they can demonstrate convincingly that someone who lives in a big house in Chelsea can apparently be resident in Monaco.

The magicians are **lawyers** and **accountants**. They're the people who, charged with coming up with clever ideas, create processes that are just within the law.

Their impact is the biggest of all the categories, because their work ensures that massive sums of money that would otherwise pay for roads, teachers and doctors are now dropped into the pockets of corporations and the wealthy.

2. The Enablers

But corporations and the wealthy need structures that allow them to operate. So the next group in the concierge class are the Enablers.

These are the **politicians** who pass legislation that benefits the rich, the **tax havens** that reduce their taxes, and the **bankers** who benefit as corporations deposit their money in offshore funds.

The politicians are hiding in plain sight. They set budgets that cut taxes for the rich but reduce the services that the rest of us use. And hardly anyone complains.

The tax havens are particularly invidious, because they exist solely to help the wealthy and corporations avoid paying taxes.

Enablers include self-serving politicians.

And the bankers provide a service no one can do without. Since they take a thin (and sometimes not so thin) salami slice off every transaction, they could sleep all day and still make money.

3. The Pushers

But none of these would be of any value if public opinion was hostile to corporations and the wealthy.

So they recruit an army of Pushers, whose job it is to persuade governments and public opinion that they're a deserving cause.

The Pushers spread the word that the rich have worked hard (don't we all?) and therefore deserve to keep their money. They promote dog-eat-dog values, and deride the idea of community or mutual support.

This has the curious effect of persuading people, including those on the breadline, that somehow their best interests are to support those with the most money.

The Pushers include the **media**, the **economists** and the **trade associations**.

They also include the **think tanks**, which consist of bright, well-educated, right-wing young people who, through selective use of research and statistics, suggest policies that benefit the Civil Resistance rich.

The Pushers willingly promote the values of corporations and the wealthy.

Alongside them are the **lobbyists**, who cosy up to governments, whispering in the ears of politicians at party conferences and over private lunches, that they should ignore the needs of the poor and needy, and provide handouts to the rich instead.

The **politicians** who, when in power are Fixers, are another group of Pushers. Breathing in the rarefied air found in private members' clubs and luxury hotels, they adopt the beliefs of the rich. And, enticed by free 'fact finding' trips, they sense there's a job for them when they leave politics. Whether in government or opposition, they speak in meetings and debating chambers, pushing the needs of business and the rich.

Below this group are the 'useful fools' who, by accepting donations from the wealthy, serve to burnish their image. This lot includes the **museums**, **galleries** and **universities** who put the names of the rich on their new buildings and campuses. By doing so, the ugly activities of the plutocrats, who looted their countries' wealth, are mitigated by their apparent philanthropy.

Some **scientists** work on behalf of the corporations, producing research reports that suit their bosses. The old saying 'He who pays the piper calls the tune' was never truer than when applied to the scientists who, over the decades, have sought to demonstrate that smoking is harmless, that vaping is good for you, that alcohol is no more than a pleasant treat, and that all pesticides are safe.

And finally, **the media** listens to the siren voices of the ultra-rich. They then package and trumpet their ideas to their millions of readers and viewers.

4. The Suppliers

Lastly, there are the Suppliers. The wealthy like to buy things. And so the Suppliers sell them vast yachts, private planes, and hulking great cars that can travel at 300 miles an hour.

The Suppliers deliver goods and services to the wealthy.

The Suppliers include the **estate agents** who sell £25 million London properties, the **retailers** who sell $25,000 handbags, and the **security firms** who will charge rich people $250,000 a year to protect their family.

That's at one end of the spectrum. At the other end, there's the murky world of the **platforms** which allow corporations to hire workers to do one-off 'gigs'.

It includes the **recruitment agents,** who hire many of the people who will work for the rich, including 'self-employed' drivers and delivery people. And sadly, the greatest number of these are the low-paid whose jobs are precarious, such as the domestic staff who work long days, worried that a single word or look could lead to their dismissal by their truculent employers.

This then is the Concierge Class, people who knowingly benefit the corporations and the wealthy, to the disadvantage of you and me.

They're a machine that provides the ideas, the publicity and the labour force to service and supply the needs of the wealthy.

It's time to understand them a little better. But first, have a quick look at the diagram below. It divides the Concierge Class into its constituent parts.

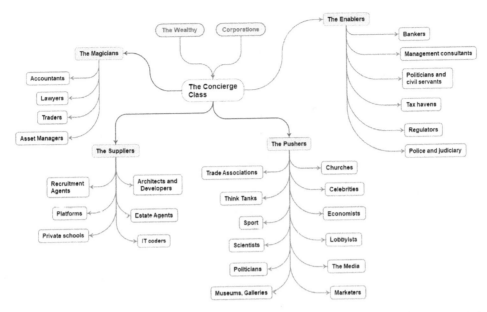

The Concierge Class: Magicians, Enablers, Pushers and Suppliers: working for corporations and the wealthy. There's a larger image at the end of the book.

The harm caused by the Concierge Class

The Concierge Class promote the values of corporations and the wealthy, namely: individualism, a small state and minimum regulation. And in doing so, they harm society. Here are some of the effects:

1. They reduce the tax take, which means fewer doctors, police officers and teachers. Our children are educated less well, and lawlessness grows. Social housing is reduced, and the poor get poorer.

2. They keep Conservative governments in power. The laws get more restrictive. Trades union action is limited, which benefits the corporations. Protest marches get banned. Crony capitalism flourishes. People who criticise the government are labelled 'anti-growth'.

3. Intolerance grows. There is hostility to immigrants, and less concern for poverty and inequality.

4. Redistribution falters. The rich pass their money on to their children and to the grandchildren. The poor stay stuck at the bottom, irrespective of how able or talented they are. Social mobility stalls.

5. The state withers, as the government continues to reduce its engagement. There's less social housing, fewer youth clubs, and meaner social benefits.

6. The UK retreats, or threatens to withdraw, from supranational groups such as the EU and the European Court of Justice. It fosters nationalism and limits the opportunities for the citizen to challenge the state.

And yet few in the Concierge Class recognise this. For them, the work they do seems far removed from its impact.

Each member of the Concierge Class is just one small cog in the wheel. The journalist who willingly acts as a voice for a right-wing politician, and the private school teacher who educates the children of the rich - they hardly see the damage this ultimately causes.

The Concierge Class is largely out of touch with the struggles of ordinary people. They live in a bubble of privilege, and have little understanding of the real world.

As time goes by, people outside this magic

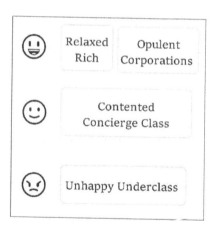

Five categories of people in the world of the Concierge Class. Some are happier than others.

circle grow to distrust social democracy, putting their faith instead in right-wing demagogues.

It ends up looking like the figure on the right, with corporations and the rich being delighted, a contented Concierge Class, and an increasingly dissatisfied underclass. It's a dangerous and unsustainable situation.

A concierge? What's that exactly?

The concierge was originally a low-paid caretaker, usually a woman, who sat in a small room at the bottom of a block of flats in Paris or some provincial French city, protecting the residents from uninvited guests, and cleaning the public areas.

There's disagreement as to the origin of the word. It could be derived from the Old French *cumcerges*, possibly from the Latin *conservus or* 'slave companion'. Or possibly it's a contraction of *comte des cierges* ('candle counting'), a servant responsible for maintaining the lighting and cleanliness of medieval palaces.

In more modern times, the concierge became the person behind a hotel desk, someone who can organise theatre tickets, arrange a taxi or suggest places of interest you might want to visit.

There are also private concierge services which, for a monthly subscription, will organise your hotel and travel arrangements. Examples include Quintessentially (average client net worth: $36m), and John Paul Group, which has over 1,000 concierges across 12 offices.

Cruise ships have also added a concierge, someone who arranges tours and events for the passengers when they visit a port.

The term was also appropriated by the corporations, to denote a higher level of service than the average customer gets. You pay extra for personalised service, and it makes you feel you're a cut above the rest. For the corporations, it's a way of earning more money, and making their product sound prestigious.

The upmarket banks such as Coutts have a concierge service for wealthy account holders, who will book tickets and arrange restaurant meals. And stores like Harvey Nichols will organise a beauty makeover for you, or take care of your shopping while you eat in one of its restaurants.

But today there's a new class of concierge. They do more than just providing a trivial booking service. And its members work not only for the rich but for the corporations as well.

And where has the Concierge Class come from? Its roots lie in the growth of the middle class, as we shall see next.

The Professional Managerial class

Back in the early 1970s, Barbara Ehrenreich was growing up as the daughter of a copper miner who'd risen in society. He'd gone to university and ended up as a senior executive for Gillette.

But he hadn't forgotten his roots. Ehrenreich's parents had two rules: 'Never cross a picket line' and 'Never vote Republican'. Each day she went to school wondering whether her parents were part of the evil 'red menace' they read about in the popular press.

Barbara Ehrenreich

Then as now, the far-left tended to refer to the working class as the group who would deliver revolutionary change. Everyone else, the Marxists decided, was the 'ruling class' or the 'bourgeoisie', united against the heroic blue-collar workers.

But as Ehrenreich grew up, she began to reflect on the educated professionals, the scientists, lawyers, academics and journalists, who historically didn't work for big corporations.

In the 1930s, these occupations had made up less than 1% of total US employment. But with the advent of the telephone, the car and then electronics, they and the growing administrative class rapidly expanded. By 1972 they'd grown to 24% of all people in work in the USA.

Ehrenreich saw that the new middle class - highly educated and with white-collar professional skills - had taken over key parts of running society in liberal democracies. This included political parties, the media, education and the civil service.

Didn't this group, which she termed the 'Professional Managerial Class' (PMC), have the potential to create a better world? These educated, intelligent, thinking people could surely end up managing society in a humane, liberal way?

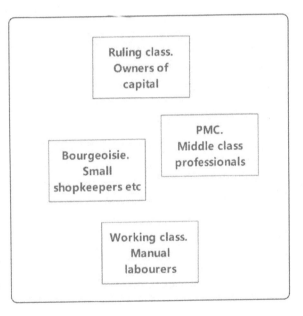

The classes, as Ehrenreich saw it.

After all, they didn't own the corporations, and they weren't in the top 1% of earners.

Sadly, it didn't happen. She concluded that the PMC were detached from the needs of the poor. She found they looked down on the working-class majority as uncultured and ignorant[2]. Through the meetings she attended, she discovered that many of the PMC viewed ordinary people as racist and homophobic.

And that brings us to The Concierge Class. They're pretty much the same folks as the 1970s PMC.

But today it's more evident that the Concierge Class spend their time working to support the corporations and the wealthy, albeit unintentionally. Maybe those old-time leftists were right?

As a group, they're socially liberal, often pushing for political reforms that make the world a more tolerant, diverse and enlightened place. So they're keen on diversity and education; and climate change is important to them. But on the flip side, critics such as Bryce Edwards say they're self-regarding and uninterested in structural change[3].

They're into 'self'. They like practising yoga and mindfulness, and learning about Eastern spiritualism.

But they're isolated from the real problems of society, and in hard times they have support of parents or savings.

In principle, they support the need for justice, equality and social mobility. But they lack any interest in the root problems of inequality, and how that might be resolved.

Traditionally, the political left and its parties sought votes from the working class and the poor, with politicians coming largely from trade union backgrounds and working-class occupations.

But this has been flipped. Politicians of the left speak with middle-class accents and increasingly get their support from the well-educated.

The left, say its critics, is both liberal and elitist, focusing more on the issues that interest the Concierge Class, rather than seeking political change that might endanger their own economic interests.

Take ESG, for example. Standing for Environmental, Social and Governance, it's a yardstick that tells shareholders how responsible a company is. The Concierge Class are all in favour of that. What's not to like?

But in truth, it's something of a smokescreen. It distracts people's attention from the underlying economic issues. It doesn't get to the root of why 14 million people in the UK are living in poverty, according to the UK government's figures. That includes 4.2 million children, which is almost one in three (29 per cent)[4].

ESG is a fig leaf that smooths over the image of polluting companies, misleading investors who want to put their money into sustainable enterprises. It does this by aggregating ESG ratings into a single score. Thus an oil company that has good social or governance policies can get a high rating, despite being a polluter[5].

And what's more, the ESG numbers are often meaningless. For a couple of decades now, corporations bought 'offsets', which meant paying a company to plant trees. That allowed the company to claim it was 'green'. As we'll see later, these offsets were found to be worthless.
But back to the Concierge Class. Some say its members a vital asset for the rich and powerful, because they create a political agenda that permits only mild change.

It sides with the Establishment, and focuses mainly on social concerns that are compatible with the status quo, either ignoring or working against the interests of working people.

But the middle class is splitting

Changes are taking place in the ranks of the Concierge Class. Due to a lethal combination of outsourcing, technology and the internet, pay and conditions have worsened for many of its members, such as teachers, lecturers and civil servants.

And as the West has de-industrialised, many graduates, especially those without family connections, find themselves unable to get on to the lower rungs of a white-collar career, and end up as baristas, shop assistants or call centre workers.

More members of the middle-class are falling from their privileged position into precarious work and housing. It's for three main reasons:

Outsourcing has been with us for decades, and has led to a race to the bottom in wages, first in low-skill work such as cleaning, and then spreading to the middle classes. Why hire a UK accountant when the work could be done in Bangladesh for half the price?

The use of **freelance 'gig' work** is now common in IT and the creative professions, and is spreading to accountancy and the law. Many lawyers now work on one of the legal platforms, earning their living on a job-by-job basis. And the rise of AI, like ChatGPT, will begin to reduce lawyers' salaries as legal knowledge becomes available at the click of a button.

As the cost of buying a house has moved beyond the reach of many, even the middle classes become reliant on **precarious tenancies** with private landlords.

Looking back, Barbara Ehrenreich was right to see the potential in the PMC, what we now call the Concierge Class. And later, she was right to be disappointed that it didn't happen.

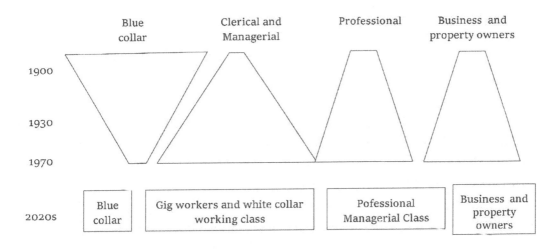

Schematic showing the reduction in blue-collar jobs in the West, the increase in the PMC, and its eventual splintering. Not to scale.

She died in 2022. Were she alive today, she'd doubtless see the Concierge Class as the same group as she saw back in 1977, but with added culpability.

But whereas she wrote off the professional managerial class as beyond redemption, that option - that luxury - is no longer open to us.

The gap between the wealthy and everyone else has grown massively greater. And like a frog in a pan of water that's slowly heating, people haven't been aware of it.

The Concierge Class, meanwhile, wields much more power. They're much more than mere managers. They're the power behind the throne. They execute the order of corporations and the rich.

In his book Capital and Ideology, Thomas Piketty refers to one half of the educated middle classes as 'the Brahmin left'. They're the educated and relatively affluent middle classes who work in journalism, public service or education.

He contrasts them with the 'Merchants', the middle classes who work for corporations, and who are more right-wing.

Both are disengaged from the struggles of the group that others have called the 'left behind'.

These groups, the Brahmin left and the Merchants, reflect the values of the group this book is concerned with, the Concierge Class. What binds them together is their lack of connection with the precariat, and their focus on cultural rather than economic issues.

The problem was also raised back in 1958 by Michael Young in his ironic 'The Rise of the Meritocracy', in which he expressed doubts about the ability of the left to maintain the support of the lower classes. The meritocracy, he said, 'have become so impressed with their own importance as to lose sympathy with the people whom they govern'.

We can't assume, as old-style Marxists did, and still do, that somehow the working class, namely the trade unions, will force the rich to transfer their wealth to the rest of us. That train left long ago.

It's up to the Concierge Class to create change. They're the group who are running the country - in favour of the plutocrats.

We need to find ways to engage with them. We have to build their awareness, demonstrate to them what they need to do, and thereby create change. It's a big challenge. But without them, nothing will alter.

And if you, the reader, are part of this class, that responsibility rests on your shoulders.

What's next?

We've examined the nature of the Concierge Class, and the risks they pose.

It's time to look at corporations and the wealthy. You might think each is different from the other. But under the skin, they're very similar, as we'll see next.

Aren't corporations and the wealthy two different things?

Corporations and the wealthy both have large amounts of money. And you might assume they have little otherwise in common.

One group consists of businesses with shareholders and directors, while the other comprises rich individuals.

But as the chart below shows, they share a set of strengths, values and aims. That leads to shared behaviours, and thus outcomes. We'll explore this in more detail.

Talk to anyone at the top of a corporation, and you'll find they have only one goal, which is to make profits. Although they preach about how they love their employees, and want to protect the environment, their real aim is to earn money for their shareholders and directors.

The wealthy share the corporations' profit motive, but they differ in one major respect - the wealthy are more right-wing.

That's because they're usually individuals, either self-made and there-fore individualist, or else with inherited wealth. As other writers have shown, they tend to be anxious about losing their money, and protective of it. An analysis by the London School of Economics found that people who won on the National Lottery moved to the right[6]. It's the way human behaviour operates.

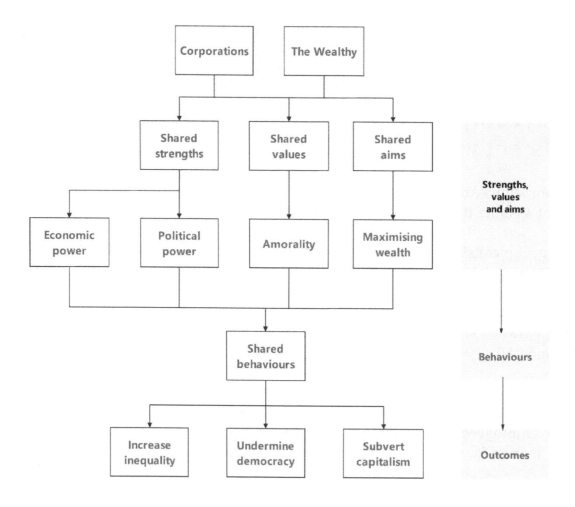

Corporations and the wealthy have similar strengths, values and aims.

By contrast, corporate senior managers are usually less extreme, being subject to their shareholders.

Directors worry about far-left politicians, because in government they'd seek to reduce the corporations' power and profit. By contrast, right-wing politicians doesn't bother businesses, because the right usually supports the needs of corporations and the wealthy.

Apart from the slight difference in political beliefs, it's hard to tell apart the wealthy and those who run the corporates.

Thus corporations and the wealthy share similar **values** and **aims**. Their priority is to protect and maximise their income, which leads to **amorality**. Ethics doesn't feature.

The two groups also have a set of shared **strengths**:

- They have **economic power**. That's to say, they have huge amounts of money in the bank, which allows them to use others to achieve their aims and to buy advantage.

- And having money gives them **political clout**. They have the ear of politicians, lawmakers and other influencers.

This leads to a set of **behaviours** - specifically the hiring of the Concierge Class to cast a magic spell over their money, fix the world so it works in their favour, and sway public opinion in their favour.

And over time the result is greater inequality, an undermining of democracy, and the subverting of 'pure' capitalism. We examine this proposition in more detail in the sections that follow.

Capitalism, in the way that most economists view it, is about perfect competition, where companies compete for your and my business. In practice, however, this rarely happens. Corporations prefer an easy life, as we all do. They'd rather buy up an irritating upstart competitor than slug it out with them in the marketplace.

Left to itself, capitalism leads to monopolies and rewards the most ruthless individuals. And that's why we have social democracy, which seeks to moderate the excesses of capitalism and provide the services that capitalists or the wealthy can't on their own provide, such as an independent judiciary, the armed services and the police.

Corporations and the wealthy inevitably seek to promote their own views, and limit the ability of governments to support the rest of the population. That behaviour should come as no surprise. If you took any ordinary individual, and put them in a position where they were earning large sums of money, they'd instinctively seek to preserve and maximise their wealth.

And so we have a situation whereby corporations and the wealthy use their shared strengths and values to increase their wealth.

Many corporations are controlled by the few

It's easy to think that corporations are controlled by the multitude of men and women in suits who turn up to the annual general meeting to vote. But it isn't true.

Amazon is owned by one man, Jeff Bezos.

Meta, which is Facebook and Instagram, is owned by Mark Zuckerberg.

Microsoft belongs to Bill Gates. And so on.

And it's not just the tech giants. Tata, the $4 billion steel company, is owned by Mr Tata. Elon Musk owns Tesla, the world's 9th most valuable company.

Owning companies, properties and shares - that's how the worlds of the rich and corporations mesh.

Some of the richest bosses don't even own the business. One of the world's highest-paid execs is Michael Rapino, the CEO of Live Nation Entertainment.

The business is owned by many investors, the largest of which is Vanguard, an investment management company. But Rapino's lack of ownership doesn't get in the way of his earnings, which stand at $139 million a year.

In other words, these organisations aren't an amorphous mass. There's a controlling brain behind each.

It's about individuals

We've seen that many corporations are controlled by individuals. And it's an important point.

Throughout the book I refer to *bankers*, not *banks*. I use the word accountants, not accountancy practices. And where possible, I talk about politicians, not governments.

I seek to focus on individuals and their personalities, rather than the institutions. Every company and profession consists of individuals; and it's those individuals who make the policies.

And it's the individuals at a lower level who willingly execute those policies. That's why the members of the Concierge Class are important.

Moving forward, we've established that corporations and the wealthy have similar aims, so let's take a closer look at each, starting with the ultra-rich.

Who are the Rich?

Have you bought a £25,000 handbag recently? If so, congratulations, you're a member of the wealthy.

And did your car cost more than £40,000?

If you answered either Yes or No to that last question, you aren't wealthy.

The right answer would have been, "I have a garage full of cars. In each of my houses. Which ones are you talking about?"

We've now established you aren't stinking rich. So let's take a closer look at those who really *are* extremely wealthy.

People who make money from the wealthy (the banks etc) call them 'high-net-worth individuals' (HNWI).

They probably think it sounds less vulgar than talking about 'our rich clients'. HNWI refers to an individual with liquid assets (cash and investments they could sell today) above a certain figure, typically at least $1 million - and that's ready money, not the value of your house and pension.

There are around 21 million very rich people around the world. And at the top of the pile are the 'Ultra-high-net-worth' individuals, with a net worth of more than $30 million.

And all these individuals need help to manage their money, their businesses and their properties. You can guess who they're going to call: it's the Concierge Class.

How did they get their wealth?

Many people assume the rich are entirely self-made. But it isn't true.

Nearly 80% of The Forbes 400 richest people either inherited their wealth or grew up at least middle-class[7].

Only 10% of Forbes 279 self-made billionaires list once lived under the poverty line or faced substantial adversity on their journey to wealth.

The exceptions include hedge fund tycoon George Soros. He survived the Holocaust and put himself through college by working as a railway porter and waiter. And there's the former Starbucks CEO Howard Schultz, who grew up in social housing.

But the usual background for the wealthiest people in the USA is a middle-class or upper-middle-class family. That includes seven of the country's ten richest people.

Jeff Bezos attended the prestigious Princeton University and then worked on Wall Street. His parents gave him nearly $250,000 to set up his online bookshop.

Mark Zuckerberg's father and mother are a dentist and psychiatrist respectively.

Bill Gates' dad founded a law firm, Shidler McBroom & Gates, now K&L Gates, and served as president of the Washington State Bar Association.

So, mostly they get a leg up, and have family money. Having wealth in your family allows you the flexibility to try something new. Failure won't ruin your life.

A middle- or upper-class upbringing provides you with investors, because Daddy and his friends will lend you money. It gives you access to advice and expertise. Overall, it increases your chance for success. And that's why rich people generally come from an affluent family.

The wealthy nepos are growing

In the old days, entrepreneurs created wealth, and created jobs in car factories and chemical plants. Nowadays, not so much.

According to the Swiss bank, UBS, the next generation of billionaires [will get their] wealth through inheritance rather than entrepreneurship. That's behind the wealthy are ageing, and are passing their money to their kids[8].

The richest woman in the world, Françoise Bettencourt Meyers, has a fortune of $91 billion, according to Bloomberg[9]. And she did nothing to earn it. She was handed it by her mother, Liliane Bettencourt, who in turn received it from her dad, Eugene Schueller, who founded L'Oréal in 1909.

Sure, Françoise is on the board of L'Oréal. But she didn't get there by grafting. She got there because she and her family own 35% of the company's shares. She's nepomonied. And there are lots like her, the undeserving ultra-rich.

Françoise Bettencourt, the first woman to be given $100bn.

Middle and upper classes pass on their superiority to their children

The children of the affluent have another advantage. They have an exaggerated belief in their competence, and think they're more able than their equally capable lower-class counterparts.

That can be misinterpreted by others as greater competence, according to research published by the American Psychological Association[10].

"Advantages beget advantages," said Peter Belmi of the University of

Virginia, who led the study. "High-earning entrepreneurs disproportion-ately originate from highly educated, well-to-do families," he said. "Our re-search suggests that social class shapes the attitudes that people hold about their abilities. And that, in turn, has important implications for how class hierarchies perpetuate from one generation to the next."

Do the rich matter?

Corporations and the wealthy have an input into the way society has run. But does that really matter?

Well, yes it does, for several reasons.

1. The needs of corporations and the wealthy are different from ours

Left to themselves, they'd organise the world in such a way that gave them maximum freedom and the biggest profits.

Apart from the most ascetic and thoughtful of us, most people would do the same in their position. It's not surprising that so many people play the lot-tery each week, because they too would love to be rich and therefore pow-erful.

2. They're stateless — and that affects their behaviour

The extremely rich consider themselves stateless, and therefore owe no al-legiance to the country and its institutions or people.

Take James Dyson, the vacuum cleaner king. He condemned the UK government's plans to extend employees' right to work from home as "economically illiterate and staggeringly self-defeating", saying it would "hamper employers' ability to organise their workforce"[11].

"Jobs will go to other, more ambitious economies," he said, ominously. "In other countries where Dyson operates, we are given the freedom to organise how – and where – our staff carry out the roles they are contracted to."

James Dyson

This came after Dyson moved his company's headquarters from Wiltshire to Singapore, a state where they execute people, imprison writers, harass lawyers, and restrict the movement of migrant workers beyond their crowded dormitories, workplaces and designated recreation centres[12].

If you, like Dyson, were to operate a global business, you might find your goal, like his, was to maximise profit. And that means choosing countries with the smallest costs and the lowest tax rates - as long as you can sell your products in countries with affluent consumers. Alternatively, you simply pretend you're located in Luxembourg (population 645,000) as Amazon does, where it pays no tax due to its somehow 'making a loss', despite EU revenues of €44bn.

3. They avoid paying tax

The wealthy are often found to have evaded the payment of tax. They do this through various legal and illegal means, such as shell companies in tax havens. As a result, the wealthy often pay a lower percentage of their income in taxes than the middle class and the poor.

People argue that taxing the rich will cause them to leave the country. But while the rich like to travel, they aren't keen to change their home. Would you really want to sit for the rest of your life on a hurricane-prone island, one which has no theatre, no nice bars and few shops? Where would your children go to school?

And I've been to Monaco. It's the most boring, soulless concrete jungle on the planet. Rich people like living in, for example, London, because it has culture, Harrods, the West End and nice houses.

The perfect tax rate for the USA rich, according to two economists at the University of California at Berkeley, is 75%, including all federal, state, payroll and local taxes. It would only apply to the top 1% of Americans, who earned more than $500,000 in income in 2019.[13]

"This estimate is the best that exists today on the basis of many empirical studies conducted over the last two decades," the two economists wrote in the book 'Triumph of Injustice — How the Rich Dodge Taxes and How to Make Them Pay'. "The tax base does not shrink much when the rich are taxed more heavily," they said.

4. Their philanthropy is overstated

The rich love to tell us how much they give to good causes. But they only give to causes that are dear to their hearts - which is why opera gets lots of money. The causes are usually anodyne and uncontroversial. And they can be self-serving or ineffectual. The rich tend not to give money to the malnourished children of Gaza or the people imprisoned behind the tall walls of the West Bank.

And the money is always *charity*. Unlike state money, to which you're entitled as a citizen, the donation can be a one-off event, or withdrawn at the whim of the donor when they move on to other, more interesting projects. That's why taxation, which is democratically mandated, and infinitely larger in scale, is the answer. When I was made redundant early in my career, my female boss said to me: "Sign on for unemployment pay today. It's your right as a citizen."

In the UK, the top 1% give only £10 a week to charity[14]. To put this in content, they're earning £5,211 a week on average.

5. They're fickle

When Ukraine was defending itself against Russia's invasion of its country, it was reliant on Elon Musk's StarLink satellites to identify where the enemy forces were. "Starlink was not meant to be involved in wars," he said. "It was so people can watch Netflix and chill and get online for school and do good peaceful things, not drone strikes." In short, the outcome of a major European war hinged on whether an entrepreneur decided to give Ukraine access to his personal possessions.

It means the rich can make decisions on a whim that affect large numbers of people. That could be closing a plant, making people redundant, or launching an unsafe product. We need systems to ensure that major decisions are taken with the involvement of all stakeholders, not one individual.

6. They're unethical and behave badly

A series of studies[15] found that higher-class individuals behave more unethically than people from lower-class backgrounds. They discovered that the rich more frequently cut up other cars and pedestrians while driving, and were more likely to engage in behaviours like plagiarism or pirating software.

The team thought several factors could explain these differences, including their feelings of independence and entitlement, lack of concern for how others perceive them, and the money to deal with the consequences of their behaviour.

By contrast, several studies have shown that lower-class individuals behave more pro-socially, offering more help and donating more money to others in need. One review suggested this is 'an adaptive strategy that helps lower-class individuals cope with threat and develop strong social networks'[16]. In other words, they're aware of their own precarity, and the benefits of community.

Whatever the causes, it suggests that corporations and the rich aren't nice people; they're dangerous and deserve criticism, not our admiration.

7. People are taken in by their wealth and power

Power is an aphrodisiac, and people are credulous. Elon Musk (him again) has 160 million followers on X, formerly Twitter.

The media said Sam Bank-Friedman (SBF) was a towering genius was. He created FTX, one of the world's largest crypto-currency exchanges, with billions in deposits, and he was ranked the 41st-richest American by Forbes.

Sam Bank-Friedman

Investors were led to believe he would bring them high returns with little risk (How often do we hear that?).

But following his fraudulent activity, FTX went bust. The collapse affected more than a million people, with investors losing around $8.9 billion[17].

SBF was found guilty of wire fraud, commodities fraud, securities fraud, and money laundering. History is rife with examples of heroes with feet of clay, and we forget so soon.

8. They create inequality

The wealthy are getting richer as the rest of us get poorer. The gap between the rich and the poor has been widening in recent decades, and this is largely due to the increasing concentration of wealth in the hands of a few.

This growing inequality has a number of negative consequences for society, such as increased crime, social unrest and a decline in social mobility.

What's to be done?

Starting here, and continuing with each remaining section of the book, we'll consider what we need to do about specific problems associated with the Concierge Class. Each section will end with 'What's to be done?'

At this point, let's simply recognise that we have to push back against the way the rich are taking an unfair amount of the wealth generated by the country.

We need to overhaul the tax system. As the old saying goes, "From each according to his ability, to each according to his need". It makes no sense that the rich should be able to evade paying tax while ordinary people struggle to pay their bills, and the state is unable to provide good quality housing or adequate health care.

But it isn't just about money. The rich are also environmentally damaging, as we see next.

The unsustainable rich

The wealthy are a problem for society because they lead an environmentally unsustainable life.

Their CO2 emissions are vast

According to a study by the Institute for Policy Studies, the wealthiest 1% of people are responsible for 15% of global carbon emissions, while the poorest 50% are responsible for only 12%.

This is because the rich consume more goods and services, which need more energy to produce and transport. They also travel more frequently and in more polluting modes of transportation, such as private jets.

A study by the University of Maryland found that the top 1% of earners in the United States produce an average of 32 metric tons of carbon dioxide per year, while the bottom 50% produce an average of only 4.5 tons. This means that the top 1% produce nearly seven times more carbon dioxide than the bottom 50%.

They pollute

The wealthy are responsible for a disproportionate share of air and water pollution. A study by the University of California, Berkeley found that the richest 10% of households in the United States are responsible for 47% of all fine particulate matter emissions, which are a major cause of respiratory problems.

The wealthy also contribute to water pollution through their consumption of luxury goods, such as yachts and private jets. Yachts, in particular, are a major source of water pollution. They release sewage, oil, and other pollutants into the water.

They make excessive use of limited resources

The wealthy consume a large share of the world's limited resources, such as water, land, and minerals. The World Resources Institute found that the richest 1% of people consume more than twice as much water as the poorest 50%.

The rich also tend to own more land, both directly and indirectly. For example, a study by the Institute for Policy Studies found that the top 1% of landlords in the United States own more than half of all rental housing.

The wealthy consume more minerals than the rest of us. That's because they use more electronic devices, cars and other products that require minerals. The World Resources Institute says the richest 1% of people consume more than 10 times more gold than the poorest 50%.

All of this has an Impact on society

The environmental impact of the wealthy has a number of negative consequences for society.

Climate change is already having a devastating impact on people around the world, and the wealthy are disproportionately responsible for this problem, because they produce excess CO_2. The climate crisis is causing extreme weather events, such as droughts, floods and heat waves. These events are displacing people, destroying homes and businesses, and causing billions of dollars in damage.

The overuse of limited resources can lead to scarcity and conflict. For example, water scarcity is a major problem in many parts of the world. This is because water is being used at an unsustainable rate, and climate change is making the problem worse.

What's to be done?

There are a number of things that can be done to address the problem of the wealthy's environmental impact.

- **Governments can implement policies that discourage the wealthy from consuming so many resources and emitting so much pollution.** This could include taxes on luxury goods, as well as regulations on the 'super yacht' industry and other polluting industries.

- **Governments can also invest in renewable energy and sustainable infrastructure.** This would help to reduce the reliance on fossil fuels and other polluting energy sources.

By taking these steps, we can reduce the environmental impact of the wealthy and create a more sustainable future for all.

Other things that can be done to address the problem of the wealthy's environmental impact include the following:

- **Educate the public about the environmental impact of the wealthy.** This could be done through school curricula, public awareness campaigns, and media coverage. If pupils were taught sociology from a young age, they would demand change.

- **Support businesses that are committed to sustainability.** This could include buying from businesses that use renewable energy, recycle materials, and have fair labour practices.

- **Advocate for policies that support sustainability.** This could include writing to elected officials, attending public hearings, and engaging in public protests.

It's not just the rich. The aristocracy has an effect, too.

I was at a trade conference when Prince Michael walked past, attended by numerous guides. He's a minor royal, a cousin of King Charles III, and is celebrated in Russia for his resemblance to Czar Nicholas II, who was his grandmother's cousin.

There was an aura surrounding Prince Michael, a stillness in the air. Everyone hung on his words, as he shook hands affably with suit-wearing people who manned stalls that promoted IT equipment.

Even I couldn't help but feel in awe at being in the presence of royalty. This was a man whose relatives were kings and queens.

Prince Michael

Slowly the retinue moved on, and the atmosphere returned to normal.

And that's the effect that royalty has. People can sneer at individual politicians, or even regard them with contempt; but the royal family is different. They stand for all the qualities of Britain and its heroic past. Or that's how it feels.

The truth is somewhat different. The House of Windsor was only founded in 1917, re-badged from the family name of House of Saxe-Coburg and Gotha, which was deemed rather too German during WWI.

Prior to that, the line only dates back to 1714, when a minor German prince-ling, Georg Ludwig, became king of Great Britain, due entirely to the deaths of others who had a higher claim to the throne.

Even I can trace my British and Irish ancestry further back than that.
But I can't become king, because that role is limited to whoever is most closely related to the current monarch.

It's a throw-back to the era when kings were 'real' rulers, appointed by God (as they claimed), but in reality were just the toughest, meanest, most am-bitious robber baron in the land.

Many people perceive royalty's role as purely ceremonial. But that's part of their disguise. It's a lot more than that. It's about the power and money they possess, the aura it bestows, and the deference it engenders.

The royal family plays a major part in maintaining the rest of us in subser-vience. The king is at the top of a pyramid that extends down through bar-ons, earls and viscounts; and then down to knights, before it gets down to the serfs, villeins and labourers (that's us).

Seven reasons the monarchy is bad for us

1. It's undemocratic: The monarchy is an undemocratic institution. The UK's head of state is not elected by the people but is determined by birth. In

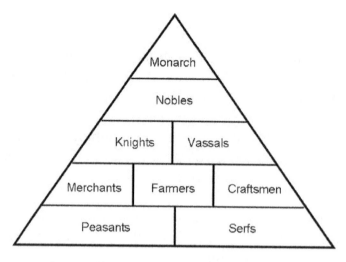

The medieval power structure. Not so very different from today.

a properly democratic society, the head of state would be elected by the people and subject to the same laws as everyone else. You wouldn't hire someone to fly a plane just because her father had been a pilot

This hereditary system goes against the principles of democracy, where all citizens are equal and have a say in who governs them. And it doesn't have to be a politician. In Ireland, as in many other countries, they've elected poets and philosophers.

2. It's costly and wasteful: The monarchy is a costly institution, funded by taxpayers. The Sovereign Grant, which provides public funding for the monarchy, totals £86 million a year. This money could be better spent on other public services, such as healthcare or education.

For those who say the monarchy brings in the tourists, the same isn't true of France, where they don't have a monarchy, and which has 79 million overseas visitors compared with the UK's 31 million.

3. A symbol of inequality and privilege: The monarchy represents a system of inherited wealth and privilege that perpetuates inequality in society. The royal family enjoys a lavish lifestyle and special privileges, while many citizens struggle to make ends meet.

4. A history of scandals and controversy: The royal family has been involved in numerous scandals and controversies over the years, which have damaged its reputation and eroded public support.

From Prince Harry wearing a Nazi armband at a fancy dress party, to Virginia Giuffre filing a lawsuit against Prince Andrew accusing him of sexual assault on Jeffrey Epstein's private island when she was 17, there's no shortage of scandals[18].

5. Lack of transparency and accountability: The monarchy is a secretive institution, and there is a lack of transparency and accountability regarding its finances and activities. The king has been claiming and profiting for years from assets known as "bona vacantia," these being houses and other assets left behind by people who died without a will or a known next of kin, and some of which has been used to upgrade his commercial properties for rent[19].

6. Potential for abuse of power: While the monarch's legal powers are limited, there's still the potential for an abuse of power. A monarch can use their position to influence political decisions or undermine democracy. We know, for example, that Elizabeth II successfully lobbied the British government to change a draft law in order to conceal her "embarrassing" private wealth from the public[20].

7. A symbol of colonialism and imperialism: The monarchy is a reminder of Britain's colonial past, which caused suffering and injustice around the world. Abolishing the monarchy would be a symbolic step towards acknowledging and addressing these harms.

The House of Lords

And before we forget, there's the House of Lords, an unelected upper house. You can't get into it unless your mum or dad is one of the 92 hereditary peers, or the prime minister appoints you - usually because you've paid their political party enough money.

The House of Commons

The elected House of Commons has changed little since the 18th century. The MPs address each other with the use of arcane titles such as 'The Right Honourable Gentleman'[21], and parliament is opened by the monarch being driven in a gold horse-drawn carriage amid much bowing and scraping. It serves to intimidate and to assert elitism. And unlike modern parliaments, the MPs face each other, as in combat, rather than a semi-circle that emphasises collegiality and compromise.

Aristocracy

And then there's the rest of the aristocracy. Just 36,000 people, or 0.6% of the population, own more than half of the rural land in England and Wales, most of which has been in their family for centuries[22].

In short, the monarchy and the aristocracy breed deference, and the wealth they own serves to perpetuate their continued existence. It does so by extracting rent from the land and property they own, supported by trusts that let them escape paying tax.

"The UK has one of the poorest rates of social mobility in the developed world," says Deloitte, not known for its socialist values, "This means that people born into low-income families, regardless of their talent, or their hard work, do not have the same access to opportunities as those born into more privileged circumstances."[23]

How does the monarchy and aristocracy relate to the Concierge Class?

The Concierge Class does the bidding of the rich and powerful. It makes them money, keeps them in power, and thereby serves to maintain inequality.

There is no group of people more evidently wealthy and in power than the monarchy and the aristocracy. Holding on to wealth and power for several hundred years demonstrates that[24].

But there's also a more subtle element to monarchy and the aristocracies, one to which I've alluded. It's the fact that they symbolise subservience. Members of the Concierge Class accept that their role is to do what the rich ask of them. Removing the bonds of monarchy would encourage a few more members of the Concierge Class to question whether what they're doing is right.

What's to be done?

To reduce the aura of privilege, we should replace the House of Lords with a more democratic second chamber.

To improve the woeful lack of social mobility we should ensure inheritance tax get paid properly. Fewer than 4% of estates currently pay inheritance tax, and the rich avoid paying it by people gifting their wealth to their children, as long as they do it seven years or more before they die. And that's easy for the rich, since less of their money is tied up in their home. That aside, any lawyer will quickly tell you eight ways to avoid paying inheritance tax[25].

We could cap the tax relief at a generous but sensible maximum of £1m, or exclude the individual's principal home. This would mean the majority of ordinary people wouldn't pay, this precluding home-owners' hostility to the tax. The tax could exclude small private businesses that would otherwise close or be sold if faced with the tax.

There are many other things that could be done, but these measures would be a good start.

The monarch and his band of aristos aren't people we normally encounter, apart from seeing them waving from a palace balcony once a year.

The corporations, on the other hand, affect us in a material way every day of our lives.

As we shall see next, the number of suppliers has shrunk in most markets, whether phones, software or supermarkets. And so our ability to control our own lives has reduced. So let's have a look at the world of the corporations.

The trouble with corporations

If I go to my local outdoor market, I can choose whether or not to buy from the bread stall.

From past experience I know whether its bread is any good, and whether the price is reasonable. If not, I can go to a shop that sells bread, or to the nearby supermarket.

Thus the market for bread operates as economists imagine it does. It has competitors, and consumers know about the quality and price of the loaves.
But in most other markets, it isn't the case. Many are near monopolies. If you want to write a document or create a spreadsheet, it's hard not to buy a

Microsoft product. And if you want to design some online graphics, it's not easy to avoid Adobe.

Platform businesses are ideally suited to monopoly. Once a company such as Google or Apples has become the dominant force in their field, such as search, the competitors wither away, because users gravitate to the biggest, most useful site. Suppliers then have to operate through the monopoly provider, which takes a cut of their earnings. And the end stage is where the monopoly stops innovating and merely relies on the income it gets from users and the smaller businesses. It's called a two-sided market.

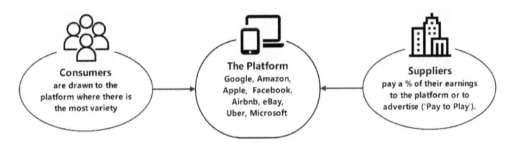

A two-sided platform

If it's not a monopoly, it's an oligopoly

Not every market is a monopoly. Often, there are just a handful of businesses, an oligopoly as it's called. Here are some of the largest oligopoly markets in the UK:

- **Supermarkets:** Four major players dominate the UK supermarket industry: Tesco, Asda, Sainsbury's and Morrisons. These four control over 70% of the market, and have a significant impact on prices and product selection[26].

- **Energy:** The UK energy market is also an oligopoly, with a few companies supplying electricity and gas. Centrica, EDF Energy, E.ON, Scottish Power and SSE are the five largest suppliers in the UK. Between them they control over 90% of the market[27].

- **Banking:** The four largest banks in the UK - HSBC, Barclays, Lloyds Banking Group, and Royal Bank of Scotland - have 75% of the market[28].

- **Telecommunications:** The UK telecommunications market is an oligopoly, with three companies controlling what phone and broadband you can have. BT, Vodafone, and Three, have over 90% of the market[29].

- **Airlines:** The three largest airlines in the UK are British Airways, EasyJet and Ryanair. They attract 60% of the passengers[30].

What effects do oligopolies have on us, the consumer?

There are six reasons why oligopolies are bad for us:

1. **Reduced consumer choice:** With fewer competitors, we consumers have fewer alternatives to choose from. It leads to less variety.

2. **Limited innovation:** Oligopolies have less incentive to innovate, compared to more competitive markets. It's a cosy world. When a firm has a dominant position, it will prioritise the maintenance of its profits rather than investing in new products or technologies.

3. **Barriers to entry:** Oligopolies often erect high barriers to entry, making it difficult for new firms to enter the market and challenge the incumbents. These barriers can include brand loyalty, patents, network effects, and economies of scale. If you wanted to launch a new breakfast cereal, you'd need a huge factory, because the supermarkets like to see the same products in each of their stores.

4. **Reduced quality and service:** Oligopolies have less incentive to maintain high quality and service standards, as they may face less competition.

This can lead to a decline in the overall quality of goods and services offered to consumers. If you've ever hung on the end of a phone line, waiting for a 'customer service' advisor to answer, you'll know the feeling.

5. **Potential for exploiting their market power:** Oligopolies often use their market power to exploit consumers, suppliers or employees. This leads to unfair practices, such as monopsony, where a single buyer has excessive bargaining power over suppliers. We discuss this later when we get to the 'gig' platforms.

6. **Higher prices:** Oligopolies have many ways of colluding with their competitors, such as agreeing to maintain similar prices. This can lead to artificially higher prices for customers, reducing their purchasing power. It's more common than you might imagine. Here are some examples:

The problem of collusion

Imagine you make widgets, and you're at a trade conference. There are only two other companies that make widgets, so you know the managers in each of them. Over lunch, the conversation gets round to pricing. You happen to have a trade price list in your pocket, and you wave it under the noses of your two fellow diners. They ask if they can see it. A conversation follows about how much better it would be if prices were relatively the same, because it would avoid unnecessary and harmful price cutting.

And so you make them copies of your price list, on the understanding that they won't undercut you. All of a sudden, there's price fixing!

There are three typical types of collusion:

- **Fixing prices:** Businesses agree to charge the same price for their goods and services. This eliminates price competition and allows firms to charge higher prices than they would otherwise be able to. The EU Commission fined MAN, Volvo/Renault, Daimler, Iveco, and DAF a total of €2.93 billion for forming a cartel and colluding on truck prices for 14 years[31]. In the USA the Department of Justice fined five vitamin manufacturers a total of $1 billion for colluding to fix prices, and fined 15 airlines a total of $214 million for fixing prices on cargo flights[32].

- **Dividing up markets**: Businesses agree to divide up the market among themselves. This stops them from competing in each other's territories and lets them charge higher prices in their own territories. Two companies that supplied drawer parts to furniture manufacturers such as Silent-Night shared out which customers they would supply, agreeing not to go after each other's clients so they could keep prices artificially high and avoid a price war[33].

- **Rigging bids**: Businesses agree to submit collusive bids on contracts. This prevents fair competition and allows companies to win contracts at higher prices than they would otherwise be able to. The UK's Competition and Markets Authority fined 10 construction firms £60 million for illegally colluding to rig bids for demolition and asbestos removal contracts. Three senior managers in the firms involved were disqualified from being directors[34].

But the trouble with corporations extends beyond the issue of monopolies. They also engage in offshoring, rent seeking, financialisation, tax avoidance, ill-treatment of the workforce, and buying political influence. We'll have a quick look at each of these next.

Offshoring

As developing countries have opened their doors to multinationals, companies that make things have moved production to the low-wage economies like India, China and Vietnam, in the search for higher profits.

They then sell the products back to consumers in the West, who get cheap products, but at the expense of lost jobs.

The loss of jobs forces Western governments to lower their corporation tax rates, in a bid to keep the remaining factories. That means less money for government services.

The alternative is to introduce import tariffs, known as protectionism. Neoliberals dislike that, pointing out that it can reduce the range of goods available, and the risk of higher prices and reduced competition.

Tariffs have to be handled carefully, not used to prop up inefficient industries and profiteering businesses, or prevent low-income countries from having reasonable access to rich countries' consumers. Equally, there are times when anti-dumping tariffs may be needed, or when policy dictates that the country needs to be self-reliant in strategic products.

So governments - and by that we mean members of the Concierge Class - have to make difficult choices that affect jobs, prices and choice. Since it's corporations and the wealthy that push for 'free trade', and since most of our goods seem to be imported from low-wage countries, maybe a little more protection for local jobs and businesses might be beneficial. You've got to ask who benefits from this libertarian world?

Rent seeking

The monopolists increasingly want you to rent their products. They can set up a 'platform business' like Upwork, where 'gig' workers pay to bid for work. Once the platform owner has built the site, they don't have to do anything in return, except take the money.

Amazon takes a percentage off sellers who use its 'Marketplace' platform. And private landlords make money off their tenants over and above the cost of mortgage (if they have one). The costs of house maintenance, which are included in the rent, help the owner to keep the house in good order, long after the tenant has left.

Microsoft, as I mentioned above, will charge you an annual fee in perpetuity for access to its Microsoft 365 software, which consists of programs whose development costs are small.

Businesses like G4S, Mitie and Sodexo manage government programmes including health and social care without putting their capital at risk. Guaranteed payments for providing the service mean they don't have to innovate or improve the service.

Other businesses get subsidies and grants. Businesses lobby governments to impose regulations that restrict others from doing business. It's known as 'privilege seeking'.

But we need to be aware that the right often apply the phrase 'rent seeking' to situations where a government applies tariffs to selected imports. Libertarians like to remove such protections, which would benefit multinational corporations at the expense of small, local suppliers. Is it any wonder that big businesses close their factories in the West, make their products in low-wage countries, and then sell their products to consumers in the West?

Financialisation

'Financialisation' refers to the growing size of the country's financial industry.

It includes private equity firms, venture capitalists and hedge funds (each of them being broadly the same thing), using rich people's money to buy companies, load them with debt, and strip out the profits.

There's also the growth in 'securitisation', which involves rich people and corporations buying and selling mortgages and loans for cars, credit cards and student debt. Securitisation of low-quality mortgages led to the near collapse of the world's economies in 2008.

The underlying problem is that financial services are taking up a growing proportion of the economy. It about making money from money, not from making goods or providing useful services. It encourages companies to take a very short-term view, which leads to reduced investment. And it gets people to take on debt, which they might not be able to repay in the event of a downturn.

Excessive financialisation helps a very few make a lot of money, which leads to inequality. And it's always what causes a crash.

They avoid paying tax

The corporations' revenues are entirely dependent on the counties where the population actually buy their products, such as the UK with its 67 million people, or the USA with 332 million.

Suggesting that the revenues are made in Lichtenstein or Luxembourg is simply a lie.

The corporations rely on the state to provide a justice system to ensure the rule of law, police officers to defend their property, and roads to carry their lorries.
They need a workforce to drive those lorries and stock their warehouses. And they expect the state to provide teachers to educate their workers, a health service to look after them if they're sick, and a state pension to care for them in their old age.

But they don't see why they should contribute. Mostly it's a defensive statement, such as the one provided by Amazon: "Amazon pays all the taxes required in every country where we operate." That's a weasel way of saying, "We pay our accountants to ensure we pay the minimum required by the law."

Piggybacking on the state

The companies depend on structures developed by the state. The internet was created by short-term public agencies: Nasa and Darpa (the USA's Dept of Defense projects agency).

The World Wide Web, which made the internet accessible, was created by Sir Tim Berners-Lee as a royalty-free system in 1989, to ensure everyone around the world could benefit from it. Without these developments, businesses like Amazon, Uber, SpaceX or Tesla couldn't have developed.

And if Elon Musk or Google had created the internet, you, me and the rest of the world would be paying them a fee every time we switch on our computers.

They exploit their workers

Driven by the need for profit, corporations will seek to minimise pay and conditions for the workforce. This is especially true in industries such as clothing manufacture or the meatpacking industry.

Major companies outsource their production. Apple designs its phones in the USA but gets Foxconn to make them in China. That way, Apple has no responsibility for the grubby business of managing a blue-collar labour force, and can switch to another country or supplier at will. IKEA gets its furniture in Vietnam, while Samsung makes its Galaxy Smartphones there, too.

Foreign companies can save almost 90% of costs by outsourcing to Vietnam, it being even cheaper than India, China, or the Philippines.

This used to be called 'lightweighting', the principle that a business limits itself to design and marketing, leaving the rest to contractors. The phrase now only seems to relate to making products physically lighter.

Marxists say 'profit is the value of surplus labour'. In other words, profits are what remains after wages and other costs, and should be shared among all stakeholders, not least the workforce.

They have political influence, and use it

The wealthy use their money to influence government policy in their favour. This can be done through lobbying, campaign donations, and other forms of political spending. As a result, the wealthy often have a disproportionate amount of influence over how the government is run.

The companies and the wealthy are in control

Corporations matter. They're increasingly monopolies, and they're taking ever closer control over our lives and habits. The same applies to the rich, whose wealth has reached unprecedented levels in the past few years.

Decisions are being made in boardrooms, and in ministerial meetings with business lobbyists, that have far-reaching impacts on our lives.
The gains are flowing away from the middle and working classes, and going to the rich.

And, as we shall see, they're doing it through the work of the Concierge Class.

What's to be done?

The government has immense power. It can break up monopolies and oligopolies, by preventing mergers and by splitting large companies into smaller ones.

It can reduce rent-seeking by taking public services back into direct control.

It can introduce import tariffs, and strengthen the power of the regulators.

But we see few signs of this happening with any vigour.

The Concierge Class lies at the heart of these problems. In corporations and in government, in think tanks and management consultancies, these individuals are pushing a libertarian agenda that benefits the few. Other members of the Concierge Class simply acquiesce, do their job, and stay quiet. But each of them has a responsibility to act in the public interest, not pander to the selfish needs of the 1%.

So next, we'll examine each category of the Concierge Class, starting with the Magicians.

But first, I have a favour to ask you.

Thank you for reading The Concierge Class.

If you found the book useful, please leave a quick review wherever you got it. Reviews spread the word, and help other readers find the book.

Here's a link: https://mybook.to/ConciergeClass

I'd welcome any thoughts or suggestions your might have about the book. You can contact me at KitSadgrove@gmail.com.

With best wishes

Kit

2. The Magicians

As we saw at the start of the book, the Magicians, are people who can make profits disappear so that the rich pay less tax. With a stroke of the pen, they'll shift revenue from the UK into Luxembourg. And they can silence critics with a single email.

They can add a fictitious £1 billion to a company's balance sheet, and make everyone believe it.

And they can magically turn a successful water company into a leaky outfit that everyone complains about - and get rewarded for it.

Let's have a look at the four main types: accountants, lawyers, traders on the stock market, and asset managers.

Why accountants aren't good at their job

Are you good at your job? Do you perform your role as people might expect, with competence and diligence, especially when it comes to the big projects?

If so, you probably don't work for one of the major UK accountancy practices.

Only one-third of 88 company audits surveyed met the required standard, according to the audit watchdog, The Financial Reporting Council[35].

The regulator also said the auditors failed to stand up and challenge their clients.

The audit industry has consistently failed to do its job properly, by failing to flag problems that led to the collapse of companies such as Thomas Cook, Carillion and Patisserie Valerie.

KPMG is the worst offender, with only 61% of the sampled audits meeting industry standards. PWC meet the standards on only 65% of its audits, compared with 76% at Deloitte and 71% at EY.

Smaller accountancy practices such as Grant Thornton met standards on only 55% of its audits, compared with 62% at BDO and 80% at Mazars.

In other words, even the best ranking practice gets it dangerously wrong in one audit in every five, while some fail once in every two audits.

Take the sad case of Thomas Cook, a travel company that created the package holiday, and almost single-handedly invented mass tourism for the Victorians.

Thomas Cook

By the early 21st century it

faced competition from low-cost airlines and online booking. It eventually collapsed with debts of £1.6 billion, putting 9,000 people in the UK out of a job, and leaving hundreds of thousands of holidaymakers stranded abroad.

But only six months before it went bust, its accountants had said it was financially sound, a 'going concern' in accountancy speak. And who were the accountants? PWC, the same crew we saw earlier.

Didn't the accountants realise that Thomas Cook would have to sell 300 million holidays a year - just to pay the interest charges and break even?

Why are accountancy practices weak at doing their audits? How could accountants give the thumbs up to Thomas Cook which had massive and growing debt?

Harvard Business Review (HBR)[36] came up with some views:

Accountants like their clients: Auditors often develop a close relationship with their clients, which can affect their objectivity. People are more inclined to protect those they know and like. In the context of auditing, this means auditors may be less likely to challenge questionable accounting practices from clients with whom they're friendly. In other words, these members of the Concierge Class don't like to rock the boat.

They need to keep their jobs: The fear of losing a client can bias an auditor's judgement. The concern is particularly prevalent where the client provides a big chunk of revenue for the accounting firm.

Take poor old Thomas Cook. Apart from auditing its books, PWC was paid £21 million for providing non-audit work over nine years. That's a lot of money. But with stunning hubris, Hermione Hudson, PWC's head of audit, said:

"I don't think doing those non-audit services would have

impacted the quality of the audit work."

In other words, 'The fact we were getting over £2 million a year in consulting fees didn't affect our judgement in any way."

They don't worry about the future: Humans tend to prioritise immediate consequences over delayed ones, especially when the long-term outcomes are uncertain. This can make an auditor less motivated to issue a critical audit report, even if they suspect irregularities. It's easier to sign off a possibly dodgy set of accounts today than to worry about repercussions in several years' time, especially since it might never happen.

It also translates as 'In a couple of years' time I'll have moved on, and it'll be someone else's problem'.

They ignore small issues which grow over time: Accountants naturally seek to accommodate, ignore, conceal or explain away minor mistakes or oversights in a client's accounts. Over time, these small compromises accumulate, leading to a significant deviation from proper accounting practices. By then it's too late, and the accountant can't own up to such longstanding falsehoods. In extreme cases, this can morph into conscious corruption. Translation: 'In the beginning, I didn't object to their little fiddles. But it's gone on for so long, and the problem has grown so big, that I'm up the creek without a paddle.'

Not everything in accountancy is cut and dried: Some things are simple, such as the rate for converting dollars to sterling on a specific day. Others allow for judgement. For instance, is the money spent on a project an investment or a cost? That affects how much profit is shown in the accounts. Translation: "The client wants to show maximum profit this quarter. So we'll choose all the most optimistic options. For example, we can bring forward sales that have been promised but haven't quite happened yet, to make the numbers look as healthy as possible. "

The audit failures symbolise the way these members of the Concierge Class have been co-opted by corporations, and are failing in their responsibilities to society.

They're mostly a combination of human weakness and venality. But those are low-level failures. It gets worse. Much worse.

The profession has its share of dodgy characters who fiddle the books to suit the needs of their corporate clients. Their toolkit includes the following:

1. Reduce your tax bill through transfer pricing
2. Inflate your expenses to lower the apparent profit
3. Use legal loopholes to avoid tax
4. Accelerated depreciation
5. Over stating the company's assets

Each of these techniques creates a lie, subverts the system, and robs the state of vital revenues.

1. Reduce your tax bill through transfer pricing

Imagine you're a UK-based business, and you have a subsidiary in Germany. At the end of the year, your accountants decide what to charge the subsidiary for support services offered by head office, such as IT or human resources. That's what's called 'transfer pricing', used for internal transactions.

But behind this facade lies one of the most potent tools multinationals use to minimise their tax bills, and thereby boost their profits. Here are some examples:

- Starbucks charges its Dutch subsidiary huge royalties for using its brand and logos[37].

- Pfizer bills its Irish division with inflated patent costs for using its drugs[38].

Why would they do that?

By overcharging subsidiaries in high-tax countries, multinationals can shift profits to their subsidiaries in low tax countries.

For example, Ireland taxes corporate profits at a tiny 12.5%, while the Cayman Islands impose no tax at all.

Firms establish an office in a low-tax country, and then use transfer pricing to route its profits to those jurisdictions through inflated charges.
Such financial engineering erodes public revenues. Estimates suggest transfer pricing bleeds countries worldwide of $500 billion in annual taxes[39]. That's money diverted from healthcare, infrastructure and education.

Starbucks: By charging its British subsidiary inflated fees to use trademarks, Starbucks shifted profits to lower-tax Holland[40]. Despite billions in UK sales, Starbucks has often paid little to no UK income tax for years, thanks to these dodges.

Google deploys similar arrangements, charging foreign subsidiaries hefty royalties to route profits to Bermuda using IP-like patents and search algorithms[41].

Apple took this to the extreme, funnelling $74 billion in offshore untaxed income as of 2012 to an Irish subsidiary that existed only on paper with no actual employees or operations[42].

It's not just the tech companies. **IKEA** slashes its taxes by charging its own subsidiaries in France and Germany for the use of its trademark[43].

Pharmaceutical giants like **Merck** and **Johnson & Johnson** move billions in profits to tax havens, using subsidiaries that hold drug patents or licences[44].

These arrangements, crafted by members of the Concierge Class in the world's top accounting firms, abuse the spirit of tax laws using legal technicalities.

How accountants enabled Microsoft to avoid billions in taxes

Microsoft established a manufacturing subsidiary in Puerto Rico, Microsoft Operations Puerto Rico (MOPR), to produce and distribute Microsoft products in the Americas.

But MOPR was more than just a simple contract manufacturer, it was a shell company strategically positioned to enable tax avoidance. Microsoft's financial engineers then orchestrated a 'licensing deal' that let MOPR use the company's assets - its source code, software processes, trademarks and patents.

By charging MOPR inflated license fees, Microsoft was able to shift billions in annual profit to the island. In just three years, the scheme provided over $4 billion in tax savings by routing global earnings through Puerto Rico[45].

2. Inflate your expenses to lower your apparent profit

Inflating your costs offers corporations an opportunity to reduce their tax bill. Known as 'expense overstatement', it comes in numerous forms.

- You can **invent fictitious companies that bill you**. A Wall Street Journal investigation found Walmart had charged shop rents to itself, thereby lowering its tax bill[46].

- You can illegally record managers' **personal expenses** like jets, holidays and parties (!) as deductible business costs[47]. Barry Minkow, pastor and fraudster, embezzled over $3 million in donations to the Community Bible Church, including charging unauthorised personal expenses on church credit cards[48]. Note: if the tax authorities spot that, they will regard it as fraudulent.

- You can classify invoices not yet paid as **'bad debt'.** You can even create fictitious customers who fail to pay.

- Or you can **sell property or other assets** to partners at below-market prices, to increase deductible 'losses'.

- If you're a film studio, you can turn hit movies into 'financial failures'. Just create a new company for each movie. Then you, the parent business, charge the film company high fees, so it doesn't make any profits[49]. That's why 'Harry Potter and the Order of the Phoenix' made a $167 million loss on paper after grossing nearly $1 billion. It also why David Prowse, the actor who played Darth Vader in 'Return of the Jedi', hasn't been paid, because the movie, which ranks 15th in US box office history, made 'losses'.

The motivating principle is the same - artificially bloating expenses to shrink taxable income.

Most accountants draw the line at wilful fraud or hiding income, lest they're found out. However, accountants well-versed in creating loopholes will come as close to the edge as audit risk allows. For multinationals seeking lower obligations, overstated expenses offer a tempting opportunity.

How Herbalife used a Chinese subsidiary to artificially increase its costs

Herbalife sells nutrition products through a network of distributors who can profit from recruiting others. This business model has drawn accusations of being a pyramid scheme[50]. But controversies around Herbalife's China revenues revealed another issue - creative accounting to understate its income.

Its Chinese subsidiary, run by a rogue manager, reported false information back to the California headquarters for nine years. The China unit artificially reduced its net income by exaggerating expenses and fabricating some vendor transactions.

This enabled Herbalife to report over $58 million less consolidated profit than it should have during this period. The goal was to avoid reaching internal targets that would have forced increased compensation to the subsidiary manager under an incentive scheme.

Fraud caused a shake-up at Herbalife

Behind the manipulation were accountants at Herbalife's Chinese unit, who kept bogus books and financial records.

Only after a whistleblower came forward did an internal audit unravel the scheme. They found the China books riddled with millions in falsified travel and entertainment expenses, plus sham vendor transactions.

The SEC fined Herbalife $20m for failing to detect the long-running fraud. The scheme highlighted how subsidiary accounts can be manipulated by insiders to understate income and taxes.

3. Use tax loopholes to lower your tax

Tax loopholes provide another route for companies to lower their taxes using methods that are technically legal, but contrary to what the government intended.

These loopholes represent exceptions or ambiguities that allow income to be exempted in ways lawmakers didn't anticipate.

For example, the **'carried interest'** loophole allows investment fund managers to categorise their income as 'capital gains' which is taxed at a lower rate than normal revenue - saving them billions[51]. This is exploited by investment firms such as private equity giants Blackstone Group and KKR. They re-name the fees they charge for helping companies succeed as 'capital gains', which are taxed at a lower rate than income. This saves them tens of billions over decades.

The **dual-capacity taxpayer rules** let oil companies classify royalties as exempted foreign income[52].

Pharmaceutical firms can deduct **"orphan drug"** credits for products with limited demand. Companies like Amgen, AbbVie and Bristol Myers have stretched the orphan drug credit meant for treatments for rare diseases. They've harvested billions for blockbusters like Humira thanks to the loophole[53].

Large technology firms like Google and Amazon have contrived elaborate **offshore schemes** to route profits through countries like Bermuda, avoiding nearly $100 billion in global taxes since 2010. We'll talk more about that when we get to Tax Havens in Chapter 2: The Fixers.
These examples reveal how companies divert earnings by exploiting loopholes. Closing them faces major resistance, but transparency and scrutiny continues to grow.

4. Accelerate your depreciation

Depreciation allows companies to deduct from their tax bill the declining value of assets like machinery and equipment over time. Accelerated depreciation turbocharges this process - enabling firms to front-load deductions and thereby minimise their taxes[54].

Under standard depreciation, companies deduct the value of an asset steadily over time matched to its useful lifespan, like a machine depreciating over 10 years[55]. But accelerated depreciation compresses deductions, claiming larger amounts sooner.

For example, a company buys equipment for $1 million. It's expected to last 10 years. Standard depreciation deducts $100,000 annually over a decade. But with accelerated depreciation, it might deduct $400,000 in year one, $300,000 in year two, and smaller amounts after that[56].

This results in greater deductions, which reduces taxable income.

Donald Trump's businesses have used accelerated schedules to rapidly deduct buildings, even as their actual value remains high[57]. Trump claimed $1.4 billion in depreciation since 2000 for his properties, despite rising market values[58].

5. Overstate your assets

This is the reverse of all the preceding wheezes. It happens when a company is failing, and needs to pretend it has more money than it really does.

As a case in point, Thomas Cook (them again) continued for many years to include over £1bn worth of 'goodwill' on its balance sheet. Goodwill is what the company says is the value of its 'intangibles': its brand name, its reputation and its customer base. It's used as an estimate of what the company thinks sales will be in future years. And putting it on the balance sheet tells investors the company has assets that exceed its liabilities (its loans, mortgages, and money owed to suppliers).

But it was evident that Thomas Cook was facing major problems, such as the decline of the High Street. So it should have reduced the value of its goodwill. When it was finally obliged to face the truth and remove that inflated asset, the company had £1.35bn of negative equity, meaning it was no longer solvent[59].

And in another case, the fashion retailer Ted Baker, which had 500 shops around the world, overstated the value of its stock - clothes and shoes - by 35%. When that was pointed out, it had to take £58m off the assets listed in its balance sheet[60]. It's like you finding you have a lot less money in the bank that you thought, and so you might not be able to pay your bills.

Accountants and the drug cartels

Accountants play a critical role in the drug trade, helping cartels to manage the business, launder cash, and avoid detection by the authorities.

The cartels generate sizeable quantities of bank notes from the sale of illegal drugs. This cash needs to be laundered, so it can be used without attracting the attention of authorities. Cartels therefore have to hire people to launder money, using methods such as:

Structuring: This entails breaking down huge amounts of cash into smaller amounts, which the cartels can then deposit into a bank without triggering reporting requirements.

Smuggling: This includes bodily transporting cash to another country, where it can be deposited into banks, paid to suppliers for money owed, or used to purchase assets such as houses.

Accountants also can help cartels manage their budgets, monitor their earnings and expenses, develop budgets, and forecast their cash flows.

Finally, some accountants help cartels to keep away from detection by law enforcement by creating a network of companies and accounting practices that make it difficult for investigators to fathom.

They may create shell companies, organisations that exist only on paper, in tax havens. They can then open bank accounts there, and move cash in and out of them without attracting attention.

Accountants who work for drug cartels are committing a crime. They can face prosecution and imprisonment, as well as civil penalties and professional sanctions, like the following:

- José Carlos Hinojosa, a Mexican accountant, was convicted of laundering cash for the Zetas drug cartel. Hinojosa helped the cartel to clean billions of dollars in drug income through a complicated community of shell groups and offshore bank accounts[61].

- At the trial of Joaquín 'El Chapo', head of the Sinaloa drug cartel, his chief accountant Jesús Zambada García gave evidence against his boss. Speaking like an accountant, he said: "The object of the business is to control the market and prices of the product that the cartel manages, and also expenses for the services that are necessary to make the product arrive at the customer."

  New York, he said, was a prize market, with delivery costs at $9,000 but a street price of $35,000. "That would produce a profit of $26,000 per kilo," he explained, "which would be $26m per tonne, and that would produce a profit per investor of $78m" - from a single shipment.

- Guillermo Pallomari was a Chilean who worked as the chief accountant for the Cali cartel. He was in charge of managing the cartel's finances, as well as delivering bribes to politicians, police officers, civil servants and military officers[62].

  Pallomari kept a ledger containing the cartel's finances, which was coded in a way that no one except he and the cartel's banker, Franklin Jurado, could decode. After he was arrested by the USA's DEA, the cartel leadership decided to have him killed. However, he was rescued by the DEA. Pallomari decided to testify against the Cali cartel in exchange for safety in the United States as part of the witness protection program.

Accountants under pressure

Few accountants are involved in the drug trade, it has to be said. But their work isn't clear cut. A survey by CIPFA, the Public Finance and Accountancy body, found that 57% of its accountants felt they'd been put under pressure, and one-third (36%) had carried out an unethical task, either partially or fully.

Another survey, across a wider range of practitioners, found that 27% of respondents had been pressured to act in a professionally unethical way[63].

The Institute of Chartered Accountants in England and Wales (ICAEW), which has 150,000 members, says accountants should raise their concern to their line manager or someone more senior in the organisation. If that fails. the accountant may have to discuss the ethical issue with the audit committee, board, auditor or their professional body. And ultimately, they may need to consider leaving the organisation and potentially blow the whistle, to ensure they fulfil their ethical obligations.

Summary

The last couple of pages have been a mildly entertaining detour into the role of the accountants who aid the Latin American drug cartels.

But we ought to get back to the more mundane - and massively important - role played by 'respectable' accountants in standard businesses the world over.

In examining how corporations and the wealthy avoid tax obligations, the consistent thread running throughout is the dubious role played by many accountants - from small firms to elite multinationals. These professionals use their unique expertise to create controversial practices.

At one end of the spectrum, accountants provide basic advice, helping to ensure that small businesses and individuals include their expenses in their tax returns. But the systemic tax avoidance analysed here is of an altogether different scale. They withhold billions from the public purse, using tax loopholes and overseas tax havens for private gain.

This industrial-level scheming depends on accountants. And auditors (accountants again) then rubber-stamp the financial statements, despite knowing they conceal more than they reveal.

Most individuals within the field don't set out to intentionally erode tax bases. But many use their expertise to achieve these problematic ends.

The American Accounting Association has published a paper called, 'Making Tax Havens Work: The Necessity of Tax Professionalism[64]', which suggests the accountants are by no means reformed characters.

And it's worth noting that accountants are the *only* professionals whose effectiveness is largely judged on how much tax they help their bosses avoid paying.

What's to be done?

We need greater public **accountability and scrutiny** of the accountancy firms that are facilitating questionable but legal manoeuvres.

Audit firms must recognise that creating tax 'products' cause reputational risks as well as undermining public budgets. In just one case, the UK government said: "We believe that PricewaterhouseCoopers's activities represent nothing short of the promotion of tax avoidance on an industrial scale[6566]."

New transparency requirements such as **mandating large multinationals to publicly disclose their profit allocations and tax payments on a country-by-country basis** could highlight discrepancies and transfer pricing schemes using offshore tax havens.

Tax authorities need stronger legal powers and more resources to combat tax avoidance tactics and access company information across borders.

Closing tax code loopholes that serve mainly corporate interests will also raise tens of billions. Addressing the "carried interest" treatment of private equity performance fees alone could generate $180 billion for the USA over 10 years[67].

Above all, **corporations** and **wealthy individuals** that benefit from avoidance schemes must recognise that their lack of contribution erodes the social contract that underpins modern civilisation. Tax is not just about cold numbers, but also ethics, values and investing in a shared future.

Who's to blame?

The UK government reckons that 30,000 individuals and 2,000 employers are involved in avoidance schemes[68]. That's just the UK.

And every one of them is a member of the Concierge Class, waving their magic wands to hide the wealth of corporations and the rich.

Step forward every accountant who has helped their client reduce their tax bill. If you were to say, 'No one need pay more than is required by law,' that misses the point about what happens if you don't pay your tax. It means the state has less money to hire teachers to educate your children, and send police officers to patrol the streets.

Lawyers: in a rich man's world

Here's a boasting lawyer: "We had another year of precedent-setting court-room victories."

Translation: 'We got more of our crooked clients off the hook.'

In one of their wins, Jeffery Ansell, a Vice President at Stanley Black and Decker, the tools business, had failed to disclose $1.3 million worth of benefits paid to four senior staff members[69].

The company's annual reports said Ansell earned an average of $167,000 a year. But the correct amount was actually $647,000.

After discussions between Covington and the USA's SEC (the USA's regulatory body), Ansell agreed to pay a fine of only $75,000. This despite the $1.3 million of false company accounts and his current ownership of $2 million worth of Stanley shares.

The company suffered no penalties, despite illegally paying top execs that $1.3 million. The SEC took into account their "self-reporting, cooperation, and remediation" (which means "It saves us time and money in court fees if you'll agree to pay a modest fine").

In another case, Covington helped Executive Health Resources, a hospital billing company, walk free after a judgement at the Supreme Court. In that case, a doctor alleged that EHR was enabling its clients to cheat the government, by charging inpatient rates for what should have been outpatient services. But after work by Covington, the court agreed that the case should be dismissed, on a technicality[70].

Most of these cases never get reported. One exception was where the company that owns betting firms Ladbrokes and Coral agreed to pay £685 million to settle an investigation into alleged bribery at a Turkish business they'd previously owned.

The company was given a Deferred Prosecution Agreement (DPA), whereby the proceedings are suspended.

Coral: Betting it would
get away with a fine.

The company thus got away without a criminal conviction[71].

The company's Chair said the firm had "changed immeasurably" since then, forgetting to mention the AUS $207,000 fine for offering illegal gambling inducements, the £5.9m UK fine for failing to have safeguards in place to prevent money laundering and harm to punters, as well as being criticised by the Advertising Standards Authority for running irresponsible advertisements[72].

It's all in a day's work for the UK's 156,000 lawyers and the 1.3 million ones in the USA.

How lawyers benefit corporations and the wealthy

The previous section you just read was about plea bargaining, where a company gets a reduced penalty (and the bosses escape jail!) by being nice to the prosecuting authorities.

But there are many other ways the lawyers earn a living (average US lawyer's salary: $126,000 a year, but much more in bigger firms. The starting salary for a *newly qualified* solicitor in London is £65,000 - £85,000).

In this chapter, we look at how lawyers can act against the public interest, by supporting the agendas of corporations and the wealthy. It's the Concierge Class in action.

Lobbying by corporate lawyers

Lawyers lobby governments to shape tax laws and regulations in favour of their clients.

Covington, mentioned above, has 1,100 lawyers and advisers 'regularly working on public policy issues' for its corporate clients, according to an article in the Law Society Gazette called 'Paid to Persuade'[73].

Charles Brasted, a partner at solicitors Hogan Lovells said: "If there are policy changes or legislation on the horizon that [our clients] are concerned about, we can help them identify those concerns, look for solutions and articulate [them] effectively to public sector decision-makers, whether it is government or a sector regulator". Translation: 'We're paid to persuade the government not to legislate against the interests of our rich clients.'

Using tax loopholes

Corporations often hire lawyers to help them find and exploit tax loopholes. This allows them to avoid paying their fair share of taxes, which deprives the government of revenue that could be used to fund important public services.

Law firm Conyers Dill, and Pearman helped the tech company Google to reduce its tax bill by $3.7 billion in one year alone. Google used a legal loophole known as the "double Irish with a Dutch sandwich" to shift profits from high-tax countries to low-tax countries. This loophole was subsequently closed by the UK government, but Google still benefits from a number of other tax loopholes[74].

Fighting the environmentalists

Lawyers working for corporations involved in oil, gas, mining and similar sectors defend their clients against allegations of pollution and environmental damage. This obstructs efforts to hold corporations accountable for their environmental impact, potentially leading to public health risks and environmental degradation.

Gibson Dunn & Crutcher has an 'environmental tort' department that specialises in defending companies against mass action claims for breaches of environmental laws. It represented food company Dole in a series of lawsuits involving thousands of Latin American workers claiming personal injuries from exposure to DBCP, a pesticide that causes impotency, and which was used on its banana farms[75].

Gibson Dunn overturned a $5.7 million fine, and obtained a confidential global settlement.

Dentons has 12,000 lawyers across the globe. In one case it tried, but failed, to win approval for Enbridge Inc to run two 'Northern Gateway' oil pipelines, 1,177 km (731 miles) long, across Canada[76].

Opposed by over half of Canadian residents, the application was finally scrapped.

Enbridge's many failings included the fact that 117 of its 125 pumping stations failed national safety rules, including no emergency shutdown at 83 of them. Its spills were numerous, including a 230,000-litre leak in Alberta.

Shell, Exxon Mobil, and Chevron use the global law firm Latham & Watkins. It, along with law firm Debevoise & Plimpton, has represented Shell in group actions brought by thousands of residents of the Bille and Ogale communities for extensive oil pollution in the Niger Delta, which they lost at the Supreme Court[77].

Enbridge oil spill

In a similar case, law firm Freshfields represented Volkswagen in the emissions scandal[78], where, you might recall, the company had fitted 11 million cars with software 'defeat devices' which cheated pollution tests. Maybe the case was so obviously criminal that Volkswagen had to pay a $4.3 billion fine in the US alone.

Three bosses were given a suspended sentence, while a low-ranking engineer got three years in jail[79][80]. The company chair, Martin Winterkorn, was indicted in 2018 on fraud charges, but six years later he still had not stood trial. He told one court he knew nothing about the devices. The prosecutors in Germany said he'd known about the devices since 2015[81], and charged him with false testimony.

Needless to say, every defendant has the right to a lawyer. But corporations often hire teams of lawyers to defend them against these allegations, and they often have the resources to drag out cases for years. This can make it difficult for environmental groups and individuals to hold corporations accountable for the damage they cause.

Using intellectual property to boost profits and create a monopoly

Lawyers help corporations to navigate intellectual property laws. But they can also use these legal protections to stifle innovation, promote monopolistic practices and inhibit fair competition, all of which are contrary to the public interest.

Companies often use the law to protect their market share and profits, and the lawyers play a major role in helping them achieve that.

DLA Piper says it has over 130 patent litigators in key jurisdictions worldwide. "We know the laws, courts, and judges in the locations where most patent disputes happen. And we develop and implement strong global patent enforcement strategies, selecting where and when to litigate to increase the chances of success[82]," they said.

Law firm Hogan Lovells has helped the pharmaceutical company Eli Lilly obtain and protect its patents on new types of insulin[83]. This has given the company a monopoly on the sale of the new insulin variants, allowing it to charge high prices for the drug[84], despite it having been introduced in 1921.

Reducing workers' rights

DLA Piper fought to allow ride-hailing company Uber to maintain that its drivers were self-employed and therefore not entitled to workers' rights[85]. The tribunal ruled the drivers were not self-employed and were therefore entitled to basic employee rights. But the battles over Uber drivers' rights have continued.

Amazon paid one law firm, Lev Labor, $371,000 in an effort to defeat a trade union organising campaign in New York. A judge found that the online retail giant violated the law on three occasions as it tried to persuade workers not to unionise[86].

Limiting the company's liability

If you're a big business, the last thing you want is pesky employees taking you to court for bullying, unfair dismissal or gender discrimination. Your lawyers will tell you the answer: put an arbitration clause in the employment contract, and get workers to sign it.

That way, if they persist with a complaint, it has to go through an arbitration company, not the courts.

Critics of mandatory arbitration say it discourages workers from bringing claims that involve small sums of money, and that workers who do bring disputes in arbitration are more likely to lose.

Additionally, arbitration awards are typically not made public, which makes it difficult to know how much money corporations are paying to settle disputes.

If you're a lawyer drawing up an employment contract for your client, why not add a clause banning them from participating in 'class action' lawsuits? These are where people band together to make it worth a lawyer's time to go to court. It can be a powerful tool for individuals to hold corporations to account. But those forced arbitration clauses make it difficult for individuals to pursue class action lawsuits.

New York lawyers Kaplan Hecker & Fink failed to win a case for Uber involving 31,000 *individual* claims against the company. It related to a clause in the firm's employment contract that drivers were required to sign, committing them to seek arbitration in the event of a dispute[87].

Reuters said that after agreeing to pay more than $146 million in 2019 to settle arbitration demands by more than 60,000 individual drivers, Uber was trying something new, but getting the same old results.

Uber "made the business decision to preclude class, collective or representative claims in its arbitration agreement with its consumers," the New York court said. Which is why it was landed with 60,000 claims.

As that same busy lawyer, you could add a confidentiality clause, which bans the employee from going public about the company's bad behaviour. It works both ways, in that it stops the company from bad-mouthing a former employee. But as we've seen in #MeToo cases, it's often used to stop former employees from revealing sexual harassment.

Muzzling press freedom

Major UK law firms, including Harbottle and Lewis, CMS, Carter Ruck and Schillings, have been accused of seeking to muzzle the press on behalf of 'organised crime, authoritarian states, oligarch proxies or corrupt corporations' via the UK court system[88], says one Member of Parliament.

In one case, MP Bob Seely said, 'there has not been a clearer case in recent times of the pro-active abuse of the law on behalf of a murderous foreign dictator.' He was referring to the plight of Financial Times journalist Catherine Belton and her publisher Harper Collins over her book about oligarchs. The defamation case was one of several lawsuits the author and publishers faced that left Belton with a £1.5 million bill.

"'These high-priced law firms, through naivety, poor judgement or simple greed, are becoming a fifth column," Seely went on.

"They are the tools by which the enemies of law-governed states, whether criminals, oligarchs, their fellow travellers or simple foreign fascists, undermine our societies and their values. And I wish they would reconsider their behaviour."

At the heart of that and similar lawsuits are the so-called 'Slapps' (Strategic

Lawsuits Against Public Participation). They usually involve ultra-wealthy people using libel and privacy laws to stop journalists or campaigners from exposing wrongdoing.

Belton had received five threatening letters in the post, from the Russian oligarch Roman Abramovich, three other oligarchs, and the Russian state oil company Rosneft. All were bringing cases against her and the publisher of her book, Putin's People, for libel.

Abramovich and other oligarchs tried to silence a journalist.

None of the suits succeeded, albeit in one case the publisher HarperCollins agreed to make a payment to charity and delete 1,700 words, which it could not substantiate, from the book.

Abramovich was later sanctioned by the UK for his ties to the Kremlin. Belton was awarded an MBE.

Abusive suits like this are designed to intimidate and silence publishers and the media.

Lawyers involved in property fraud

Transparency International (TI) has claimed that dozens of UK law firms are providing corrupt individuals with services that enable them to move, hide and defend their ill-gotten gains with impunity.

TI's report, At Your Service, reveals the role played by UK service companies in corruption and shows how law firms, unwittingly or otherwise, support corrupt individuals[89].

TI analysed 400 cases of high-level corruption and associated money laundering over the last 30 years covering 116 countries of origin. And it identified 582 firms and individuals offering such services in the UK, including 81 law firms.

It took a close look at 293 suspicious property transactions, worth more than £4.4bn. They involved cases relating to 'politically exposed' persons from high-corruption-risk jurisdictions. It also included cases where people were charged with, convicted of, or alleged to have committed corruption offences.

The report found that 56 law firms were involved in 132 of these transactions, which were worth more than £3.2bn. They either offered conveyancing services to the buyer, or were responsible for forming and maintaining the business that was used to make the purchase.

They varied in size from major international businesses to those employing fewer than 10 members of staff. It's unclear whether any of the reports had been submitted by the companies in response to the activity they had carried out for the buyers.

32 law firms were also found to be involved in 'Laundromats' – a series of large corruption schemes uncovered by the Organised Crime and Corruption Reporting Project. Many of them are globally renowned firms with offices around the world. These payments came from shell companies with accounts at Baltic banks that have now been closed.

TI said corrupt individuals were also able to use law firms' services "to defend themselves and their commercial interests, and to cleanse their reputations."

Email theft

A prominent British barrister, Hugh Tomlinson, used emails stolen from his client's opponent to prove his case[90].

It started with a spat between the sheikh of a small but powerful UAE emirate (Ras Al Khaimah, population: 192,000) and an Iranian-American businessman, Farhad Azima.

Tens of thousands of Azima's emails, personal photographs, voice recordings, videos and WhatsApp messages were hacked and then illegally uploaded to the internet. Since the information was now publicly available, the emirate was free to use it in London's High Court.

Remarkably, the English legal system allows a judge to accept hacked emails as evidence in court in the interests of justice, unless persuaded to exclude it.

According to the Bureau of Investigative Journalism (BIJ), there is no suggestion that Tomlinson had any involvement in the hacking of Azima's emails, but was aware that they were the product of a hack, and would have been professionally obliged to deploy them if instructed to do so.

Tomlinson told the court the emails had been sent unsolicited by an "anonymous source" to the offices of Stewarts Law – a London law firm that later represented the emirate.

Also in the picture was Dechert LLP, a global law firm, retained by the emirate. One of Dechert's lawyers then joined Stewarts Law - hence its involvement in the case.

The BIJ also alleged that lawyers from a "top City firm" held a secret perjury school" in the Swiss Alps to prepare false witness testimonies about how they got hold of the illegally obtained information.

As with many members of the Concierge Classes, here's how the lawyers appear to see themselves: "We're professionals, doing a job. Sure, we get the odd slightly dodgy client, but it's swings and roundabouts. You take what you can get. We stay within the law. It's not up to us to decide who our clients are. We're agnostic on that. And it's our job to keep the clients from doing something really stupid."

Needless to say, that narrative isn't adequate.

Just the top of the iceberg

So far, most of the lawyers we've looked at have worked for the top law firms. Can we expect them to have a social conscience or political awareness? It's doubtful.

The odds of a solicitor getting to work in a big law firm (in the UK, that's one with more than 250 practitioners) are around 31%. So, two-thirds of solicitors work in smaller practices[91].

But what proportion of these are engaged in socially useful legal activity? There's a clear need. To take just issues relating to women:

- In more than half the countries in the world, it's lawful to discriminate against women.

- Almost 250 million women experience physical or sexual violence from an intimate partner each year.

- In the UK, a woman is killed by a man every 2.6 days on average.

- Two-thirds of women in prison have suffered domestic abuse.

- Britain has the most expensive childcare in Europe.

And those are just a handful of statistics about women.

So, do lawyers support those without ready access to justice?

A survey of lawyers found that larger firms (which we'll categorise as those with a pro-bono co-ordinator) spent only 1.4% of their time on pro bono work.

Those without a co-ordinator (the smaller firms) spent 3.9% of their time doing non-paid work. It means smaller firms have a slightly bigger conscience[92].

But neither suggest the lawyers are aware of social welfare issues.

And how do they feel about themselves? 99% of lawyers in law firms feel their work provides them with a strong sense of purpose. Well, pat yourself on the back, guys.

Similarly, most legal and tax professionals feel that their work has a positive impact on their community and wider society. They're "proud of how their companies and firms contribute to the greater good in their communities and society at large[93]." This came down to four elements:

- Having a direct impact on society
- Enabling a civilised and orderly society
- Knowledge sharing and empowerment

Somehow, it's a bit unconvincing.

We can't expect lawyers to shoulder the problems of society. But of all the professions, they're the most qualified to create a better society. And from the evidence we've looked at, they don't do that. Like other members of the concierge class, they aren't engaged; they don't care.

The exceptions

120 lawyers have stated publicly they'll refuse to prosecute climate protesters such as Extinction Rebellion, Insulate Britain and Just Stop Oil, as well as refusing to act on new fossil fuel projects. The group, Lawyers Are Responsible, is made up of barristers, solicitors and academics.

Barristers are duty-bound by their Standards Board to accept a client, irrespective of whether they disagree with the client's views or actions. Some of the signatories have reported themselves to the Bar Standards Board for going against the rule. It's thought to be the first time in legal history that barristers have engaged in a collective act of civil disobedience[94].

But The Secret Barrister, an anonymous legal author with over 515,000 followers on Twitter, said: "I prosecute when I'm instructed to prosecute. And defend when I'm instructed to defend. I don't only act for people I like. Or in whose cause I "believe".

What's to be done?

As skilled members of the Concierge Class, lawyers should reflect on whether they're doing enough to make the world a better place. They need to be aware of colluding with corporations and the wealthy. And they should spend time supporting those who would otherwise be denied access to the law.

They need to take personal responsibility for the clients they accept. This includes doing due diligence not just on the client's ability to pay, but on the nature of the job and the client's ethical background. Lawyers have to be brave enough to turn away jobs.

It's not a matter of denying someone justice, because another lawyer will take them on. But some lawyers are already refusing to take on the abusive suits known as Slapps.

The wider responsibility, meanwhile, rests with the practice partners, to create an ethical work environment.

Higher up the ladder are the regulators; and beyond them to government, who need to ensure that everyone has appropriate access to the law, and that the legal system is not abused by those with money.

Stocking up on the money

The son of a postman, Gary Stevenson grew up as a poor child in a small terraced house in Ilford, East London, with trains running past his window. From where he lived, he could see the huge towers of Canary Wharf, London's financial district. Everyone in his neighbourhood dreamed of working there.

Stevenson was expelled from school at age 16, for selling cannabis. But he was clever at maths, and got a job as a trader at Citi Bank, then the largest bank in the world.

By his second year, at age 23, he was making Citi £12 million a year, and getting a £400,000 bonus. And that was despite one trade where he lost the bank $8 million when "the Swiss National Bank did something that surprised me". By his fourth year, Stevenson was Citi's most profitable trader.

But he resigned shortly afterwards because, in his words, "People from my background were getting poorer, while the rich were getting richer."

He'd come to realise that "No matter how smart you are, no matter how hard you work, if you come from the wrong family, you'll probably never own property. That's feudalism. We're going back to a world of aristocracy."

Capitalism, he said, "should be a system where, if you work hard and you're talented, you should be able to have a nice secure comfortable life, if you want it.

"That's capitalism. That's what people where I come from believe. But it's not possible any more. It's an inheritance society."

Gary Stevenson: "People from my background were getting poorer, while the rich were getting richer."

Now this former trader spends his time explaining to people why the system is rigged. And nowhere more so than on the stock markets.

What's the function of the stock market?

Talk to an investor or a financier, and they'll tell you the stock market provides capital for new investment, and that leads to growth.

But that's not so. The stock market consists of:

- Rich people betting on the value of businesses: will their value go up or down? They convert their spare cash into shares, in order to get a dividend every 90 days.

- Other rich people manipulating the price of their company shares, with the aim of making more money.

- Funds buying companies, hollowing them out, and selling them off, again with the aim of making a short-term quick buck.

That's it. Let's take the key issues in turn.

1. The stock markets don't help to grow businesses

As I said, people think the purpose of the stock market is to raise money for new businesses and provide investment money for existing businesses, thereby helping to support the growth of companies. But that ain't true.

According to the London Stock Exchange, new businesses accounted for only 2% of all transactions on the UK stock market in 2022.

And "Secondary capital raisings" - that is when *existing* businesses offer *extra* shares for sale - that accounts for only around 30% of all transactions on the UK stock market.

In other words, 70% of all transactions are merely devices that allow the rich to make money.

But wait, are the "Secondary capital raisings" - transactions, remember, that allow listed companies to get additional capital - are they really useful? According to EY, here are the stated aims of secondary raisings:

Growth investment (e.g., new product development, market expansion, acquisitions)	50%

Repayment of debt	25%
Strengthening the balance sheet (e.g. increasing liquidity, reducing leverage)	25%.

But what do these jargon-laden terms really mean? Let's unpick them one at a time.

The biggest section, **'growth investment'**, includes acquiring other businesses. In other words, you buy up your competitors, your suppliers or the businesses who buy from you. That gives you an easier life because you're more in control of the market. Less competition.

Or you decide to buy a business in another sector, rather than create your own business in that area. It's a self-preservation strategy rather than so-called 'growth investment'.

Now look at the second and third items: **repaying debt** and **strengthening the balance sheet**. I'll let you into a secret. They mean the same thing. It's all smoke and mirrors.

'Increasing liquidity' means 'putting more cash into your bank account'. It's the same as you or me asking the bank manager for a loan because we're short of money. Meanwhile, *'reducing leverage'* means 'cutting your existing debt by taking on more shareholders, to whom you will have to pay dividends every year'.

But let's say you're a founder. You sell some of your shares in a 'secondary raising'. The result is you reduce your shareholding at a time when the business is growing. So you get cash for yourself. Nice work.

2. Buybacks are massive - and they're a con

Remember I said 70% of stock market activity was nothing to do with raising new money?

Well, part of that 70% involves a 'buyback'. That's what happens when a company uses its profits to buy its own shares.

Why would you do that? Answer: it reduces the number of shares on the market. That boosts the 'earnings per share', which is 'profits divided by the number of shares', which is a measure of 'yield' - the percentage return you'll make on investing in that company.

Seeing an increased yield will make it more desirable to investors, which will push up the price of the shares still more.

But companies that do a buyback aren't thinking about small investors. No, it's for the benefit of the asset managers who own most of the shares, and the directors who also have been given shares.

In other words, by getting the company to buy back its shares, the directors personally gain. Hmm.

In recent years, buybacks accounted for 75 percent of what US non-financial companies did with their profits.[95] In other words, the profits didn't go to improving staff wages or conditions, investing in new equipment, or creating new products. They benefited the shareholders and directors.

In recent years, HSBC created a £5 billion share buyback program, GSK went on a £3 billion buyback spree, and Shell acquired $9 billion work of its own shares.

Between 2015 and 2017, the top five US buyback spenders in the restaurant industry spent 172 percent of their profits on buying their own shares. In other words, they borrowed money, over and above their profits, to buy their own shares.

If these companies had instead directed those funds towards worker wages, low-wage workers would have seen a dramatic increase in their pay. McDonald's would have been able to pay all of its 1.9 million workers almost $4,000 more if the company had put the money it spent on buybacks into staff wages. Similarly, if Starbucks had reallocated money from share repurchases to pay packets, every worker would have received $7,000 more.

Companies are rarely transparent about their buyback motives. This makes it difficult for investors to assess the true impact of these actions on the company's long-term prospects.

Overall, buybacks reduce a company's cash reserves, limiting its ability to invest, and thereby potentially contributing to economic downturns.

3. Shareholders aren't local. Nor are they individuals

Foreign investors own the majority (66%) of shares on the UK stock market. The largest proportion of foreign ownership comes from North America (46%), followed by Europe (29%).

The largest US investors in the UK stock market include BlackRock, Vanguard Group, and Fidelity Investments, businesses that buy up companies with the aim of squeezing more profit out of them.

UK-resident individuals own only 12% of the UK stock market, while institutional investors, such as pension funds, mutual funds, and insurance funds have only 13%[96].

So the stock market isn't about local owners, nor about individuals. It's about the world of global investment.

4. The stock market encourages short-term behaviour

If people can buy and sell shares in your business, it means you serve two masters: the customers and the investors. Every 90 days, you have to send your shareholders a report detailing what profits you're making for them. If they don't like it, they'll sell the shares.

Then the price of your company's shares will drop. Other investors could buy your business cheaply. And you might lose your job, like a football manager whose team isn't performing well.

So the directors of publicly quoted companies spend their time trying to boost profits, in order to appease the shareholders, protect their own jobs, and increase the value of their own shares.

This usually means cutting costs, which means reducing staff numbers, investing less in new plant and equipment, cutting back on new products, and reducing the quality of the existing ones.

All of a sudden, publicly quoted companies look less like grown up management, and more like life in the Roman arena (short and brutal).

It encourages risky and criminal behaviour

So far, we've looked at the stock market as a *system* for making rich folks richer, whether through IPOs or buybacks.

We've also noticed that it has nothing to do with supporting jobs or the economy, and indeed undermines the long-term vision needed to create a stable economy.

But it gets worse, because imagine what can happen if a 23-year-old (like Gary Stevenson at the start of this section) is given huge amounts of money to makes bets on currencies, shares, or the future price of beef. It's like leaving a child in a sweet shop.

Not only that, but the 23-year-old can use borrowed money to make bets. It's called 'leveraging'. In UK regulated markets, you can put down £1, and bet £30. The trouble with that is it magnifies your risk.

If you put down £200, you can bet £6,000 on, say, the future price of gold which is (let's say) currently £1,000 an ounce. If the price of gold rises, you can make a great profit. But if it falls to £900 per ounce, you've just lost £600, and the broker will come knocking on your door for their cash.

Not only that but for some 1:30 is far too dull. Trade on GoFX, and you can borrow 1:3,000.

So is it any wonder that traders can get into trouble? Let's look at some real-life examples, which risked destabilising the markets.

1. Nick Leeson, a trader at **Barings Bank**, a British merchant bank, carried out unauthorised trading to hide losses from his superiors. It led to the collapse of Barings Bank, which was at the time one of the oldest and most respected banks in the world. The collapse of Barings Bank cost investors billions of dollars and resulted in the loss of thousands of jobs.

2. Jérôme Kerviel was a trader at **Société Générale**, a French bank. Kerviel hid his losses, and eventually amassed a massive portfolio of futures contracts that exposed Société Générale to significant risk. This led to losses of €4.9 billion for Société Générale, which was at the time one of the largest banks in France.

3. A group of traders at **JPMorgan Chase**, known as the "London Whale," engaged in risky trading practices that led to losses of $6.2 billion for the bank. They would place large-scale bets on the creditworthiness of

European sovereign debt, and these bets ultimately turned sour when the sovereign debt crisis in Europe worsened. The bank was fined over $900 million.

And then there are traders who act illegally for their own benefit. Several investment banks, including Barclays, HSBC and UBS, manipulated the Libor interest rate for their own financial gain. When this was discovered, the regulator fined the banks $9 *billion*, and some individuals were sent to prison. Tom Hayes, a UBS trader, was sent down for 14 years, while four Barclays Bank traders received sentences of between two and six years.

Plus, there's the added problem of computerised trading, where the use of algorithms can cause additional volatility. Currently, 60-75% of trading is done by algo trading, with no human involvement[97]. Sure, there are 'stop' mechanisms, and extreme falls will eventually be corrected by investors snapping up a bargain. But does that make you feel any more secure, knowing that a bunch of computers, all set to roughly the same 'buy' and 'sell' points, are making the decisions?

What does all this mean? And what's the role of the Concierge Class?

In summary, the stock market is mostly a device for rich people and the directors of corporations to make money. Almost none of it goes to investing in better products or reducing a company's environmental impact.

The annual return on the UK stock market over 20 years has been 7.5%. Over the last 119 years, UK stocks have made annualised returns of 5% over and above inflation[98]. So, over the long run it's a safe bet. And it's also a space where wealthy people can make huge gains (see 'buybacks' above).

The people who benefit most are the rich - the corporate directors and people rich enough to hold shares. At the end of 2020, shares in quoted UK-domiciled companies listed on the London Stock Exchange were worth a total of £2.2 trillion[99]. Of this, by far the biggest amount was held overseas, £1.2 trillion. So the money doesn't go to insurance companies or local people, but to faceless people 'abroad', many in tax havens.

And who's making this happen? What part does the Concierge Class play? Answer: there are countless people in the middle, earning fat fees and large salaries.

Those who also benefit, and make a nice living from it, are the Concierge Class. They're the stock brokers, who buy and sell shares on behalf of people and institutions. But a great many other people are also involved, such as investment bankers, auditors, analysts and portfolio managers. All of these people are hard at work, checking the numbers, booking the trades, ensuring it's all technically legal, and keeping records. These are the Concierge Class.

They include the accountants who explain to company directors why they should buy back the company shares, and the 'activist investors' who target businesses with the aim of enforcing cost reductions once they've bought enough shares.

Thus the stock market forces CEOs to focus exclusively on shareholders, at the expense of other stakeholders - communities, workers, and those concerned about the environment.

And what's the outcome? The stock market has almost no relationship to the real world. It's a way to make money out of money. It benefits only the rich and the Concierge Class who make it happen.

What's to be done?

Too few people explain what is really going on in the stock markets, and fewer still want to.

There's almost complete obfuscation, despite (or perhaps because) it's about the rich getting richer.

Even the traders don't understand the impact of their actions. And the media don't explain it, because their readers either know how the circus works, or would find it boring and beyond their comprehension.

You, the reader, are the rare exception.

Traders are gamblers. They get high on risk. Raising questions about the ethics of trading would be greeted with bemusement. But creating awareness is important, because unless members of the Concierge Class are confronted with these questions, they can't change.

The issues should be aired in the media, whether in the mainstream press or on social media. And that requires people with an understanding of the markets to stand up and be counted.

Regulation has greatly tightened since the last crash, but the financiers will always push for looser controls; and many politicians are ready to acquiesce. **Legislation needs to be tightened,** and **regulators given more power.**

Minimum capital requirements need to be set (liquidity), in order to cover potential losses.

We need to **tilt the economy back towards the productive sectors** that actually make things, and **encourage real-world companies to invest in their business**.

The government should limit or **put an end to open-market buybacks[100]**.

It should restrict or end **stock-based compensation**, whereby directors are paid a bonus if the share price increases. It encourages them to boost the share price, rather than focus on the underlying business.

Asset managers: milking the state

Want to know how to create money? Here's the formula:

1. Get some rich people to put money into an investment pot. It avoids having to use your own money.

2. With £100m in your pocket, go and buy a public service, such as Thames Water, the Dartford Toll crossing, Gatwick Airport or student accommodation.

3. Now burden that business with the £100 million you paid to buy it, which it'll have to repay like a mortgage, every month.

4. Then reduce the company's maintenance budget, and increase the price of the services it provides.

5. The profit is now going up nicely. Increase the dividends you pay to yourself and your investors.

6. After a few years, sell the asset to another investment business - for much more than you paid.

7. That's it. Your investors get a nice profit on the capital they originally put in, and they've had fat dividends each quarter. Meanwhile you've taken 1% of every bit of profit, which amounts to millions.

But, you ask, what happens to the 'asset', for example Thames Water? Well, maybe not so great. It's carrying not only the debt you added, but also the purchase cost the new owner has dumped on to it. So its monthly payments are higher still. Less money for replacing the old Victorian sewers.

Its pipes are leaking like a sieve, due to the lack of maintenance and under-investment while it was under your ownership.

And the consumer is paying higher bills for the water that comes out of their taps, because you jacked up the price. But hey, that's not your problem.

It's a bit of magic you've conjured up. You used other people's money to buy an asset, milked it for ten years, and sold it.

And that, briefly, is how asset management companies work.

But note that the rich didn't have to do anything. They simply put some cash into the fund.

It's members of the Concierge Class, the fund managers, who did all the work.

In one incident, Thames Water was fined £4 million for spilling 79 million litres of untreated sewage across an area of 6,500 square metres at New Malden.

And the profits have come about by degrading the business and impoverishing the users.

It's one thing to damage a company. But asset management companies are doing the same to public utilities, as we're about to see.

What's the scale of the problem?

In a word, enormous. the "Big Three" asset management firms—BlackRock, Vanguard and State Street—have over $15 trillion of managed global assets, an amount equivalent to more than three-quarters of US gross domestic product.

In the UK, BlackRock owns part of South West Water, Severn Trent, Bristol Water, and United Utilities which provides water across North West England[101].

According to the Investment Association, UK asset managers hold assets worth £1.6 trillion in the UK, £40 billion of which are in UK public infrastructure. That includes utilities, transport, telecommunications and renewable energy. They also own buildings that relate to public health, schools and higher education.

This results, it says, from 'the growing reliance on market-based finance.' Translation: 'Although government could buy this infrastructure more cheaply, it doesn't want to be seen to borrow money, even though it costs the taxpayer more in the long term.'[102]
Investment companies like assets because they generate regular predictable income through rent, tolls or user fees.

The businesses usually appreciate in value over time, keeping pace with inflation. If inflation goes up 3%, you just charge your users an extra 3%. And so the value of your asset grows by a similar amount. It's like when your landlord puts the rent up each year.

Great for them. Not so good for us.

But it's not just water companies. 863 care homes that look after vulnerable children are fully or partially controlled by investment companies, a number that's doubled in the last five years.

These companies now provide nearly one in four places in English children's care homes. And they're eye-wateringly expensive at £21,000 a child per year[103].

Private equity and investment groups had been attracted to this sector by the growing demand for children's care, especially for youngsters with complex needs.

Councils are legally obliged to find suitable specialist care, education and accommodation for children who require the state's support. It therefore provides investment companies with a reliable income, and the opportunity to raise their prices[104].

In response, the Department for Education (DfE) said that "profiteering in the children's homes market is wholly unacceptable".

There's also a problem with homes for the elderly. Those that are run for profit deliver worse care than voluntary and public sector operators. Studies have found that for-profit operators have on average fewer staff hours per resident and worse indicators for quality of service[105].

And now the investment companies have their eye on the home rental market. In parts of the USA, they've been buying up to two-thirds of properties for sale in some counties in Mississippi. Iowa and Texas, outbidding would-be homeowners with cash offers and fast-track purchases. Only later do the renters realise the limiting conditions and additional costs and fees imposed on the house and its maintenance[106].

Back in 2018, the late Jack Bogle, who founded Vanguard, said there was a risk that "a handful of giant institutional investors will one day hold voting control of virtually every large US corporation." To which we might add 'and UK companies'. He prophesied that the impact of this 'growing dominance' would be 'major issues in the coming era[107].'

It's not investment as we know it

When financial companies talk about 'investing' in a business, what they really mean is: they buy a business or a chunk of it, in order to extract the profit, month after month. It's not the same thing as investing in R&D or developing new products.

Asset managers simply want to make a profit. That's their only concern. They don't love the businesses they buy. They don't admire the staff who work in them, or respect their customers. Their needs aren't aligned with the needs of ordinary people or the governments that serve the population.

Investment managers expect to sell their investments before too long, and make a capital gain. That enables them to invest in yet more activities. And their investors will want their money back after less than a decade.
Most of the funds that are used to invest in infrastructure and property are short-term 'closed funds' that last a fixed period, usually ten years

Thus, asset managers have an inherently short-term perspective on the businesses they acquire or invest in. But all fixed assets like buildings, bridges and roads are long-term products that need constant maintenance and long-term investment. Sadly, asset companies aren't inclined to renew and repair, knowing they'll be selling the asset in a few years[108].

What's to be done?

Unlike the stock market, 85% of the UK assets controlled by management companies[109] come from UK pension funds and insurers.

And that means pension funds are supporting the asset managers to damage the economy, privatise public assets, increase the cost of services, and reduce the standard of services. Pension fund managers and trustees should decide not to invest in such ruthless behaviour.

The government could ban investment funds from making short-term investments in long-term infrastructure. Asset managers could threaten not to invest in the UK, but their competitors will continue to invest. The right-wing pundits will complain that the government is discouraging investment, and get the news media on their side. That would be politically damaging for the government, but the result would be worth the sort term storm.

Alternatively, the government could buy back the utilities and other public assets. That would cost money, but it would pay for itself[110].

Alternatively, the government could simply privatise the assets and offer to pay a smaller amount of money to the owners, such as what they originally paid for it (bearing in mind they'd had constant dividends).

That might result in lawsuits against the government, and also would mean that investors would require a higher rate of return for any future investments, because they'd fear their assets could be taken away from them. This means that in future the government would be paying more to loan to borrow money.
The government has to accept that it needs to invest public money in publicly owned assets. Building and owning its own care homes, for example, will save money in the medium term, because the income from the homes will pay for itself.

What's next?

That's been an exciting whirl through the make-believe world of Magicians. What a life they lead, making money appear and disappear, and casting a spell over judges and government officials, so that criminal clients become kindly, well-meaning types who love their grannies.

We've seen 23-year-olds investing vast sums of money on the roulette wheel that's the stock market, and stony-faced men milking former state assets.

Let's move on to a more sedate bunch of people, the Enablers. Let's face it, dictators and oligarchs would be stymied if they had nowhere to safely stash their money.

And if tax havens didn't welcome corporations, they'd have to keep their money under the mattress.

Businesses also need supine regulators who'll only tap them on the wrist for polluting rivers with excrement. And they need a justice system that lets them off when they've committed a crime.

So let's look at the Enablers, starting with the bankers and traders.

3. The Enablers

The Enablers smooth the rich people's path. They create laws, act as regulators, and provide no-questions-asked bank accounts.

Even apparently impartial judges fall under their sway. And it's all legal, not least because the Concierge Class decide what's legal and what isn't. Let's start with the investment bankers.

The next banking crash isn't too far away

Two years after the great banking crash of 2008, the fashion magazine Esquire went to interview some bankers in the City of London. Much had changed. No longer were they the 'champagne-swilling, Porsche-driving, red-braces-wearing, coke-snorting alpha dogs'. Now they were 'battered, bruised and desperate to keep their jobs'. At least, that was the headline.

And yet, as the magazine discovered, the rich were still happy. Investment banker Euan Rellie let reporter Miranda Collinge into a secret:

> "Really rich people love a recession, because they're still rich and everything else is cheap. The restaurants aren't full, so you

can book. You can rent private planes; you can buy yachts cheaply. It's actually not a bad time to be really successful and rich."

And over a decade later, it's truer than ever. "Rich people have never been wealthier, and are spending more than they were before the pandemic," experts told the Business Insider website[111].

And the people who make it happen are the bankers.

Maybe we need some definitions here. Bankers come in two main types: retail and investment. If you can find a local branch of NatWest or Barclays, which they're shutting as fast as they can, you might meet a retail banker, someone who will explain ISAs to your mum.

These *retail banks* are the sensible twin sister. They make money by charging you a fee on your overdraft, on your credit card transactions, and on interest from your car loan. Lots of small, relatively safe transactions, to lots of ordinary consumers.

By contrast, the flashy *investment banking* sister lends big money to corporations, and trades on the stock exchange. Investment bankers can make a lot of money - and if the market crashes they can go bust.

So each has their own role to play.

Most retail bank transactions are mundane, although a minority act as money launderers for the criminal classes and the plutocrats. We'll meet some of those when we talk about the estate agents later in the book.

But the investment bankers cater exclusively for big money. And that's why they're members of the Concierge Class.

In the section on the stock market, we saw how the rich can make money by betting on company shares. But they trade a lot of other things, too. They can gamble on the world's currencies, deciding on which will rise and which will fall.

One month ago, 1,000 South African Rand (ZAR) would have bought you $52. Two weeks later, it was worth $55. So if you'd bought a million ZAR with dollars, and then traded them back, you'd have made $3,000 in two weeks, without getting out of bed.

For the average person working in a shop in Johannesburg, or indeed the rest of the world's eight billion people, the changes in exchange rates are pretty irrelevant. The only people who get really interested are the rich, and the bankers who do the trades for them.

And that's how the investment bankers join the Concierge Class. Let's dig a bit deeper.

Investment banking harms society and ordinary citizens in several ways:

1. Supporting offshore tax evasion

Some of the money laundering we just discussed goes through tax havens. The Panama Papers, a massive leak of 11 million confidential documents from law firm Mossack Fonseca, exposed the use of tax havens by wealthy individuals and corporations to evade taxes and hide assets.

The Panama Papers revealed that a number of major banks were involved in setting up offshore accounts for wealthy individuals and corporations[112]. These banks included:

- **HSBC:** Over 2,300 offshore businesses were linked to the bank.

- **UBS:** UBS was another major player in the offshore banking industry, with over 1,500 businesses.

- **Credit Suisse:** Credit Suisse was also heavily involved in offshore banking, with 1,200 companies.

- **Deutsche Bank:** Deutsche Bank was another major player, with over 800 accounts.

- **Royal Bank of Scotland:** Royal Bank of Scotland had 600 businesses.

- **Barclays:** Barclays had more than 500 offshore companies linked to the bank.

The banks were involved in setting up offshore accounts for a variety of reasons, including:

The former offices of Mossack Fonseca in Panama City. The company is now dissolved. But others will take their place.

- **To help wealthy individuals and corporations avoid taxes:** Offshore accounts can be used to hide assets from tax authorities, allowing individuals and corporations to evade their tax obligations.

- **To launder money:** Offshore accounts can be used to launder money from criminal activities, such as drug trafficking and corruption.

The passports of at least 200 Americans were included in the documents, along with 12 current or former heads of state.

The Panama Papers revelations had an impact on the offshore banking industry, leading to a number of investigations and regulatory reforms. However, offshore banking remains a major industry, and there are still concerns about the use of offshore accounts for illicit purposes.

2. Promoting risky financial products

Investment banks have a history of pushing complex and opaque financial products that can lead to market instability and economic crises. These products, such as derivatives and collateralised debt obligations (CDOs), often involve excessive risk-taking and can magnify losses when markets turn sour.

The 2008 financial crisis was largely caused by the widespread use of these products. They led to the collapse of the housing market and the subsequent financial crisis. It had a devastating impact on the global economy, leading to widespread job losses, business failures and economic hardship.

Almost every major recession and crisis is brought about by the foolish banks. And when it happens, it's due to lax controls.

When Silicon Valley Bank (SVB) collapsed, it was the biggest bank failure in the US since the financial crisis. And as it happened, other countries' systems became vulnerable as investors (call them by what they are: rich people) began to panic.

Then Credit Suisse investors started to pull their money out of that bank, fearing it was likely to go bust. The Swiss Central Bank pumped in SFr50 billion ($57 billion) of guarantees into it. And still its price continued to fall.

Headquarters of Credit Suisse. Who'd have thought they laundered drug money, managed the accounts of Nazis and human traffickers, and destroyed documents relating to Russian oligarchs' loans?

By now investors had pulled SFr100 billion ($114 billion) out of the bank. So the government forced Credit Suisse to accept a take-over by UBS, Switzerland's biggest bank.

UBS demanded Switzerland give it access to a *further* SFr100 billion from the Swiss National Bank, *and* guarantee losses of up to SFr9 billion, *and* write off SFr17 billion of Credit Suisse's government bonds.

This means the biggest Swiss bank is now vastly bigger - and therefore more risky than before. It's holding double the whole annual output of the entire country[113].

Only quick work on the part of US, Swiss and UK governments stopped this pack of dominoes from collapsing.

But just two weeks later, Time magazine glibly said "Economists say this time is different and caution against comparing the bank failures to those of 2008[114]." To other observers, it was a hair-raising moment. Once again bank profits go to shareholders while the state pays for the losses.

3. Lobbying for its own interests

The bankers lobby for policies that favour themselves and thus their wealthy clients, but which increase the risk of another financial crisis.

A long time ago, in the 2008 bank crash, the German government had to bail out its banks at a cost to taxpayers of €70 billion. Ireland, not a big country, had to inject €42 billion. And the UK government (that's you and me) paid out a massive £1.162 trillion (of which £456 billion is still owed[115]).

As a result, governments around the world have sought to increase the amount of cash held by the banks, to ensure that we should never again pay for bank bailouts. The 'Basel 3' plan was designed to increase the amount of cash held by the banks by an average of around 20%. But due to the EU legislators agreeing to numerous exemptions, that number shrank to 4% by 2030 (rising to 7% by 2033).

The banks achieved this by organising 200 meetings with the MEPs responsible for banking reform. Experts from civil society, on the other hand, only had four meetings with MEPs.

The net outcome was a watering down of how much cash banks needs to hold. That allows them to lend more money and therefore make more profit. Reducing the 'cash-to-total loans' ratio means more risk of bank failure, which lead towards another crash. That would mean households and businesses unable to get loans or even cash, which would make a recession much worse. Inevitably, taxpayers would have to bail out the banks again.

4. Supporting bad corporate behaviour

Investment banks tend to prioritise short-term profits over long-term value creation, encouraging unethical business practices. And they aren't fussy about who they lend to.

A report by the International Labour Organisation[116] found that UK banks had been involved in financing the exploitation of labour in the global cocoa industry. The report found that banks had provided loans to companies that were using child labour and forced labour to produce cocoa.

Barclays Bank provides over £3 billion in loans and underwriting to 9 companies whose weapons, components, and military technology are being used by Israel in its attacks on Palestine[117].

The Financial Conduct Authority (FCA) has criticised the UK banks for greenwashing and conflicts of interest on their environmental loans[118]. These are deals that link borrowing costs to sustainability targets. The regulator says polluting companies use these to burnish their reputation without setting meaningful climate goals. Bankers have an incentive to do these deals as they count towards their annual green financing targets, which is sometimes linked to executive pay,

5. Exacerbating environmental problems

Investment banks play a significant role in financing fossil fuel companies and other environmentally harmful industries. Their support for these industries contributes to climate change, pollution, and other environmental threats.

JP Morgan Chase is putting hundreds of millions of dollars into the deforestation business, including massive cattle ranches in the Amazon. Industrial agribusiness makes big profits for the bank, the largest in the US and the sixth largest in the world. The Rainforest Action Network says that Chase has loaned companies half a billion dollars for building cattle ranches directly linked to illegal deforestation in the Amazon[119].

A report by Feedback Global says the UK's 'Big 6' banks (Barclays, HSBC, Santander, Lloyds, NatWest and Standard Chartered) provided at least $77 billion in financing to 55 of the world's largest big livestock and animal feed companies between 2015-2022.

At the time of writing, these banks also owned nearly $1.2 billion in shareholdings in these companies[120]. Meat and dairy accounts for around 14.5% of global greenhouse gas emissions, according to the UN's Food and Agricultural Organization.

6. Money laundering

Money laundering involves moving money made from crime into

untraceable 'shell accounts', then using it to buy property or other assets, which they then sell, so the new cash is clean.

When adjusted for each country's GDP, Britain ranks second only to the United States in levels of money laundering. On average, this illegal activity costs the country's economy more than £100 billion in lost taxes every year[121].

The International Monetary Fund (IMF) estimates that money laundering accounts for 2-5% of global GDP. Globally, this translates into a massive sum. As a result, money laundering has far-reaching socio-economic consequences, in lost support for social welfare and state services.

The question is whether the bankers do sufficient due diligence on the borrower. Anti Money Laundering (AML) processes can be quite straightforward. It starts with a simple Google search.

Mostly the banks just want to know whether the borrower can repay the debt. They'll look at the client's bank balance and say, 'Yes they can.' And so the borrower gets the money. But what if the money has come from unethical or illegal sources? Driven by the lure of profit, many investment bankers ignore its source.

7. Having a cavalier attitude towards charities

Sophie Epstone, who founded and runs Trekstock, a charity that helps people in their 20s and 30s deal with cancer, says Barclays shut down the group's account.

"We believe that we complied with all their requests," she says, "but despite that the account of 15 years was just frozen. No warning, and all our direct debits cancelled just like that.

"You can't imagine the impact of this. We were in the middle of major projects, including upgrading a room at a large cancer hospital, and we were no longer able to pay our commitments or staff."

"I keep getting told that it is the bank's mistake and they rectified it. I then get a letter saying that the matter is ongoing. The account is now back up and working but who is going to compensate us for the lost time and expense?[122]"

It isn't an isolated case. The Guardian newspaper quoted Paul Latham, a Charity Commission director, as saying: "Charities are on the frontline of the current cost of living crisis, providing vital support to people across the country. What we have heard since the open letter was published has further reinforced our view that there are widespread problems in the way banks engage with their charity customers."

8. Closing bank branches

Banks are rapidly removing their branches from small and medium sized towns, leaving small traders and the elderly vulnerable. According to the Office of National Statistics, the number of bank and building society branches in the UK fell by 34% between 2012 and 2021[123].

In the parliamentary constituency when I live, there are no branches of Barclays, HSBC, Nat West or Lloyds Bank. In fact, there are only two banks, both TSBs, in the entire constituency. I like to carry a small quantity of £1 coins, to give alms to the homeless people and beggars I encounter when out walking. I also like to leave a tip for servers in cafes. But without access to cash I'm frequently without coins.

It's understandable why the banks would want to close their branches. People are relying less on both physical cash and traditional bank branches. Cash is used for only 14% of all payments in the UK, according to the trade body, UK Finance[124].

But the independent Access to Cash Review[125] highlighted the risks to millions of people of "sleepwalking" into a cashless society. Research by the Financial Conduct Authority (FCA)[126] found that many depend on cash, especially the digitally excluded, older people, those who are ill or disabled, the poor, and those without a car.

Many small businesses also rely on branches, according to a report from the Federation of Small Businesses[127]. And the Scottish Affairs Select Committee reported that whole communities – especially in rural areas – are affected when the last branch in a community disappears[128].

And post offices have been closing. The number has halved from 25,000 in the mid-1960s to 11,415 now. Only 1% are run by Post Office Ltd.

It epitomises the way the world has moved. Many parts of our society are now managed by large organisations, whose objective is to make money. They don't have to pay for any costs that don't appear on their profit and loss account. Such costs, so-called 'externalities' (in this case, anxiety, stress, time wasting and transport costs), are born by individuals and the welfare state.

Post offices are mostly run by small businesses, which are liable to close.

Once again, it's the Concierge Class who make it happen

Anyone with managerial responsibility in an investment bank bears some responsibility for the problems caused by bankers.

That might come as a surprise to some individuals who, on a day-to-day basis, simply procure money for businesses and rich people.

But bankers are salespeople. They have to find and win over clients - people who want to sell part or all of a company, buy a business, or get more capital. So investment bankers do a lot of schmoozing and networking, working hard to win the prospect's trust. They have to be likeable.

And in doing so, they inevitably ignore the problems the client's organisation causes. Does the client treat its workforce well? What about the pollution it causes? Is it simply a rent-seeker, a business that merely makes money by milking an asset, without giving anything back?

Do its products or services benefit its users? Here's one company: "We have strong foundations, and a strategy for accelerated growth. We are transforming our business to build a sustainable enterprise of the future." That's BAT, the cigarette company. Tobacco kills 76,000 people in the UK every year, according to the NHS[129]. It may be the worst case I can think of, but most businesses are exploitative in one way or another, some more so than others.

Does the business pay its fair share of taxes? Can it demonstrate a serious commitment to making the world a better place? And if so, what percentage of its profits are allocated to that?

In short, investment bankers should refuse to work for bad companies and the greedy rich. "That's an impossible task," I hear you say. "Bankers don't have that kind of mentality." And that's my argument, precisely. The Concierge Class is amoral and unthinking. And because of that, they do damage.

What's to be done?

As I've said, bankers are responsible for the ills they cause. Most of them wouldn't recognise that statement because it's not part of their mindset. But it's true.

The finance industry plays a pivotal role in rigging society in favour of the wealthy, creating pollution, the climate crisis and environmental damage.

Bankers help to create low-paid jobs, harm many who live in the developing world, and cause pain for everyone but the very few 'winners'.

The biggest responsibility, meanwhile, lies with government. There's a constant tussle between regulators who want to reduce the risks that bank lending poses, and the bankers and right-wingers who want to be free to do what they want - which means lending to the max.

It's therefore imperative that the world's regulators **keep a tight grip on banks' liquidity** - how much cash they have in the tills to cope with future losses.

Time after time, whenever the restrictions on banks are lifted or oversight is reduced, there's a crisis of potentially catastrophic proportions. In recent years it's been 1983, 1975, 1980, 1990 and 2008[130]. It won't be long before the next one.

The regulators need to have **strong audits** to stop banks like Credit Suisse from getting involved scandals that included (deep breath) "money laundering for Japanese gangs and Bulgarian drug traffickers, kickbacks in Mozambique, tax evasion in the United States, spying on former employees in Switzerland, dealing with African dictators, and jobs-for-business-deals with Chinese officials in Hong Kong[131]."

Why legislation fails us

Back in 1862, Jeremy Bentham called for 'the greatest amount of good for the greatest number of people'. That's a pretty fundamental idea, but one that's somewhat lacking in our legislation.

He also called for social welfare, the separation of church and state, freedom of expression, equal rights for women, the right to divorce, and the decriminalising of homosexual acts. He wanted to abolish slavery, capital punishment and physical punishment, including that of children.

But back to 'the greatest good for the greatest number'. How do we achieve that? Answer: through legislation.

The government has the over-archiving job of achieving that. Its job is to create a just society, through means such winners as fair taxation and decent public services.

And this boils down to politicians creating laws that benefit the majority of the people.

So it feels really strange that we live in a country where two million people go without food for at least one day a month. Britain's five-year-olds are among the shortest in Europe, due to malnutrition[132][133]. And people can be made homeless in 30 days.

So let's take a look at how this is being caused by politicians and the other members of the Concierge Class involved in government action: the civil servants and special advisers (Spads).

Between them, they pass pro-capitalist legislation in several ways:

1. Cutting taxes
2. Reducing state spending

3. Deregulating industries
4. Privatising state assets
5. Promoting 'free trade'
6. Hampering trade unions
7. Preventing the creation of council housing
8. Giving financial benefits to corporations and the rich

1. Cutting taxes

Right-wing politicians like to introduce tax cuts, which typically benefit the rich. They say it stimulates growth.

But there's no evidence that UK growth increases when taxes fall. This is shown in the Figure below, which compares the growth in Gross Domestic Product (GDP) with taxation as a percentage of GDP over 30 years. The correlation between these two measures is negligible (-0.10), indicating that they're unrelated[134].

Just to re-phrase the economics jargon: when taxes go up or down, it has no effect on output.

Additionally, work by the LSE shows that reducing taxes specifically for the rich has no impact on growth. It examined[135] the effect of tax cuts for the rich on inequality, growth and unemployment across 18 OECD countries over a period of 50 years. It showed that reducing taxes for the rich produces higher rates of inequality in the long run, but has no effect on economic growth.

2. Reducing state spending

Right-wing politicians like to reduce state spending, believing that government expenditure distorts the free market and hampers corporations.

We examine this proposition in more detail in Chapter 4, The Pushers, where we discuss the opinions of economists. For now, here are just a few bullet points about state spending:

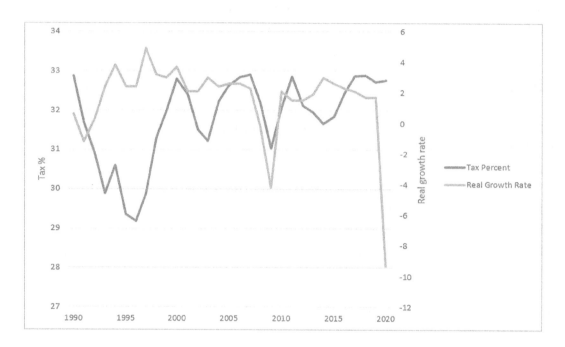

Economic Growth doesn't correlate with taxation. UK 1990 to 2019. Source: Office of National Statistics and OECD. Acknowledgement: Paul Whiteley, LSE/University of Essex.

- **Cuts to benefits increase poverty for vulnerable individuals and families.** The Institute for Fiscal Studies found that the number of children living in poverty in the UK increased by *half a million* between 2010 and 2015. The cuts to Universal Credit were a major factor in this increase[136].

- **Reducing public services disproportionately affects low-income communities.** For instance, cuts to public transport make it more difficult for people without cars to access essential services such as jobs, education and healthcare.

- **Government spending on infrastructure, education and research stimulates economic activity and creates jobs.** For example, increased funding for training leads to a more skilled workforce.

3. Deregulation

Deregulation isn't always a bad thing. It would be hard nowadays to imagine the UK having only one telecommunications company, BT, and specifically one that was owned by the state.

The proponents of deregulation say it leads to more competition, which creates more efficient businesses, so prices fall, and consumers benefit.

But when politicians deregulate industries, it often causes standards to fall, whether your bus service is less frequent, or your food having more additives.

And often deregulation simply doesn't make sense. Trains and buses were traditionally operated by a company either wholly owned by the state, or one that was licensed to provide the service, either with or without a subsidy.

A deregulated bus service run by Stagecoach. The Souter family that owns it is worth £730 million.

But in recent years, many such markets have been deregulated, by paying the operator with the lowest bid to provide the service with little regard to its quality.

In 1986, the UK's bus services outside London were deregulated to open the market to competition from private operators. No licence was required.

Local authorities were no longer allowed to subsidise fares. National and local bus operations were sold to private owners. Local authorities could only fund concessionary fares, and they could only tender for services that private operators didn't provide[137].

Since then, as governments have recognised the mess they created, legislation has gradually moved back towards putting back the system to where it was. But funding for buses in England is almost £400 million a year lower than it was ten years ago, according to the Campaign for Better Transport[138], causing major difficulties for those without a car.

A quarter of all regional bus routes is run by Stagecoach, a company whose behaviour has been described as 'predatory, deplorable and against the public interest.'

Many markets are natural monopolies, so opening them up to competition doesn't make sense. The British Royal Mail is charged with delivering letters to any address in the country, from Land's End to the most remote Scottish island home.

When deregulation allowed competitors into the market, the private firms weren't required to carry the same obligations. And taking revenue from the Royal Mail reduced the revenue that it previously used to subsidise the unprofitable distant deliveries.

The issue applies to all kinds of policy making. The main argument used by the advocates of Brexit, whereby UK voted to leave the EU, was that it would reduce the amount of regulation imposed by the EU on businesses. As a result, they said, the country would flourish.

But several years later, two-thirds of the British public thought Brexit had damaged the economy. Even among Leave voters, only one in five think the change has been positive.

Making life easy for businesses can have unexpected negative effects. In the 1980s, both the UK and US governments decided to deregulate the financial services industry, in the interests of fostering competition. They dismantled the legislation that had separated investment and retail banks, which had been put in place after the crisis of the Hungry Thirties (1929-1939) following a banking crisis.

Removing the protections meant the failure of an investment bank could put ordinary consumers at risk of losing all their savings.

And sure enough, that's what happened. In 2008 the UK government had to spend £107 billion to prop up the Royal Bank of Scotland and Lloyds Banking Group. And then in 2010, it had to fund Northern Rock and Bradford & Bingley (another £37 billion) as they headed towards bankruptcy. Total guarantees added up to over £1 trillion at the time of peak support[139].

Why do politicians forget the lessons of history so soon? Answer: because the Concierge Class do the bidding of corporations and the wealthy - people who want to loosen the regulations in order to maximise their profits.

4. Privatisation

A close cousin of deregulation is privatisation.

For right-wing politicians, it's a matter of faith that private businesses are more efficient that state-run ones. As a result they like to sell state businesses to the private sector, often at a big discount.

Yet it often leads to higher prices and lower quality services for the public.

That's because private companies prioritise making profits, which often means they cut corners and let standards slip. If the newly-private business fails, the government often has to clear up the mess. This is known as 'privatising profits and socialising losses'.

Sold off by the government, Royal Mail, whom we mentioned above, has paid out over £884 million to shareholders in the last three years. And in the last year alone, three of the top directors were paid nearly £4 million between them, with company profits of more than £750m lost to the public purse[140].

Water was once considered a public health necessity, rather than a commodity. But governments gradually reduced funding for the water authorities, and stopped them from borrowing money to fund investment. This resulted in lower standards of water cleanliness. The authorities were then privatised in 1987.

Most of the English water companies are now owned by private equity firms which engage in tax avoidance and load the businesses with debt[141]. Currently, a majority of people want water, energy, rail, buses, Royal Mail and the NHS to be run in the public sector[142].

5. Promoting 'free trade'

Free trade aims to remove import tariffs. This makes it easier for countries to trade with each other, and lets corporations make more stuff in low-wage nations. It's a purer form of capitalism, says its adherents. But while Western consumers have got the benefit of cheaper goods, workers have lost much of their well-paid and secure work.

Free trade creates more jobs in the developing world, but they're often sweat shop roles (for instance Bangladesh), made in authoritarian countries (China), or where there is with weak protection for employees (92% of countries in the Americas violate the right to strike[143]). The profits are usually made by multinational corporations, whose profits go either home to the West or to a tax haven.

6. Hampering the trade unions

The United Kingdom has the most restrictive anti-union laws in Europe. Between 1980 and 1993, Conservative governments passed six pieces of legislation limiting unions' power to go on strike[144]. Picketing has been restricted, political action banned, and losses solidarity strikes outlawed. Unofficial strikes have been made illegal, meaning spontaneous action can't happen, thus handing still more power to the employers.

Additional Acts, such as the Trade Union Act 2016, restricted industrial action still further. As a result, the number of days lost to strikes plummeted, due to legal impediments.

But productivity fell compared with pre-1980 UK levels and those attained by competitor countries, indicating that strong trade unions don't inhibit productivity growth but quite the reverse[145].
For a ballot to be legally valid, at last 50% of workers must vote. Thus if 100 workers are eligible to vote, and only 49 turn out for the vote, workers can't take industrial action even if all 49 vote in favour.

Given that workers such as train drivers or nurses are dispersed all over the country, are working on different times and days, and aren't necessarily engaged with their union, the difficulty of getting a 50% turnout is immense.

If the dispute involves workers in 'important' public services, the vote has to reach a 40% support among *all* workers eligible to vote, as well as the 50% turnout threshold.

So if 100 workers are eligible to vote, at least 50 have to vote, and at least 40 have to vote in favour. If 50 voted and 39 voted in support, it wouldn't be legal to take industrial action, even though the vast majority of voters wanted it.

A union has to give the employer two weeks' notice of the intended ballot, one measure among many which requires extra administrative hurdles for the union.

A union must elect an official supervisor for its picket, who has to give the police their name, contact details and the location of the picket. On the picket itself they must be easily identifiable (such as through wearing an armband), and must carry a letter of authorisation from the union to be shown to employers on request.

63% of Britons supported walkouts by health care workers. But strikes are difficult to run.

So a picket could be declared illegal if any supervisor slips up, by forgetting the letter or mislaying it[146].

In periods of strike action involving sectors such as paramedics, border security and rail workers, the UK government can set minimum service levels. This limits the right of a workforce to go on strike[147].

In such case, employers can issue a 'work notice' to unions, setting out who must work during a strike. Employees could then be sacked if they refuse to work.

Employers can sue a union for losses if they don't take 'reasonable steps' to ensure work notices are adhered to. This means unions will be required to actively encourage their members to break their own strikes.

The UK government says the legislation is intended to protect the lives and livelihoods of the public by providing access to certain services during strikes. Opponents see it as a ruse to make strikes less effective.

Unions have their flaws. But they even up the unequal balance of power between the employer and the workforce. And while strikes can be disruptive to the public, they're sometimes the only action a workforce can take when all attempts to gain agreement have failed.

The politicians have created these restrictive laws to undermine the power of the employees, and they're in marked contrast to more progressive European countries where the freedom to combine is accepted.

7. Preventing the creation of council housing

In 1980, the then conservative Prime Minister Margaret Thatcher knew that home owners were more likely to be conservative voters, and so she created the 'right to buy' legislation, which allowed council house renters to buy their house at up to 50% off, and get a 100% mortgage to pay for it. As people said, 'You'd be made not to do so'.

Under that legislation, two million homes have been sold. But 40% of Overall them are now rented privately, as the owners bought bigger houses or died.

The law discourages councils from building new social homes. That's because they'd have to sell them at up to a 50% discount, and keep only one-third of the sale price.

3.8 million people are on the UK's waiting list for social housing, according to housing.org.uk.

19% of the population now lives in a private rented home, which means they could be made homeless if they lose their job or the owner decides to sell the property. There are now 1.6 million households on housing waiting lists.

With fewer homes, local authorities now have to put tenants into landlords' houses, at much greater cost.

And as the New Economics Foundation has pointed out[148], the loss of the more affluent tenants - those who could afford to buy their house - has added to the stigma of council housing.

There's now a housing crisis, brought about with the connivance of those members of the Concierge Class who voted for this policy, and have since failed to change it.

8. Giving financial benefits to corporations

The UK government plans to give £2.2 billion of new money to the private water companies to 'accelerate their investment' on infrastructure to 'tackle pollution and increase the country's water resilience'[149].

This is despite the fact that these companies are profit-making organisations, charged with the simple job of providing clean water. The same businesses paid out £1.4 billion in dividends in the latest year, up from £540 million the previous year, despite rising household bills and a wave of public criticism over sewage outflows[150].

Oh, and there's another £469 million of state investment to "develop new large-scale water infrastructure, including transfers, recycling, and reservoirs". Again, this is money going to private corporations.

In short, the state is handing public assets over to private companies, and then paying for the mess this creates.

And members of the Concierge Class are responsible for that.

More than just legislation

But it isn't just about legislation, which can be debated in public, and is therefore at least transparent.

There's also the problem of hidden influence. Politicians can easily get too close to corporations and the rich, particularly if they're lobbied, or are politically sympathetic to them. Two key issues are: engaging in corrupt practices, and benefiting from the revolving door. We'll look at each in turn.

1. Corruption and 'Crony Capitalism'

Get too close to the rich, and you can find yourself doing them favours.

Corruption has many negative consequences for democracy. It leads to a loss of public trust in government, undermines the rule of law, and leads to bad decisions by government.

- **The PPE Medpro scandal:** The UK government awarded a £100 million contract for personal protective equipment to PPE Medpro, a company with no prior experience in the sector, and which had been in existence for only 30 days before being awarded the contract.

  The company was owned by Lady Mone, a Conservative peer who had donated money to the Conservative Party. The contract was awarded without a competitive tender, and there were allegations that Lady Mone had used her connections to secure it.

- **The Greensill Capital scandal:** The government awarded a series of lucrative contracts to Greensill Capital, a financial services company with close ties to David Cameron, the former Prime Minister. The contracts were awarded without proper scrutiny. And the company then went bust.

- **The awarding of peerages:** It's alleged that the government has awarded peerages in exchange for donations to the Conservative Party. For example Peter Cruddas, a Conservative donor, was awarded a peerage after donating £3 million to the party.

And too many MPs seem to have their snouts in the trough:

- Over the past decade, financial institutions that hired a former UK Chancellor benefited on average from a 59% increase in meetings with government departments. And almost three quarters of all past and present Bank of England decision-makers have held roles in private finance[151].

- Financial institutions and individuals closely tied to the sector collectively spent £2.3 million directly on MPs throughout 2020 and 2021, partly as payment for second jobs and speeches, and partly as donations, gifts and hospitality.

- The same institutions and individuals donated £15.3 million to political parties throughout 2020 and 2021.

- A fifth of peers in the House of Lords have registered paid positions at financial institutions, including over half of peers on the committee responsible for investigating matters related to economics and finance.

2. The Revolving Door

The 'revolving door' phenomenon, where individuals move from high-level government positions into lucrative corporate roles, and vice versa, can lead to conflicts of interest and undue influence.

Every single former Chancellor of the Exchequer in the past 40 years has gone on to take up paid positions in the financial sector after leaving public office.

1. Former Chancellor **George Osborne** was appointed as a senior advisor to BlackRock, the world's largest asset management firm. His move to a company with significant financial interests in the UK meant questions were asked about the propriety of his new role.

2. **Tony Blair**, a former Prime Minister, has done extensive consulting work for JP Morgan, a global investment bank. His involvement in securing contracts for JP Morgan with governments raised questions about his exploitation of privileged access gained during his time in office.

3. **Barclays Bank** recruited former senior officials from the Financial Conduct Authority (FCA), the UK's financial regulator. Some saw this as an attempt by Barclays to gain insider knowledge and influence regulatory decisions. They also snagged Katharine Braddick CB (Companion of the Order of the Bath), former Director General of Financial Services at HM Treasury as Group Head of Strategic Policy and Advisor to the Group CEO at Barclays Bank.

4. Accountancy giant **Deloitte** has hired many former government officials in recent years, Margaret Hodge MP accused Dave Hartnett, the second most senior official at HM Revenue and Customs (HMRC), of having "no shame" after taking a job as an adviser to accountancy giant Deloitte.

These examples highlight the revolving door phenomenon and the potential for conflicts of interest when government officials and politicians move into corporate roles.

The electoral system

As the figure below shows, it took 866,000 votes in the 2019 election to elect one Green Party MP. But the SNP needed only 26,000 votes. Meanwhile, 644,000 people voted for the Brexit party without gaining a simple MP.

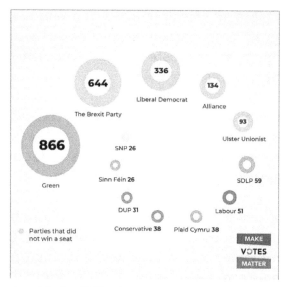

A widely differing number of votes are needed to elect one MP from different parties.

In short, the voting system doesn't accurately translate parties' votes into seats.

Proportional representation ensures it takes the same number of votes to elect an MP, irrespective of which party they belong to.

The UK's 'first past the post' electoral system favours the right-wing, as do all majority voting systems. In such cases, the governments are always more right-wing than the voters.

Proportional representation, by contrast, more accurately mirrors the voters' views, and is not biased to left or right[152]. If it were introduced in the UK, right-wing parliaments would be elected less often.

The role of the Concierge Class

As we've seen, strategies to cut government spending and boost the private sector end up benefiting corporations and the rich, at the expense of the rest of is.

And all of this is done by the Concierge Class, in this case the politicians, their advisers and the civil servants.

But it's not just the legislation that causes the problems. There are also the 'sins of omission', the things politicians *don't* do.

These sins are everywhere you look, with queues at food banks, the waiting lists for a hospital appointment, and millions of people living in expensive and insecure private rented housing.

Much of the support for the vulnerable has been swept away, and again it's the Concierge Class that's implemented this.

When they cut taxes for the wealthy and corporations, they reduce the amount of revenue needed for essential services, such as education, healthcare and infrastructure. It leads to a decline in the quality of life for everyone.

And finally, the extent to which *civil servants* are culpable needs to be debated. Most would say they're merely 'following orders', which was the claim made by the servants of fascism in the 1940s.

As we'll see throughout this book, and especially in the Culpability Index at the end, we all have to reflect on the degree of our involvement with the systems that facilitate inequality. We need to understand our complicity, and decide how to stand up against corporations and the wealthy.

What's to be done?

The root problem is that many citizens no longer trust the mainstream social democratic parties, knowing they haven't solved the problems of precarious housing, insecure jobs and stagnating wages.

Far-right politicians take advantage of this, positioning the centrists as focused on environmentalism, trans rights and support for ethnic minorities.

It's therefore up to the progressive politicians to deal with the real economic problems that most people encounter - everyone, that is, but the Concierge Class who are protected from worry by secure jobs and homes.

This means introducing legislation that supports the majority, rather than the rich and the middle classes. We need laws to reduce precarity in jobs and housing.

For secure housing we need legally-controlled, **affordable, long-term tenancies**. This requires legislation and a massive programme of **house building by the state**, not the house builders.

For secure jobs, we need legislation to make it less attractive for corporations to move jobs to **low-wage economies**, laws to **protect 'gig' economy workers**, and a **ban on zero-hours contracts**.

Politicians in government need to **question the benefits of free trade**. They must ensure that **corporations and the wealthy pay their fair share of tax**, including a land or wealth tax. As the graph below shows, the UK has led the way to the bottom in corporation tax. But as the IPPR report points out[153], cutting corporation tax hasn't shifted the UK from having low rates of investment and productivity.

Procurement laws should be amended to prevent failed private sector suppliers from bidding for new government contracts.

We should introduce **proportional representation**, to ensure every vote matters, amend parliament's second chamber, and change the discredited honours' system.

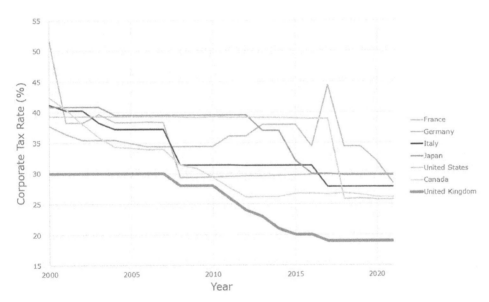

The fall in corporate tax rates. Source: IRPPR

And, as individuals, we need to hold politicians accountable for their actions, demand they represent the interests of all people, and require them to uphold the highest standards of ethical conduct.

Heaven is a tax haven

The tropical breezes blow through palm trees as billionaires sip cocktails on the white sand beaches of the Cayman Islands (population: 45,000). But this Caribbean paradise is more than just sunshine and paradise - it's one of the biggest tax havens in the world.

Tax havens allow companies and the rich to stash their money in shell companies and secretive trusts, avoiding billions in taxes back home.

From Bermuda to Switzerland, tax havens provide a financial underworld where rich people put their money beyond the reach of tax authorities. Shell companies conceal the true owners, and creative accounting reduces the apparent profits. Tax haven abuse has become standard practice for the tax dodgers.

The sums are eye-popping. Over $32 trillion currently resides in tax havens, much of it illicit[154]. And more streams in every year.

The losses are staggering. Unpaid taxes linked to havens could total $500 billion annually[155]. Globally, economists estimate trillions are siphoned away. And all the while, ordinary taxpayers face higher rates to fill public budget holes.

Coyly known as 'low-tax jurisdictions', tax havens in places like the Marshall Islands, and the British Virgin Isles charge little or no taxes plus ironclad secrecy[156].
And despite being on the EU black list as non-cooperative for tax purposes[157], they're approved by the UK's stock exchange[158]. That makes it so much easier to launder your money by routing it via these tax havens.

But exposure looms. Leaks have already peeled back the curtain on secret tax deals and shell companies created by accounting giants like PwC and the dodgy law firm Mossack Fonseca[159].

Examples of tax havens

The Caymans have over 600 banks and trust companies[160] cementing its status as the premier haven for hot money.
Officials demur when probed about dubious money flows, citing privacy laws to reject enquiries[161].

Estimates suggest two-thirds of the world's hedge funds now call the Caymans home[162] – not for the snorkelling, but for sheltering wealth far from tax authorities' reach.

There are great beaches in the Caymans tax haven. But not much else. It's no bigger than Bognor. Almost no theatre. Dull scenery, apart from, yes, the beaches. Life isn't cheap: fish fingers are £8.50. Healthcare and social services are limited.

Switzerland, meanwhile, is the gold standard for ultra-private banking. For generations, discreet numbered accounts, Swiss secrecy laws, and corporate-friendly cantonal tax incentives have attracted legitimate and illicit capital alike. Despite the recent erosion of its bank secrecy model, assets in Swiss banks still exceed $2.4 trillion[163].

While the days of total bank secrecy have passed, Switzerland still offers unparalleled opportunities for the wealthy to quietly minimise their tax burdens.

There are 33,000 shell companies in Switzerland, according to a survey[164] by NGO Public Eye. Geneva is the leading location, with one letterbox firm for every 37 citizens in the canton. Under pressure, the Swiss government is trying to introduce transparency, but it's coming up against obstructions.

Switzerland's lawyers are fighting back, saying the draft law is guilty of over-reach and is vague. Attorney-client privilege is not defined clearly enough, they say.

And so much paperwork would be involved! The corporate, commercial and real estate lawyers, "will face an unbearable amount of new, very complicated and time-consuming compliance work," complains Miguel Oural, chair of the Geneva Bar Association.

The government has also underestimated the difficulty of implementing and enforcing the law, according to Geneva Lawyers' Supervisory Board which oversees Geneva's 2,700 lawyers, but has fewer than 10 staff.

"The canton needs to give us the resources," says Shahram Dini, a lawyer and its president. "Either the controls are done by us and the canton gives us the money, or the canton refuses and a federal inspector comes and does this," he says. "It's the choice between bad or worse."

And if you're a member of Asia's billionaire class, Singapore has emerged as the tax avoidance haven of choice.

It charges little or no tax on capital gains or property, offers rock-bottom corporate rates around 8.5%, and ensures rigorous bank secrecy[165],

How the wealthy hide their fortunes offshore

Few examples shine light on this underworld like the Panama Papers, leaked documents that exposed how the rich use shell companies and offshore accounts to dodge billions in taxes[166].

An anonymous whistle blower handed over 11.5 million documents, totalling 2.6 terabytes of data, detailing financial and legal information on 214,488 offshore entities.

They came from the office of Panamanian law firm Mossack Fonseca, one of the biggest managers of offshore tax schemes.

The Panama Papers revealed how iconic business figures like Jackie Chan and people close to Vladimir Putin have used networks of anonymous companies in places like the British Virgin Islands or Switzerland to disguise wealth and avoid taxes[167].

Some shell companies existed only on paper, while others engaged in sham transactions to get money offshore. Mossack Fonseca maintained a clandestine portfolio of over 200,000 of these façade companies for the wealthy to mask their assets[168].

Even fictitious billionaire names like Harry Potter and John Grisham were given offshore companies, hinting at the lengths individuals will go to obscure their earnings[169].

Real billionaires like the Rothchild family had dozens of trusts and offshore accounts[170]. It's estimated the Panama Papers exposed over $2 trillion worth of anonymous offshore wealth[171].

How billionaires exploit offshore trusts

Casino billionaire Sheldon Adelson, who died in 2021, used foreign trusts and accounts to avoid his tax obligations. At one point, Adelson had at least nine offshore trusts and over 30 offshore company holdings[172].

In total, these offshore trusts allowed Adelson to direct over $7.9 billion into opaque foreign investments to avoid US tax obligations[173].

Had this income been reported as ordinary investment gains, it would have been taxed at over $2 billion.

Richard Covey, a lawyer who pioneered the trick, reckons these tax shelters may have cost the federal government more than $100 billion since 2000.

Adelson isn't alone among the billionaire class in exploiting offshore trusts and accounts to lessen tax bills. By one estimate, offshore wealth now surpasses $21 trillion among the globe's richest individuals[174].

James Simons contributed $2.1 billion to charity, and was the sixth-largest benefactor of U.S. political causes, giving more than $26 million, nearly all to Democrats.

James Simmons

But at the same time he shirked paying his fair share of taxes.

Bloomberg puts Simons' net worth at $15.7 billion. But because Simons' trust had accumulated so much money, and for so long, it was incurring a multibillion-dollar U.S. tax liability nearing 80 percent, according to an accounting document found in the files of offshore law firm Appleby.

This includes more than $200 million in interest charges for the delayed payment of taxes.

Renaissance Technologies, which he founded and which became one of the world's biggest hedge funds, agreed to pay the USA's IRS £7 *billion* in unpaid taxes[175], after a decade-long fight.

Legal but divisive

Tax havens exist in a contentious grey zone. Their defenders claim that charging no corporate taxes is the right of any country, and encourages investment.

However, critics argue financial secrecy and tax avoidance deny other countries revenue and undermine fairness[176].

This debate intertwines issues of transparency, privacy, public budgets, and inequality.

Supporters contend tax havens offer jurisdictions for creating legitimate, regulated trusts and companies, not just tax dodges.

However, the Pandora Papers exposed how prominent politicians like Tony Blair and King Abdullah II secretly owned houses and yachts via offshore companies in these havens[177].

And critics highlight how tax havens enable money laundering and corruption.

Who's to blame?

The big four accountancy practices have offices in 43 of the 53 tax havens. KPMG has 80 offices in tax havens, while Deloitte has 75. Each of the big four has over two offices in each of the tax havens where they have an office[178].

Below, for example, are PwC's offices in the British Virgin Islands, the world's largest tax haven.

And for every accountant in a tax haven, there are many more in New York,

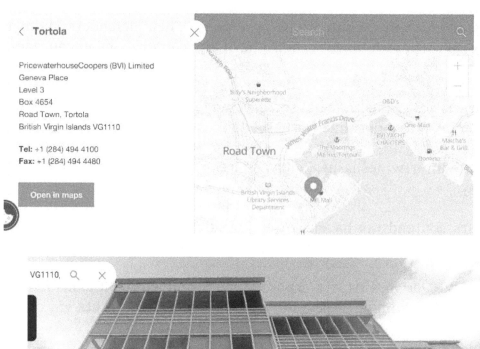

PwC's offices in the British Virgin Islands tax haven.

London and every other major city in the world, chatting to their colleagues in the tax havens.

Richard Murphy of Funding the Future, formerly Tax Research, appeals to the accountants saying:

> "My challenge to every partner in the Big Four firms (and those accountants and auditors outside that group that copy them), is ... to ask them what are they going to do to end the threat to democracy that their firm's operations in tax havens represent?
>
> If these firms shut down their offshore operations, then this problem would be well on its way to being solved. So why won't they take that necessary action?"

What's to be done?

1. The accountancy practices should, as Richard Murphy says, shut down their tax haven offices.

2. Accountants should refuse to help clients stash their money in these tax evasion hideouts.

3. Governments and supranational organisations should work for greater transparency in the tax havens. We need to know how which individuals and businesses are storing their money there, and how it was earned.

How central banks support the wealthy

The Bank of England is a Goldilocks institution. It doesn't like the economy to be too hot or too cold.

But to guide the economy it has very few tools at its disposal. It can lower or raise interest rates, which should boost or reduce economic activity. And it can increase or lower the amount of money it lends to the banks, for the same reasons.

But it doesn't care whether these actions harm ordinary people. That isn't part of its brief. Or it doesn't see that as an issue to be addressed. It's only what's good for 'the economy'.

And this goes to the heart of how the country is run. It's managed by the Concierge Class, for the benefit of corporations and the rich, as I hope to show.

Look at the people who work at the Bank of England. The average salary is £62,189. Seen from the perspective of someone who works in McDonald's, it's a lovely amount. But it doesn't get the bank's employees into the 1% of earners. For that, they'd need £183,000 a year.

The Bank of England. People from the Celtic regions of the country might ponder why it's not called the Bank of Britain?

But it puts them squarely into the Concierge Class, far removed from the concerns of the average person. And they're comforted by an annual bonus of up to £22,500 a year, on top of their salary.

And then there's their attitudes. On a podcast, Huw Pill, the Bank of England's chief economist, said: "Someone (by which he means ordinary people) needs to accept that they're worse off and stop trying to maintain their real spending power by bidding up prices ... through higher wages[179]."

He went on: "We're all worse off, and we all have to take our share." This from a man who earns £190,000 a year, and allegedly lives in a £1.5 million home in London.

He also seemed to misunderstood that, at the time of writing, inflation was caused not by wage increases but external events, specifically Russia's invasion of Ukraine, and the ensuing huge increase in the price of fuel, accompanied by massive rises in food and almost everything else.

The fact that ordinary people are the most vulnerable to price rises, and would be desperate for their wages to keep pace, was clearly not on his mind.

In other words, when times are hard, he thinks the poor will have to suffer the most, for the benefit of everyone else.

Amanda Gearing of the GMB union, said it was "absolutely outrageous to be honest, asking some of our lowest paid workers in this country not to take a pay increase when inflation is so high".

"People can't afford to live, they're not able to pay their rent or put food on the table," she said[180].

How to manage the economy

As the UK's central bank, the Bank of England's job is to maintain the country's financial stability. That means four things:

1. Mostly, it's about inflation, which it hates. That's its priority.

2. When the economy is in trouble and at risk of recession, it will grudgingly seek to boost the economy.

3. At a time of real crisis, it will put cash into the coffers of the retail

banks' (NatWest etc), to stop them going bust, and to encourage them to lend money to companies and individuals.

4.   And finally, it acts as a regulator, for example by ensuring that the retail banks have enough cash to cover their bad loans.

Deflating the economy

Imagine the economy is roaring, and people feel good. There are plenty of jobs and businesses are investing. But prices are rising. Things are costing more. So the central bank decides to deflate the economy.
It seeks to reduce the supply of money or make it more expensive to borrow money. This includes:

- Raising interest rates
- Selling government bonds
- Increasing reserve requirements for banks

These actions make it more difficult for businesses and consumers to borrow money, which can lead to a decrease in spending and investment. This can slow down economic growth and lead to lower prices.

Deflation affects the wealthy and the poor differently

Inflation hurts the poor and benefits the rich. That's because the cost of staples like bread and rice increases during inflation, which hurts the poor most.

Wealthy people own their home, and so they're protected from interest rate rises. But inflation causes landlords to increase rents, which hurts the poor.

While deflation can sometimes reduce inflation, it also has a number of negative effects on the economy, including:

- Increased unemployment
- Lower wages
- Reduced business profits
- Increased debt burdens
- Decline in asset values

These effects disproportionately harm the poor, who are more likely to be unemployed, have lower incomes, and are more indebted.

Here are some specific examples of how deflation can affect the wealthy and the poor:

- **Unemployment:** Deflation leads to increased unemployment as businesses cut back on spending and investment. This disproportionately harms the poor, who are more likely to work in low-wage jobs that are more easily eliminated.

- **Lower wages:** Deflation leads to lower wages as businesses try to reduce their costs. This further hurts the poor who, as we said, are more likely to work in low-wage jobs.

- **Reduced business profits:** Deflation tends to reduce business profits, as businesses sell fewer of their goods and services, or have to cut their prices. This can make it more difficult for businesses to stay afloat. But it hurts small firms harder than multinationals, because the small guys have fewer ways to cut back, and less money in the bank.

- **Increased debt:** To make ends meet, both companies and the poor will take on loans. When they can't afford to repay the loans, there will be increased bankruptcies and bailiffs knocking on the door.

- **Decline in asset prices:** Deflation causes a decline in the value of assets, such as the price of shares and houses. This is more likely to affect the wealthy, who own a larger share of assets. But if you had £1.2 million worth of shares and now they're worth only £1 million, it's not as though you can't afford to buy your child a new pair of shoes.

Overall, deflation can have a number of negative effects on the economy, and these effects disproportionately harm the poor.

So, curbing inflation is a good thing. But deflating the economy to bringing down inflation hurts ordinary people.

Here's how the central bank boosts the economy

At other times, the economy is doing badly. This can happen because:

- There's a big increase in the cost of raw materials, or energy prices.
- Or the economy has been booming, so people and companies have been taking on debt to buy things. Then the markets decide shares and houses are over-priced, get scared, and things go into reverse. People find they're overstretched and can't pay their debts.

There's a downward spiral. Time for the bank to leave the bat cave.

There are two things a central bank can boost, to get things moving:

It can cut interest rates: When the economy is doing badly, the central bank usually cuts interest rates. This makes it cheaper for businesses to borrow money. Supposedly this should lead to increased investment and job creation, which benefits the economy as a whole. However, it primarily benefits wealthy people and corporations, who are more likely to own businesses and assets that will appreciate in value when interest rates are low.

It can increase the amount of activity in the economy by making it easier

to lend and borrow: The bank can increase the amount of money - cash and balances in bank accounts - in circulation. These are the assets that households and businesses use to make payments. It does this by buying government bonds back from commercial banks, and by lowering the interest rate it charges commercial banks for loans.

When the economy is weak, businesses are reluctant to invest and consumers are hesitant to spend. This can lead to a recession. By increasing the money supply, central banks seek to make it easier for businesses to borrow money and for consumers to spend. This boosts economic activity and thus helps to create jobs.

But in practice, when it's easier to borrow, the rich scramble to buy more shares, houses and land, which pushes up their price, making it hard for ordinary people to buy them. And it can lead to inflation, which erodes the value of savings and hurts low-income households.

Pumping money into the banks

Imagine that things are really bad. Interest rates are near zero, economic growth is stalled, and businesses are failing. Faced with this problem, the bank can't reduce interest rates any further.

What it can do, however, is to pump money into the banks. That will stop them going bust. And because they have cash, they will lend more to people and businesses.

The central bank sometimes does this though what it calls quantitative easing (QE).

QE is the most obscure term I've ever come across. If I was prone to conspiracy theories, I'd assume it was designed to obfuscate.

But anyway, the central bank buys back government bonds from the commercial banks that hold them. This puts cash into the banks' tills.

Now flooded with cash, the banks can lend businesses money. It's supposed to boost investment. But QE boosts the value of assets such as houses and company values, and pushes up stock market prices. This increases inequality, as the wealthy own a disproportionate share of houses, companies, and company shares.

These interventions usually trigger a boom in the value of stocks and bonds — but the rise in asset prices often isn't accompanied by an increase in economic production.

Talking about the most recent use of QE, Francisco Ferreira, director of the International Inequalities Institute at the London School of Economics (LSE) said: "Instead of leading to more economic output, a bulk of the sudden infusion of money into the financial system led to a dramatic rise in asset prices, including stocks, which benefited the rich."

The elephant in the room

Being able to buy a house is dear to most renters' hearts, especially the young. But house price inflation puts it beyond the reach of many.

Yet house prices are excluded from the bank's reckoning. So it doesn't consider what effect its decisions would have on people who rent.

So why does the bank's yardstick, the Consumer Prices Index (CPI), not include house prices? Well apparently, inflation is regarded as a measure of the costs of buying goods and services for immediate consumption. And the economists regard houses as a long-term investment, not something you quickly consume such as bread or fuel.

The myth is that housing shortages has driven up house prices. But research by the Bank of England shows that it's the bank's monetary policy (low interest rates) that has pushed house prices out of reach[181]. By focusing on low interest rates, the bank drives up house prices, because borrowing is cheap.

What does this all mean?

Whether the Bank of England either inflates or deflates the economy, it's corporations and the rich that benefit. The poor suffer the most.

The people who work in the bank have no tools to help ordinary people. Or to put it another way, they choose not to find new tools.

And it's the Concierge Class who make and implement the bank's decisions. There's an ugly arrogance and complacency at Threadneedle Street, one that comes from being cosseted by dated and erroneous economics, and a lack of concern for ordinary people.

What's to be done?

The Positive Money pressure group says there are other, better options the bank could take[182].

The Treasury and the Bank of England should take into account the impact of their policies which result in property price inflation and deepen inequalities. It points out the policies transfer wealth to homeowners, landlords and the asset-rich, and away from the young, renters and low paid workers. The organisation says the bank should:

- Limit house price inflation to sustainable levels. It could do that by controlling mortgage lending, for example by managing the loan-to-value ratio by lenders.

- Move financing towards public investment in housing, and increase the amount of affordable and social housing.

- Introduce policies to shift credit away from speculative property investment and towards consider productive investment in the real economy.

- Publish alternatives to QE, including the Bank directly financing government spending and giving money directly to citizens.

If you spend your life, as Bank employees do, talking with bankers and the rich, it's perhaps unsurprising that they have little understanding of the real world.

At the end of this book, we examine the steps that those who work at the Bank should re-evaluate the pain they cause to ordinary people.

I've paraphrased some of the organisation's wording to add clarity. Therefore it may not fully accurately represent the organisation's views.

The management consultants' playbook

I once went for a job interview at PwC, the management consultancy. A dozen of us shortlisted candidates were taken to a secluded manor house in the countryside, where we spent for a couple of days engaged in discussions, interviews and presentations.

It was all going rather well for me, as I thought. Impressed by my apparent eloquence, my fellow applicants asked me to manage one of the sessions in front of a flip chart. There I dutifully engaged the more reticent members and invited the opinions of the group, before summing up the session. Easy, I thought, job done. I looked forward to a life of having major clients hang on my every word, before I jetted off to another all-expenses paid international project.

On the final day we were sat round the lunch table, at which I sensibly drank only water. The conversation came round to the NHS, where the PwC consultant extolled the benefits of privatisation. It would rescue patients from the inefficiency of the public sector, he said, and hand them into the care of the infinitely more effective private corporations.

I gently challenged the consultant, pointing out that the corporations' track record was not unblemished. He fell silent. After lunch, one by one, we went into one of the offices to be told our fate. In the minibus afterwards, it turned out I was the only one to fail.

So my dream six-figure salary never happened, though I eventually worked for a consultancy that helped companies reduce their environmental footprint.

But let's have a look at what the consultants do, and see how they affect the rest of us.

1. They help corporations make more profit

This usually means improving 'operational efficiency', which involves cutting costs. Here are some examples:

Privatisation

Consultants generally recommend the privatising of public services, such as education, healthcare and transport, on the grounds that private companies can do the work more cheaply (and with weaker trade unions).
But this often has the opposite effect, leading to higher costs, a worse service

and complaints from users and the public. Deloitte was criticised for its role in advising the UK government on the privatisation of the National Health Service, specifically its in-house bank of doctors and nurses who can work flexibly. It led to concerns that healthcare would become less accessible and affordable for ordinary citizens[183].

Outsourcing

The NHS National Blood Service outsourced its IT services to IBM in an attempt to save £30 million over five years. However, the outsourcing deal went sour, with the service plagued by system failures, data breaches, and poor customer service.

The failures led to delays in blood testing and cancellations of donor appointments, raising concerns about patient safety. In 2015, the NHS was forced to terminate the contract with IBM and bring IT services back in-house.

Royal Mail outsourced some of its blemished postal delivery services to TNT Post in a bid to reduce costs and improve efficiency. However, the outsourcing process was marred by delays, disputes, and poor communication, leading to disruptions in mail delivery. Customers faced delays of up to two weeks, and businesses reported losses due to late deliveries. The problems persisted for several years, damaging Royal Mail's reputation and causing financial losses.

Birmingham City Council turned its cleaning and maintenance services over to ISS Facility Services in a cost-cutting measure. However, the outsourcing deal led to a decline in service quality and complaints from residents. Cleaning standards fell, staff morale plummeted, and the council was forced to intervene on multiple occasions to address issues. The outsourcing decision was widely criticised, and Birmingham City Council ultimately decided to bring the services back in-house.

The UK's Ministry of Justice outsourced its electronic tagging service to Serco and its tagging by to G4S. The move was intended to save money and improve efficiency. However, the outsourcing contract was plagued by problems from the start, with G4S being taken to court for fraud. struggling to recruit and retain staff, leading to chronic staff shortages.

This resulted in delays in court hearings, increased risks for prisoners and staff, and a rise in prisoner complaints. The Ministry of Justice was forced to intervene and provide additional support to G4S, undermining the cost-saving rationale for outsourcing[184][185].

Offshoring

Consultants often recommend that corporations offshore their jobs to low-wage countries in order to reduce costs.

The Tony Blair Institute estimated that more than 5.9 million jobs – equivalent to 18% of the UK's workforce – could be headed offshore. This followed the discovery during the pandemic that many people could work from home, and if so one in five jobs in the UK can now be classified as "Anywhere Jobs".

This leads to job losses and wage cuts for workers in the UK and other developed countries. Aided by McKinsey & Company, the US giant retailer exported its jobs to China, leading to the loss of thousands of jobs in the United States. However, some of these jobs are now being re-shored due to automation and weaknesses in global distribution chains.

2. They help corporations expand their reach

Corporations engage consultants to identify and help them enter new markets, both domestically and internationally. Bain & Company helped Amazon expand into India and China. That may have been good for Amazon, but not so good for the employees who went to work in its warehouses, the local booksellers who went bust and the bookshop employees who lost their jobs.

And with transnational corporations, suppliers and employees are always at risk of them walking away. In India, Amazon India decided to shut down its food delivery and edtech businesses due to an economic slowdown[186]. That meant firing 10,000 people.

3. They help corporations raise capital

Management consultants help corporations raise capital from investors, both through IPOs and private placements. Goldman Sachs helped Alibaba Group raise $21 billion in its IPO in 2014. So who benefited? The business did: The IPO raised capital for Alibaba Group, which the company used to fund its growth and expansion plans. It was able to invest in new businesses, such as cloud computing and logistics. It also expanded into new markets, such as Southeast Asia and India.

The shareholders won: Alibaba Group's founder and CEO, Jack Ma, sold a portion of his shares in the IPO and made billions of dollars. Nice for him.

The underwriters won: companies like Goldman Sachs and Morgan Stanley earned big fees for their role in helping Alibaba raise capital. Goldman Sachs earned an estimated $200 million in fees from the IPO.

But did that help the employees of AliBaba? The new hires won, if they got better jobs than before. But working for a public company is unsettling. Every 90 days the AliBaba managers have to report to their new shareholders how much profit they've made. Shareholders are notoriously impatient and fickle. So management has to constantly find ways to make more profit. And the easiest way to do that is to costs, by reducing head count. Bye-bye employees.

And sometimes corruption takes place: Bain & Company was paid $10 million by the South African Revenue Service to help collect taxes. But the company was accused of corruption and was eventually fired.

4. They help corporations buy other companies

Management consultants Bain helped private equity firm 3G Capital to merge Heinz and Kraft foods. The cost of buying the businesses was $36 *billion.*

The aim was to slash costs, and get rid of staff, and thus make large profits.

It was supposed to be about that buzz word 'synergy', but everyone knew it was about getting rid of duplicate jobs and factories, and force better deals from suppliers and stockists.

The plan was to extract a huge $1.5 billion in cost savings. But in reality there were fewer savings to be had, and so the new owners had implemented extreme cost-cutting measures that decimated its supply chain and reduced innovation[187].

The end result weakened businesses and caused damaging job losses, all in the pursuit of profit.

5. They impose austerity measures

Management consultants often disadvantage ordinary citizens by promoting austerity measures. They frequently recommend that governments cut spending in order to reduce budget deficits. This leads to cuts in the public services and social programmes that ordinary people need.

McKinsey & Company advised the Greek government on how to cut spending in order to meet the terms of its bailout agreement[188]. This led to massive reductions in education, healthcare and social welfare.

But the consultants ignore the real problems

The 'Centre for Policy Impact' (CPI) is a trojan horse outfit which offers to:

> 'act as a learning partner for governments, public servants, and the diverse network of changemakers leading the charge to re-imagine government so that it works for everyone.'

It's paid for by Bain Consulting Group, the management consultancy. It thinks government is stuck with "a flawed "industrial" mindset that seeks to manage and control". It says "our models of government are ill-equipped to tackle some of the most urgent issues we face as a society.[189]" And it talks about empathy, authenticity, trust and curiosity.

Sadly, it doesn't talk about the real problems: lack of money to meet the community's needs, brought on by years of tax cuts which have meant increasingly impoverished local authorities. To which we could add cuts to education and health, and legislation that increased the number of people in precarity and their children in poverty.

And meanwhile by 'engaging' with politicians and civil servants CPI builds a relationship with them that allows Bain to embed itself within government and grab more work that involves 'listening', 'empathising' or 'learning'.

It could be so different

At various times, trades unions, NGOs and the government have examined alternatives to the sorry round of redundancies, offshoring and outsourcing that the consultancies proffer.

The Lucas Report of 1976 was a pioneering effort by workers at the arms company to retain jobs by proposing alternative, socially-useful applications of the company's technology and their own skills. It remains "one of the most radical and forward thinking attempts ever made by workers to take the steering wheel and directly drive the direction of change[190][191]."

With a positive mindset, this kind of fresh thinking could be Act applied across all organisations.

Who wins?

The winners in all this are the management consultants. The practices, nowadays separated by a "Chinese wall" from their accountancy parents, hire bright graduates and set them to work. Typically they advise corporations about tasks for which the client has no in-house expertise. There's a consultancy playbook which provides standard solutions based on cutting staff costs, gobbling up other businesses, and offshoring work to low-cost countries.

A McKinsey song, reputedly sang at a consultants' Christmas party, starts like this[192]:

> If you aim to get the best result
> And maximum performance you want to see,
> Then you really should consult
> A Management Consultancy.
> McKinsey management consultants are we.
> We take all our clients' money.
> We can earn many a million
> Because our clients have no vision.

What's to be done?

For the individual consultant, it's a matter of recognising the work they're being asked to do, its frequent lack of effectiveness, and its damaging impact on the weaker members of society.

But the profession mostly attracts unthinking people.

- There are the fresh-faced graduates who are quickly absorbed into the practice, and adopt the attitudes of their bosses.

- There are the amoral and right-leaning consultants who are inured to self-reflection.

- And there are the drudges who do the background research and collect the information for their sharper brethren.

We aren't likely to change any of them.

That being the case, clients need to wean themselves off reliance on management consultants, and build in-house expertise. This particularly applies to managers in government bodies, such as the NHS, which spends £300 million a year on hiring external consultants[193]. One of the many drawbacks about using consultants is that you don't acquire and embed knowledge into your own organisation.

Management consultants have a standard playbook that they bring out each time. It's one of the following: cut staff; remove or add layers of management; diversify; get rid of non-core businesses; re-structure the business; or merge with/acquire another business. And mostly they're brought in to justify what management already intends to do.

Re-thinking how organisations work, and assessing the social value they produce, requires the Concierge Class to step off the treadmill and have a radical think about their role in undermining society.

A slap on the wrist by the regulators

Trade associations complain about over-regulation, 'red tape' and 'hampering competitiveness'. They also say regulators are risk-averse. But they would, wouldn't they? It's in their interests to say so. What they really want is freedom from regulation.

It's true that regulation can get out of date or be badly designed. But in general, regulation is what creates an even playing field, and sets standards for consumer protection.

Here's a press release from The Managed Funds Association. It "wants the UK Financial Conduct Authority (FCA) and the UK Prudential Regulatory Authority (PRA) to enhance the UK capital markets by eliminating redundant securitisation due diligence regulations. ... This will increase capital investment in the UK and optimise risk management on behalf of UK investors."

This jargon translates as: "Please stop requiring us to hold so much cash as a protection against future losses. This will let us make more money".

And that creates a higher risk to the public, because in the next downturn we'll discover that the finance companies don't have enough cash in the bank to cover their loss-making investments. As Warren Buffett said: "Only when the tide goes out do you discover who's been swimming naked".

How to neutralise a regulatory body

One of the best ways to hamstring a regulatory body is to gradually deprive it of funds.

Since 2010 the budget of the UK's Health and Safety Executive (HSE) has been cut by over 50% in real terms. The jobs of 500 front line inspectors have gone[194]. And job cuts have hit certain specialisms hard, such as personal protective equipment (PPE). So there's a greater risk of accidents happening.

Similarly, funding for environmental protection services provided by the UK government's Environment Agency (EA) was cut by 50 per cent over ten years, according to Prospect, a trade union which represents professionals in the public sector[195].

And Labour Party analysis of official figures shows that raw sewage discharge in England and Wales has more than doubled in five years, to public outrage[196].

Capture

Regulators easily get captured by the industry they're supposed to regulate. A few years ago, the UK government announced it planned to reduce the Department of Transport's budget by 37%. And that was at a time when its Vehicle Certification Agency (VCA) was already getting 70% of its income from car manufacturers.

These same manufacturers pay the VCA to certify that their vehicles are meeting emissions and safety standards[197]. So is it any wonder it hadn't spotted that Volkswagen had installed illegal software to cheat emission tests, allowing its diesel cars to produce up to 40 times more pollution than was permitted?

Some regulators have implicit understandings with the companies they're supposed to supervise. They and the companies they regulate see these relationships as 'sensible', 'light touch' or 'pragmatic'.

But critics regard that behaviour as 'regulatory capture'. In many cases it's made worse by their dependence on their industries for the information they need to do their jobs[198].

Martin Stanley, of civilservant.org.uk, says evidence of regulatory capture includes:

The VCA is supposed to regulate vehicle testing. But it gets 70% of its money from the car manufacturers.

- Quality and safety regulators giving advance notice of inspection visits

- Frequent staff interchange between regulator and industry

- The reluctance of either party to be strongly critical of the other

- Both regulator and industry engaging in increasingly introverted consultation processes, baffling to the outside world.

Pseudo-regulation

If a newspaper ad strikes you as untruthful, or a TV commercial is offensive, who should you complain to? Answer: Call the ASA. That's the Advertising Standards Authority. Last year it received 32,000 complaints.
But the ASA isn't a regulatory body. It has no legal powers. And it's funded by the advertisers whose work it assesses.

They seem to be a bit coy about their success rate. From the evidence of previous years, it rejects around 95% of complaints.

Osborne Clarke, a law firm, mused whether the ASA regime "is out of step with the zeitgeist and needs to review the Code and/or the make-up of the Council that adjudicates on complaints?" Are the "soft" issues of alarm and distress are not being addressed in a way that reflects current attitudes and mores? they wondered[199].

Mark Tallon, chief executive officer at the European food law consultancy Legal Foods, said the ASA wasn't fit for purpose.

"They are not a statutory regulator so they have no powers in terms of taking a company to court or issuing an improvement notice," he said. "The only way they work is by causing brand damage by issuing a ruling on their website. And because they aren't a regulator there's nothing forcing them to act if they're made aware of non-compliance[200]."

He also didn't like that, in the case of complaint by a competitor, the ASA says it "will not act until we're satisfied that you've attempted to resolve the complaint with the advertiser.

The aim is for disputes to be resolved in a fair and prompt way, in the spirit of fair competition and with the minimum of formality and cost..."

Tallon said "No company will do this as it is time consuming, likely to lead to bad blood, and, most importantly, it should not be their responsibility.
On another occasion, green activists

Life sparkles at the ASA's offices. But it's controlled by the advertising industry.

from Adfree Cities criticised the ASA after its council overturned a draft ruling against Land Rover[201]. One member, Robbie Gillert, claimed the watchdog was "too slow, too reluctant to investigate and lacking any enforcement teeth if they do."

Another self-regulating industry body is the Gambling Commission. One critic among many is MP Carolyn Harris, who co-chairs a cross-party group of MPs investigating gambling regulation. "This is the gambling industry marking their own homework," she said.

Whether or not any of these criticisms are valid, the point is that any self-regulating body that's funded by its industry members will always stand accused of being captured, and under the control of the corporations.

Counter-regulation

Governments use counter-regulation as a way to make markets more efficient and competitive, and also to reduce regulation. They do this by increasing transparency, promoting competition, or empowering consumers. Here are some examples of counter-regulation in action:

- The European Union promoted competition in the telecommunications industry, by allowing consumers to easily switch between providers.

- The UK introduced gave consumers the right to cancel contracts within a cooling-off period and receive compensation for poor service.

Counter-regulation can be a more effective way to reduce regulation than simply repealing regulations. This is because counter-regulation addresses the underlying causes of regulation, such as market failures or information asymmetries. However, there are also risks associated with counter-regulation:

- **It can be complex and difficult to implement.** Counter-regulation often requires careful design and implementation to be effective.

- **It may not be effective in all cases.** Counter-regulation may be ineffectual in addressing market failures or information asymmetries (where the consumer knows less than the companies).

- **It may be opposed by interest groups.** Interest groups that benefit from regulation may oppose counter-regulation.

And needless to say, the proponents of counter-regulation are often those who want a small state, and who think that giving the consumer enough information will solve the problems. But this leaves the consumer unprotected when it comes to complaints and unfair dealing.

What's to be done?

Regulators need to be aware of the aims of lobbyists and the corporations that hire them. The regulators must represent only the best interests of the citizens who use the services of the companies they're regulating. They should be transparent in their dealings, and be evidence-based in all their dealings.

Regulators must also be conscious of the attitudes of politicians who may seek to persuade them to weaken their oversight.

Self-regulation will always be prey to the charge that it's an industry stitch-up.

The members of the Concierge Class who work at any of the regulators need to speak up for regulatory independence, and prevent capture and interference.

And all of us need to withstand the 'small state' forces that seek deregulation, and push back against them.

Justice - but only for some

Have you ever been summonsed to appear in court for having committed an offence?

I have. Aged 23, young, feckless, broke and disorganised, I'd failed to respond to a Notice of Intended Prosecution, and the follow-up letters. It related to a car I'd driven which had multiple defects.

In the court there were two types of people, I discovered. Some had middle-class accents. They were the ones in charge: the lawyers, magistrates, police, and the clerks. Well-dressed, they spoke clearly and confidently across the courtroom to each other.

And then there were the defendants. They muttered their brief answers, staring at the floor. Speaking in a regional accent, they were in the dock for failing to pay a fine, for drugs offences, or for committing minor criminal damage. They looked thin and poor.

I got let off with a fine and a promise to sort my car out.

But the day remains with me. It was where two unequal worlds met: the justice system.

And it's got worse since that day, many years ago.

Let's look at how inequality has seeped into the law. We'll review six different aspects of the judicial system:

1. Leniency towards corporations
2. Tolerance of crimes committed by company directors
3. Acceptance of tax evasion
4. Low sentencing of white-collar crimes in the courts
5. Uneven police behaviour
6. Prison policy

Let's start with the corporates.

1. Leniency towards corporations

Three companies: Deutsche Bank, Eni (the world's seventh largest oil company) and the drug company Novartis all share an ugly track record. According to the International Consortium of Investigative journalists (ICIJ), they're all repeat offenders.

Each has engaged in bribery schemes.

They've promised not to offend any more, and paid to settle their cases.

They were subsequently accused of similar offences. And in each case the authorities let them settle out of court[202].

Eni settled twice, Novartis four times, while Deutsche Bank escaped prosecution five times on charges of bribery, tax fraud and antitrust charges.

Corporate settlements save the authorities time and money, in return for a fine. But it lets the companies off the hook.

"The proliferation of US-style corporate settlements is quite alarming," said Peter Reilly, a law professor at Texas A&M University. "The rule of law is being undermined, and governments are failing to protect the very people they are charged with protecting — something that both undermines basic fairness and ultimately weakens a democracy."

2. Tolerance of crimes committed by company directors

A pitifully small number of individuals are prosecuted for white-collar crime.

HMRC, the UK's tax authority, is just one such area of inactivity. At the time of writing, only 11 affluent people were prosecuted by HMRC in the last 12 months. Its charges against wealthy taxpayers have dropped by two-thirds in recent years.

Dan Neidle, the founder of Tax Policy Associates and a former partner and head of tax at Clifford Chance, one of the largest legal firms in the world, claimed that HMRC is pursuing less risky civil penalties and settlements as opposed to riskier and more costly criminal actions.

"When it comes to civil law and punishments, people calculate the risk," he said. "[But businesses] don't make any kind of equation with criminal prosecution; [they] just don't go near it".[203]

When a company director is prosecuted, they get off with remarkably lenient sentences for the damage they've caused. To take just three examples:

- **Fred Goodwin**, the former CEO of Royal Bank of Scotland was fined £340,000 for his role in the bank's collapse, which cost taxpayers £45 billion. He wasn't jailed. And he has a £545,000 annual pension[204]. The -Financial Services Authority cleared Goodwin of any wrongdoing over the collapse of RBS. It tells people that company directors can avoid responsibility for their companies' failings[205].

- **Kweku Adoboli**: A trader at UBS was sentenced to seven years in jail in 2012 for committing the UK's biggest fraud, which caused his employer, UBS, a loss of £1.5 billion. But he was released after serving just two years.

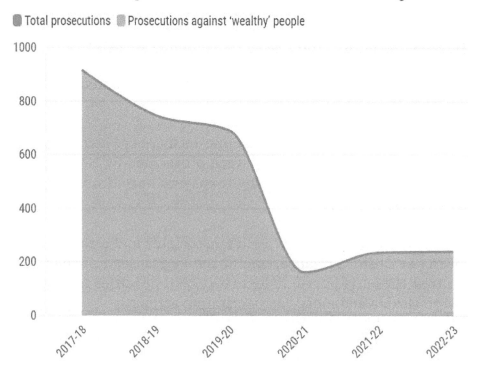

Prosecutions brought as a result of HMRC criminal investigations

● Total prosecutions ● Prosecutions against 'wealthy' people

Source: HMRC responses to freedom of information requests sent by TBIJ

- **Stephen Hinchliffe:** The former chair of the Facia retail group was sentenced to 15 months in jail in 2007 for conspiracy to defraud. But the sentence was suspended and he didn't serve any time in jail.

Fraud now accounts for 40% of all UK crimes, but the level of prosecutions is low.

Failure to prosecute fatal workplace accidents

The same is true for fatal accidents. 140 people die in UK work accidents each year. The Crown Prosecution Service (CPS) has been able to prosecute companies under health and safety legislation since 2008. But since then there have been fewer than 30 convictions for corporate manslaughter[206], and these have all been against small companies.

This is because corporate manslaughter requires a failing by senior management, and it's easier to attribute failings to senior management in small businesses, where they're engaged in day-to-day control. Fines can be more than £20 million, but so far fines for corporate manslaughter have been a lot lower.

3. Acceptance of tax evasion

There's a growing consensus that the UK is failing to adequately prosecute tax evasion. This has been highlighted by a number of recent reports, including one by Transparency International, which found that the UK was the second worst G7 country for tackling tax evasion[207]. There are several reasons for this:

- **The complexity of tax laws:** Tax law is complex, which makes it difficult for both the authorities and the public to understand. It's easier for criminals to hide their activities.

- **The lack of resources:** The UK's tax authority, HMRC, is understaffed and underfunded. It has limited resources to investigate and prosecute tax evasion.

- **The lack of political will:** To some people, tax evasion looks like a victimless crime, just a matter of accountancy. It's committed by well-spoken people - the Concierge Class. And many influential people commit it, and they have a personal stake in letting that continue.

As a result of these factors, the UK loses around £20 to £80 billion a year (estimates vary considerably). It's money that could be used to fund public services, such as education and healthcare.

TaxWatch says that over the past 11 years there have been 88,000 criminal prosecutions for benefits crimes, 23 times more than for tax crime of all types (4,000)[208].

Patriotic Millionaires UK is a group of very rich people pushing for higher taxes on the wealthy. They say imposing a 2% tax on those with more than £10m of assets could raise £22 billion a year, or £420 million a week. "That could pay for the average salary cost of more than 600,000 nurses a year – more than three-quarters of the UK's nursing workforce," the group said[209].

A YouGov survey reported in the Guardian found three-quarters of Britons support a wealth tax[210], while the Patriotic Millionaires group says 68% of the richest people support that[211].

4. Low sentencing for white-collar crime in the courts

The courts treat white-collar crime more leniently than other types of crime.

- A study by the UK's Centre for Crime and Justice Studies found that people convicted of white-collar crime were more likely to receive non-custodial sentences than people convicted of other types of crime.

- Studies have also found that white-collar offenders were more likely to get shorter prison sentences than offenders convicted of other types of crime[212][213].

- A study of 14 judges in New York City revealed they believe that sentences shorter than those given to street criminals are not less punitive. Let's untangle what that means. The judges thought that a one-year prison sentence for an upper-class or middle-class citizen was tougher on them than a three- or four-year sentence would be to a street criminal[214]. In other words, street criminals should get sentences three or four times harder than ones meted out to middle-class criminals.

That sounds like a value judgement in favour of 'good chaps', rather than one based on evidence.

- And a Finnish study[215] shows that that those who commit financial crime are less likely to go to prison compared with other non-violent crimes (despite the fact that fraud costs about 1.5% of GDP). Only 11% of defendants are imprisoned, half or one-third of the rates for non-violent drug or property crime respectively.

There are many reasons why the courts treat white-collar crime more leniently than other types of crime:

- Judges see white-collar criminals as less harmful than other types of criminals. For example, they may see a corporate executive who's convicted of fraud as less harmful than a violent offender.

- Judges think white-collar offenders are being more likely to be rehabilitated. For example, they may regard a corporate executive who's convicted of fraud as more capable than a violent offender of changing their behaviour and not committing future crimes.

- White-collar criminals are often wealthy and well-connected. That gives them access to a better quality of legal representation and thus more likely to receive a lenient sentence.

But these all boil down to favouritism for the white-collar criminal, despite the much greater losses they cause.

The lenient treatment of white-collar crime has benefits for corporations and the wealthy.

- It's easier for corporate execs to engage in risky behaviour, as they know they're unlikely to face serious consequences if they're caught.

- It's simpler for wealthy individuals to avoid punishment for their crimes, because they can afford to hire expensive lawyers and thus use their wealth to influence the criminal justice system.

But there's a wider issue: the lenient treatment of white-collar crime leads to a loss of faith in the criminal justice system, as people may feel that the system is biased in favour of the wealthy and powerful.

Once again, the law seems unsatisfactory when it comes to prosecuting corporations and the rich. But what about the police?

5. Uneven police behaviour

In this section, we'll look at some topical issues relating to the police: 'stop and search', the 'county lines' drug distribution network, and how the police handle protests.

Stop and search

While the courts go easy on white-collar criminals, the police seem to focus on arresting people of colour, in particular through the 'stop and search' procedure which allows an officer to stop someone if they have 'reasonable grounds' for suspecting that they will find stolen or prohibited articles.

The most recent figures show the police have conducted over half a million 'stop and searches' annually in England and Wales. And according to the Metropolitan Police Service, only 2% of its stop and searches result in a conviction.

GB sprinter Bianca Williams and her partner Ricardo, a Portuguese top athlete, were stopped arrested, and handcuffed. As the driver, he was told he smelled of cannabis (he's teetotal and doesn't take drugs).

They were kept handcuffed for 45 minutes while the officers carried out a search looking for weapons and drugs. They found nothing. When they were finally released, details of Zuri, their three-month old son, were stored on a police database that records information on children who become known to the authorities.

Bianca Williams with Dos Dantos. He's been stopped more than 20 times.

Dos Santos had been stopped more than 20 times by Met officers, including once six weeks earlier. When he bought a new BMW X4, he was stopped nine times in the space of six weeks.

Following an investigation, the Independent Office for Police Conduct (IOPC) concluded that five of the officers should face allegations of gross misconduct, and for breaching professional standards of behaviour and equality and diversity.

Four were also alleged to have breached standards for use of force; and three were alleged to have breached standards for honesty and integrity[216]. In other words, they lied.

There's a footnote to this story. Shortly after the two of the police officers were sacked, a JustGiving page raised £52,000 for the guilty officers in 14 hours[217]. Several of the donors said they were police officers.

At the time of writing, 24 officers in the Met have been dismissed for gross misconduct in the past 12 months, and three others would have been had they not already left the force. Around 355 officers are currently awaiting misconduct hearings.

To be fair to the police, it's a tiny number out of the 34,026 serving Metropolitan officers.

County lines

As with 'Stop and Search', the UK police's 'country lines' operations attract criticism. This is the programme that says drug dealers in large cities establish networks to supply drugs to users in towns and rural areas. They use other people, mostly those who are young or otherwise vulnerable, to transport, store and sell the drugs. It's a focus for police work, in that cutting the distribution will result in fewer addicts.

But a report by the Institute of Race Relations (IRR), says the government's claim that county lines is the "most violent and exploitative" drugs distribution model, requiring a multi-agency approach, is unproven[218].

"There is a dearth of evidence to support the contention of an increase in the use and supply of [Class A] drugs as a result of 'county lines'," said the study. The county lines operations are based on unproven assumptions and "racialised tropes" that criminalise Black boys and young men, it says.

Policing protests

Policing protests is another are of contention. Paul Stephens, a retired detective sergeant with 30 years' service in the Metropolitan Police, said the force uses resources and tactics against peaceful climate activists similar to those used to counter violent criminal organisations[219]. The Met, he says:

> "are overstepping the law in their eagerness to protect

'business partners' who are actively increasing the risk to life by pumping more CO_2 into the atmosphere or supporting those that do.

"It is not the rank and file so much, many of whom I know to be well read on climate science, it is the senior command who hide behind their duty to uphold law in favour of their duty to protect human rights, and quite frankly, should raise their vision, recognise what we face, show some integrity and speak truth to power."

6. Prison policy

So far, we've seen that the justice system is tolerant of corporations' crimes, and tough on protests and on low-level drug offenders.
But now we've got past the courts and the police, at the extreme end of the justice system lie the tall gates of prison.

The UK's prison policy gets criticised for a number of reasons, including:

Overcrowding: The UK has one of the highest prison populations in Western Europe, with over 80,000 people in custody. This has led to overcrowding in prisons, which makes it difficult to provide prisoners with adequate access to education, healthcare, and other rehabilitation services.

Lack of focus on rehabilitation: The UK's prison system has traditionally focused on punishment rather than rehabilitation. It's led to a system that's more likely to make people worse than to make them better.

Scandinavian countries have a lower prison population than the UK, and a lower recidivism rate. That's because they have a more rehabilitative approach to prison, which focuses on providing prisoners with the education, skills and support they need to avoid re-offending[220].

Use of short prison sentences: The UK has a high rate of short prison sentences, which are often ineffective in reducing re-offending. Shorter sentences mean that prisoners have less time to complete rehabilitation programmes and are more likely to be released back into the community without the skills and support they need to avoid re-offending[221].

Disproportionate impact on certain groups: The UK's prison population is disproportionately made up of people from minority groups, people with mental health problems, and people with substance misuse problems. It suggests that the criminal justice system is not working fairly, or is wrongly directed[222].

High recidivism rate: Over half of all UK prisoners re-offend within two years of release. That's a waste of money and resources, and it means that victims of crime are more likely to be suffer again.

Imprisonment of black people. The incarceration rate for people of black and ethnic minorities in the UK is double that of white people. 27% of the prison population in England and Wales is from a minority ethnic group, compared with 13% of the general population. This means that people from minority ethnic groups are more than twice as likely to be imprisoned as white people.

The disproportionate incarceration of people of black and ethnic minorities is has a number of contributing factors:

- **Socioeconomic factors:** People from minority ethnic groups are more likely to be living in poverty and to be unemployed. These factors are associated with an increased risk of offending.

- **Policing practices:** There is evidence that the police are more likely to stop and search people from minority ethnic groups. This can lead to more arrests and convictions for minor offences, which can then lead to longer sentences for subsequent offences.

- **Sentencing practices:** As the table below shows, judges are more likely to impose custodial sentences on people from minority ethnic groups[223], for drugs and sexual crimes.

- This is even true when the offence is the same and the offender has no previous convictions.

The disproportionate incarceration of people of black and ethnic minorities has a number of negative consequences. They include:

- **Social exclusion:** People who have been imprisoned are more likely to be unemployed and to have difficulty finding housing. This can lead to social exclusion and make it difficult for former prisoners to reintegrate into society.

	Volume of Cases	% White	% White Imprisoned	% BAME	% BAME Imprisoned
Acquisitive violence	1,424	73%	**85%**	27%	**78%**
Drugs Offences	4,367	73%	**45%**	27%	**66%**
Sexual Offences	3,297	86%	**58%**	14%	**70%**

Case volumes, % of self-reported White and BAME offenders and % imprisoned, and adjusted imprisonment Odds Ratios from higher-order offence-group regression models, for selected offence groups. Source: UK Ministry of Justice.

- **Family and community breakdown:** Imprisonment can have a devastating impact on families and communities. Children who have a parent in prison are more likely to have mental health problems and to experience educational difficulties.

- **Cost:** The cost of incarcerating someone in the UK is estimated to be around £40,000 per year. It's a significant cost to the taxpayer, and is money that could be better spent on other public services.

Who's to blame?

So, if the criminal justice system seems to benefit corporations and the rich, who, if anyone, is to blame?

Who exactly is supporting the corporations and the white-collar workers? Perhaps a better question might be: who is *not* guilty?

The police find complex white-collar crime hard to unravel, often involving many countries, and requiring IT and forensic accounting skills.
The CPS finds it hard to prosecute large companies for fatalities, with senior managers being far removed from the site of the accident.

And the judges are clearly lenient on white-collar criminals.

Some of the police's programmes, such as 'stop and search' and the county lines programme, seem focused on low-level crime where the mules get arrested but the drug lords stay out of reach.

The police are over-worked and under-resourced, and many are dispirited. They spend much of their time on social welfare problems rather than on the prevention of crime. And they've lost the support of many sections of society, because crimes such as burglary are under-investigated, and police tactics are seen as racist.

Meanwhile the government uses 'tough on crime' legislation to boost its popularity with voters, rather than investing in the community.

Most of these groups - the senior police officers, the government, the CPS and the judges - are members of the Concierge Class, and are culpable.

What's to be done?

The judicial system needs a complete overhaul, from top to bottom. Here are some of the main issues:

The CPS

White-collar crime needs prosecuting.

The police

We need more resources for the UK police forces. The police also need additional skills to identify white-collar crime. And senior management in the police must set goals that focus just as much on corporate crime rather than on low-level drug offenders and what are seen as racist 'stop and searches'.

Sentencing policy

- Government and the judges should reduce the use of short prison sentences

- We need to legalise soft drugs, and provide better support for addicts

- In sentencing, there should be a focus on rehabilitation rather than punishment

- The government should invest in education, healthcare, and other services for offenders in prisons and the community.

- Government should learn from the Scandinavian countries' more successful approach to prison policy.

Black and ethnic minorities

- **Address the underlying socioeconomic factors:** The government should invest in programmes to reduce poverty and unemployment among minority ethnic groups. This would help to reduce the risk of offending in these communities.

- **Change policing practices:** As mentioned above, the police should reduce the number of 'stop and search' exercises of people from minority ethnic groups. They should also provide more training for officers on understanding people from different cultural backgrounds.

- **Change sentencing practices:** The government could change sentencing guidelines to ensure that they are not unfairly biased against people from minority ethnic groups.

Moving on

That brings us to the end of our look at The Enablers, the people who manage the system for the corporations and the wealthy.

Whether it's the judges failing to punish the guilty corporations, or politicians creating laws that benefit the rich, nothing happens that hasn't first been put in place by the Concierge Class.

Next, we assess the Pushers. They may lack the Enablers' power to change the law, but they have their own special skills. They're all out there, scribbling for the newspapers, lobbying for their masters, and preaching from the pulpit.

4. The Pushers

We're now moving into the arena of propaganda. It's where plutocrats, corporations and even countries (United Arab Emirates) buy newspapers and football teams to improve their image.

They donate to universities and art galleries, to whitewash their tarnished identity. And they finance murky think tanks to spread their neoliberal message.

We'll start with the news media.

The media megaphone

The media is largely owned by corporations and wealthy individuals.

Despite the 'lamestream' name-calling by the far-right media such as Fox News (prop. Rupert Murdoch), most of the major media is controlled by corporations and ultra rich people. So it's not surprising they support the agendas of the rich.

- **The Daily Mail** is owned by Jonathan Harmsworth, a viscount. We'll talk some more about the Mail in a moment.

- **News Corp**, which owns Fox News, the Sun, The Times, and TV stations in Australia and elsewhere, belongs to Rupert Murdoch. We'll come to him soon.

- **The Washington Post** belongs to Jeff Bezos, who owns Amazon, has assets worth $162 billion, and is the third-wealthiest person in the world.

- **Bloomberg Media** is owned by the eponymous Michael Bloomberg. Bloomberg is a multi-millionaire who made his money creating software for financial trading platforms. He ran for the US presidency, spending $935 million of his own money on the campaign.

- **Forbes Media** is owned by the Forbes family, who made their money from trading opium and tea in the 19th century.

- **Gannett** (which is an unfortunate homonym of 'gannet', the eponym of 'greedy'), is the largest newspaper publisher in the United States. It's owned by Gatehouse Media, which borrowed $1.8 *billion* from Apollo Global Management, a private equity company, to buy it. Its CEO, Mike Reed, earned $7.7 million in 2021.

- **The Telegraph** is jointly controlled by RedBird, a US based investment firm that owns companies worth $8.6 billion, and IMI, owned by Sheikh Mansour bin Zayed, whose family own the United Arab Emirates, a feudal country that has no democracy, tortures its citizens, and stoning is legal.

- **The Guardian** is an outlier among this group, being both left of centre, and having been put into an independent trust, the Scott Trust, that guarantees its financial independence.

Let's have a look at the kinds of things the billionaire-, plutocrat and corporation-owned media say:

The Mail

Over the years the Daily Mail and the Mail on Sunday have constantly published articles that benefited corporations and the wealthy:

- 'Now let's turbocharge growth with tax cuts' [tax cuts primarily for the rich].

- 'Mail poll shows voters want tax cuts' [Only 37% wanted that].

- 'The Leftie lynch mob' [those opposed to the sale of the publicly-owned Channel 4].

- 'Defiant union leaders are threatening to plunge Britain into a second 'winter of discontent' with mass strike action that involves two million workers, bringing the nation to its knees'.

The Telegraph

Owned until recently by the reclusive right-wing Barclay brothers, The Daily Telegraph and Sunday Telegraph have long supported plutocrats and corporations, and been opposed to trade unions and the needs of ordinary people and the poor. Here are some examples:

- 'Militant trade unions have trashed the economy – for nothing'.

- 'Tax cuts are more than possible'.

- 'Minimum wage harming job opportunities for young'.

- 'Let the markets decide when it comes to minimum wages'.

- 'Windfall tax putting billions of pounds of investment at risk'.

- 'Worry over zero-hours contracts and insecure work is 'misplaced'.

The Sun

- 'The trade union bullies plot more strikes, their contempt for the British people becomes increasingly clear.... Blinded by self-interest, gripped by left-wing ideology and consumed by greed, they have lost all concept of public service'.

- 'The mob of environmentalists from Just Stop Oil plonked themselves on top of tankers at the oil terminal during the dawn raid'.

When corporations and wealthy individuals own media outlets, they influence how the news is presented.

And while circulations have massively fallen, the printed media still plays an influential role in shaping public opinion and influencing government policy. The media's complicity in supporting corporate and plutocratic interests is a serious problem. It leads to policies that benefit the wealthy at the expense of the public interest. And it does so in a number of ways:

Promoting policies that favour the owner: The media often lobby for policies such as tax cuts, deregulation, and the privatisation of public assets.

Attacking opponents: It's normal for the media to attack opponents of corporate and plutocratic interests, such as environmentalists, trade unions and consumer advocates.

Disseminating misinformation: The corporate-owned media often skew comment about corporations and the wealthy, such as downplaying the negative impacts of climate change and exaggerating the benefits of tax cuts.

Sensationalism: The media often focuses on sensational stories, rather than on stories that are important to the public interest. This can distract the public from important issues and make it more difficult for people to make informed decisions.

Here's a list of the top newspapers in the world by circulation, along with their owners, and the prices they paid for them:

Newspaper	Owner	Price (if applicable)	Year
The Sun	News Corp (Rupert Murdoch)	£750 million	1988
The Daily Mail	Jonathan Harmsworth	£1.9 billion	1999
The Mirror	Reach PLC	£90 million	1985
The New York Times	The New York Times Company	$1.1 billion	2020
USA Today	Gannett	$2.8 billion	2019
The Wall Street Journal	News Corp	$5 billion	2007
The Telegraph	RedBird IMI	£600 million	2024

Who's the biggest mogul of them all?

Jonathan Harmsworth owns Britain's biggest daily newspaper, the Metro, and the 2nd highest, the Daily Mail. He also owns the best-selling Sunday paper, the Mail on Sunday. His Mail Online has a massive global online with 24.7m monthly unique visitors who ogle the bikini-clad celebrities as it rattles out its right-wing opinions.

Harmsworth also owns a 25% share in the country's third biggest daily paper, The Evening Standard[224]. The majority share is owned by former KGB chief Alexander Lebedev who, on leaving the Russian security service, inexplicably managed to buy what is now one of Russia's largest banks, the National Reserve Bank, which in turn owns 11% of the main Russian national airline Aeroflot, 44% of the Ilyushin aircraft industry, and large parts of Gazprom, the largest natural gas company in the world and the largest company in Russia by revenue[225].

The Mirror, which used to be centre-left, is now owned by Reach plc, whose shares in turn are owned by a number of investment companies, the biggest of which is the investment company M&G. Its CEO, Jim Mullen, was formerly the CEO of Ladbrokes, the UK's largest gambling firm.

So, who in the media are members of the Concierge Class?

Owners: At the top of the pile are the owners. They may not visibly direct the publication, but their views are widely known in the trade. Journalists and editors write what the owners expect to see.

Politicians: The papers invite right-wing politicians to write shouty populist articles.

The editor comes next, with strong opinions about what the readers want to hear. Editors are appointed by the owner, and will be hand-picked for their right-wing views.

The columnists are the people who most diligently serve the corporations and the wealthy. Here's' a quick sample:

- Alistair Heath: "Only a bonfire of human rights law can save the Tories from extinction."

- Celia Walden: "Sex education in schools is so warped we've forgotten to teach kids how to have babies."

- Michael Deacon: "Pro-Palestine protesters tear down hostage posters for one reason – they need to hide the truth".

- AN Wilson: "These organisations [the National Trust and the BBC] are riddled with the progressive drivel of the age."

- Richard Littlejohn: "The loudest howls of protest are -coming, inevitably, from [Brexit] Remainers - big business, the Blob, the Labour Party, the Greens, and the BBC."

They're professional rabble-rousers whose job it is to find enemies, invent causes and inflame the readers with their exaggeration. These days, their job is to create a fake culture war that the right believes is a vote winner.

The journalists go out and find the news or, more often, re-write press releases sent out by the lobbyists. They chat with politicians to procure a headline from them, usually anonymously.

Less than one in five (19%) journalists went to a comprehensive school, and 51% attended a private school. Almost all (92 per cent) went to university[226]. So it's clear that journalists are core members of the professional middle classes, and are therefore most likely to lack solidarity with ordinary people.

And finally there are the **headline writers**. They seek the biggest claim that could possibly attach to an article, often to work their readers into anger or despair.

News reporting and discussion

Let's ignore the columnists for a moment. They're something of an outlier, because most of the news content in the mainstream media tends to offer reasonably factual, albeit partial, reporting. This is especially true of the serious newspapers such as the Times, the Telegraph, the Guardian and the Independent; and the TV companies: BBC, ITV and Channel 4.

But here's the issue: the TV stations and some of the broadsheet newspapers are *socially* centre-left, but *economically* centre-right.

In other words, they're concerned about climate change, poverty, diversity, racism and homophobia.

But they don't analyse the underlying cause: that society is skewed in favour of the rich and the corporations. As a result, a growing number of people live in poverty, with insecure housing and jobs.

And when people see the political parties don't have meaningful solutions, they vent their anger on immigrants and ethnic minorities. Crime grows. And the media tuts. But it doesn't argue for action to re-balance the economy, including a fair levying of tax, controls on offshore havens, and a programme for council house construction.
It's almost unheard of for news programmes to take seriously radical programmes (which some might call sensible or obvious) such as taxation of the rich, adequate benefits, a universal basic income, and proper penalties for white-collar crime.

Such suggestions are regarded as overly radical. And the reason for this is central to my argument: that the Concierge Class are in charge of the public discourse. The journalists come from secure backgrounds, and have absorbed the values of the middle and upper classes.

In short, they buy into positive social values, but their economic outlook is inherently opposed to substantial change. They'll wring their hands and wonder 'What is to be done?'; but their mind is pre-set to support only minor changes to the status quo.

And regrettably, it's only economic change that will create a fair society.

Social media

The social media's circulations have soared as newspaper circulations have dropped, both as a result of the internet.

The main social media are controlled by just two men, Elon Musk and Mark Zuckerberg. The algorithms of their apps are designed to promote posts most likely to arouse engagement and strong emotions. As the old media magnates used to say: 'If it bleeds, it leads.'

It's an environment perfectly designed to whip up anger, fear and hostility. And it's where conspiracy theorists hang out, pumping out false stories about how vaccinations contain microchips, will permanently alter your DNA, or cause autism[227].

And as we'll see when we get to Chapter 5 - The Suppliers, within these organisations are IT developers working to make the social media algorithms ever more emotionally arousing.

Where are people getting their news from?

As the internet has grown, so the newspapers, the traditional news outlets, have either failed or are a small shadow of their former selves. The regional press in particular has withered, leaving many parts of the country without a local news source.

Into this gap has come the websites, funded by rich, right-wing individuals and institutions.

One such example is 'Real Clear', a large news organisation whose sites cover a range of niches including energy, religion, education and politics. It claims to be independent, but is funded by right-wing mega-donors.

One of its largest funders is Donors Trust, a non-profit 'dedicated to the ideals of limited government, personal responsibility, and free enterprise'[228].

Global Disinformation Index (GDI), a British NGO that advises advertisers and search engine companies, labelled Real Clear Politics as a high-risk news site for disinformation.

Real Clear reckons the rich pay enough tax.

And therein lies the problem. In an era where people don't pay for their news, they get it either from the babble of social media, which is infiltrated by bad actors, or by sites that get cash from the wealthy and the corporations.

What's to be done?

We can do a number of things to address the problem of the media's complicity in supporting corporate and plutocratic interests.
As individuals we need to be aware of the ownership of news media outlets in order to be a critical consumer of news. By knowing who owns a news media outlet, you can better understand the potential biases that may exist in the news that is reported.

We need to support independent media outlets. They're less likely to be influenced by corporate interests and are more likely to report on stories that are important to the public interest.

And as a society we need to educate the public about the ways in which the media can be biased. This will help people to be more critical of the information they're presented with and to make more informed decisions about the issues that affect them.

Governments and supranational organisations like the EU need to require owners of social media, such as X (formerly Twitter) and Facebook, to minimise hate speak and the spread of disinformation.

Governments and the EU also need to require Google and Facebook, which reproduce the news sites' stories without payment, to pay the news gathering media for their articles[229].

And the members of the Concierge Class, who are paid good money to write the articles that foster fear and resentment, should refuse to do such work. They need to reflect on society's underlying unfairness, and push for change.

Shameless marketing

You don't have to look far to find harmful products and deceptive advertising, or both. And at their heart lie the marketers, creating products and advertising them.

These members of the Concierge Class are found in the offices of manufacturers and service companies, and also in the creative department of their ad agencies.
If you're a marketer, you have an array of tactics to persuade people to buy the products. You can exaggerate the product's benefits, make false claims about its performance, or use misleading packaging.

I've worked for ad agencies in London. One of them specialised in commercials that had jingles, which we used to promote the sale of chocolate bars, fizzy drinks, and breakfast cereal. It meant you could surround the products with a warm and fuzzy feeling that made people well-disposed to them.

Like the majority of ads everywhere, the products we advertised weren't for the essentials of life, and the food products we promoted were always ultra processed and sugar-heavy.

These days, marketing people are using cuddly animals to make their products look harmless and appealing. Insurance is sold by meercats. Football clubs have furry mascots. And toilet paper ads have a puppy. They're often plump, with big eyes and a baby face, designed to make us think of babies, pull at our heart strings, and open our purses. The world is being infantilised by the Concierge Class.

Tenuous claims

When promoting unnecessary or even undesirable products, it's hardly surprising that the marketers come up with falsehoods and tenuous claims.

The Advertising Standards Authority (ASA) banned ads by the oil giant Shell which suggested it was a green business. The ASA said the campaign failed to make it clear that Shell's business was still primarily based on fossil fuels. The body also found that the campaign was likely to mislead consumers into believing that Shell was a more environmentally friendly company than it actually was[230].

The ASA also banned a Lucozade campaign that claimed the drink could improve cognitive function and athletic performance[231].

The watchdog said the campaign was misleading because there was no evidence to support these claims.

The product consists mostly of carbonated water and glucose syrup (a cheap sweetener, regular consumption of which may increase your risk of obesity, high blood sugar, poor dental health, high blood pressure, and heart disease).

Lucozade also has the artificial colours Sunset Yellow and Ponceau 4R, which are linked to hyperactivity in children.

The brand has form for making false claims, The ASA banned Lucozade Sport Low Calorie Isotonic Sports Drink ads claiming it was a healthy drink that could help people lose weight. The watchdog ruled the campaign was misleading because there was no evidence to support the claims.

Lucozade ad

Airlines frequently make false claims. Ryanair's 'Always Getting Better' campaign was banned because it implied Ryanair was a customer-friendly airline that was always improving its service. The ASA ruled that the campaign was misleading and banned it.

Marketers also exploit people's vulnerabilities

This applies particularly to products for children. It includes using techniques such as appeals to fear, emotional triggers, and peer pressure to manipulate consumers into making purchasing decisions. An app designed for children by Weetabix was found to exploit children's credulity and made them feel inferior if they didn't ask their parents to buy Weetabix's products. And it could lead them to think they were failing in some way if they didn't eat Weetabix[232].

Promoting Unrealistic Ideals

Marketing often portrays unrealistic and unattainable ideals of beauty, body image, and lifestyle. This can lead to body image issues, low self-esteem, and a sense of inadequacy among consumers, particularly young people. Such portrayals can also reinforce gender stereotypes and promote unhealthy social comparisons.

Brits watch two and a half hours of broadcast TV daily. Americans encounter 3,000 advertisements each day, and spend two years of their life watching TV commercials. Many of those ads show idealized female beauty. The models are slim, tall, and light skinned. Women in magazine features and press ads may have their waist digitally reduced.

"Women and girls compare themselves to these images every day," said author and ad critic Jean Kilbourne. "And failure to live up to them is inevitable because they are based on a flawlessness that doesn't exist."

The American ideal of beauty has become so pervasive that 50% of three- to six-year-old girls worry about their weight, according to the Harvard University's school of health[233]. And on the island of Fiji, the arrival of television heralded a boom in dieting among women and girls who before then hadn't considered there might be something 'wrong' with them.

Marketing campaigns can encourage **excessive consumption and materialism**, which then causes damage to the environment. It promotes non-essential products, and the need to acquire possessions. Add all the wasteful packaging and it adds up to a toxic brew.

Do we really need the Fascination watch from Graff Diamonds, price $40 million? Or a McLaren Elva car, price tag $1.8 million? Or a Gucci Diana small crocodile tote bag at £28,990? And those are just the expensive products. Many children's bedrooms are littered with cheap plastic toys that have little play value and are soon discarded.

And it's not only the advertising. Product development is part of the problem. If you sit in the original Mini, you'd be surprised at how tiny it seems, especially when compared with the bloated version now seen on the streets. Nowadays it's common to see tank-sized cars transporting a small child to school.

And the essential element to all this product development and advertising is the marketers, because marketing is the essential machine for driving sales. Without them, most of us never think about buying the products and services put in front of us every time we visit social media, watch television, or walk down the high street.

There's a growing awareness about the ills of marketing. 32,000 people complained about a poster campaign for Protein World that showed a woman in a bikini with the headline that asked 'Feeling objectified yet?'

Needless to say, some advertisers relish the publicity that an ASA ban brings, and probably the increased sales.

Yet few in the marketing world consider whether the products they're touting are bad for society or the planet, and whether they should be encouraging people to consume.

Meanwhile the owners of the brands mentioned above get richer. Back in 2013 the Japanese drinks firm Suntory bought Lucozade and another soft drink, Ribena from GlaxoSmithKline for £1.35 billion, which just goes to show how profitable these products are.

And Shell, recognising the public's hostility to oil and gas companies, splurges on 'greenwash' advertising campaigns. Meanwhile, the huge profits it makes, $5bn (£3.9bn) in just 90 days at the time of writing, don't add to its charm.

What's to be done?

The people who work in the ad industry are few in number, well paid, and have an impact far beyond their numbers. It's thanks to their unceasing work that people are turned into mindless victims, buying gadgets, devouring ultra processed food, and hardly daring to go out unless they're wearing the right brand of canvas shoe.

As a result, the average citizen is disengaged from the need to create a better society.

Like bankers, advertising and marketing people will always be amoral, always pushing the envelope of what's acceptable.

Any member of the Concierge Class in the advertising profession who has doubts about the benefits they bring to the world by promoting processed cheese and plastic toys should apply their skills to better ends.

But that's a minority. Ultimately, it's up to the government to install regulators with the power to limit the scale of advertising, and fine wrongdoing.

Let's have a look now at the new kids on the block, the social media influencers.

The new influencers

Want to make money on the side? If you're a celebrity, just lend your name to a dodgy product and you'll rake it in.

In the 1930s and 1940s, tobacco companies paid Hollywood stars up to $75,000 a year to promote specific brands of cigarettes[234].

But have things improved? Not with the arrival of Facebook and the other social media channels, and the troop of wannabe influencers.

Many of the endorsements are fairly harmless. But some, less so. Remember former football player and TV presenter Gary Lineker endorsing Walker's Crisps? A study involving 181 children were shown adverts for Walkers crisps, featuring Lineker.

The children were offered two bowls of crisps to eat, one labelled `Walkers' and the other marked 'Supermarket'. Both bowls contained Walkers crisps, but after watching the Lineker advert, the children ate considerably more crisps from the bowl labelled 'Walkers crisps than those who didn't.[235] The take-home message is: if you're a junk food company, hire a celebrity and get kids to eat more of your product.

And it works for adults, too

The Kardashians have been promoting various health and beauty products on social media, including vaginal steaming, flat tummy teas, and maternity shapewear.[236]

Kourtney Kardashian, the eldest sister, encourages Kim, Khloé, and Kris to do yoni steaming. In case you didn't know, it involves directing herb-infused steam into your vagina, a practice that has been criticised by gynaecologists.

The family's influence is vast, and even their casual conversations can inspire the masses. Flat Tummy Co, a company that produces teas, shakes, lollipops, and gummies, has been endorsed by both Khloé and Kim, who claim the products speed up metabolism and reduce bloating and cravings. Critics, however, argue that it reinforces unhealthy eating habits and a negative body-image.

'Waist trainers' and maternity shapewear have also been promoted by the

Kardashians, but they often fail to mention the potential side effects of wearing these products. Health practitioners warn that waist trainers can weaken abdominal muscles, lead to back pain, poor posture, heartburn, a weakened pelvic floor, and organ damage from over-compression.

The Kardashian's weight loss drug, Ozempic, is a diabetes-turned-weight-loss injection created by Danish pharmaceutical company Novo Nordisk. It's intended to treat Type 2 diabetes, but can also help shed pounds. However, taking a pharmaceutical drug for anything other than its intended use could be dangerous, as it could cause inflammation of the pancreas, gallbladder problems, low blood sugar, acute kidney injury, damage to the eye's retina, increased heart rate, and suicidal behaviour or thinking.

SugarBearHair vitamins are marketed as a way to rejuvenate and strengthen hair and nails. The sugar-filled gummies look like little bears. How cute!

Kim Kardashian's skincare line SKKN offers a 'more is more' approach to skincare, encouraging customers to use multiple skincare products throughout the week, at a cost of $700. Experts, however, suggest that multiple steps aren't necessary, and that the most important thing is to learn what works for you.

The first two ingredients are sugars. There's a clue in the name.

Want to know how to invest your spare cash? Kim Kardashian will do it for you. She has set up SKKY Partners, a private equity firm that will invest your money. Kris Jenner and Kardashian's mother, Kris Jenner, will also be partners at the firm.[237]

So, welcome to the Concierge Class, Kim, Kris and Khloé!

What's is all about? And what's to be done?

The celebrity Pushers promote false, materialist values, and distract people from recognising how society really works. Their words are then amplified by the news and social media.

Like their Concierge Class colleagues in marketing and the media, the influencers don't have an awareness beyond their own simple need to earn.

Governments have made a start by requiring influencers to state when a post is a paid-for placement.

But we need to understand the underlying systemic issue here: we're being fed unhealthy corporation-led narratives, fronted by members of the Concierge Class.

We need to educate our families and our children, and help them understand they're being manipulated.

The lobbyists who pervert democracy

If you're scrolling through X, formerly Twitter, you might come across posts with hashtags like 'Save My Vape' and 'Back Vaping, Save Lives'.

They appear to have been posted by ordinary members of the public, concerned to protect vaping. But in reality they're run by right-wing think tanks and lobbyists that oppose tobacco regulation and want to influence government policy[238].

Some of the posts come from The World Vapers' Alliance (WVA). The organisation says it "amplifies the voice of passionate vapers around the world" and that over 50,000 "vapers... are fighting with us". But it doesn't provide evidence to support that claim.

In fact, WVA was set up by, and receives funding from a pro-tobacco lobby group, the Consumer Choice Center (CCC), which gets funding from British American Tobacco (BAT)[239].

Organisations like WVA have pushed their posts to millions of Facebook and Twitter users.

Leaked emails and documents showed that BAT 'played a central and hands-on role in orchestrating, directing, and funding WVA'. The *Daily Beast* found that WVA "acknowledged internally that it was presenting a false outward image" and that in the Netherlands it was engineering "seemingly organic letters". These were from fake 'supporters' who wanted e-cigarette regulations rolled back, and which were sent to members of the Dutch and European parliaments.[1]

Such is the world of the lobbyists. This particular strategy is known as astroturfing, running an orchestrated PR campaign that appears to be from members of the public, but is on behalf of a lobby group's client. 'Astroturf' is a brand of plastic outdoor carpeting designed to look like grass, so it isn't what it claims to be; and the word is also a play on the word "grassroots".

The front groups

These front groups are an effective tool in the lobbyist's arsenal. They appear independent but are, in reality, funded and controlled by corporations or wealthy individuals, providing a façade of grassroots support for a particular agenda.

Amid the US opioid crisis, the pharmaceutical sector deployed front groups to veil their role, advancing their interests at public health's expense.

WVA has made 6,317 posts, supported vaping, under the guise of being a grassroots organisation.

Funded by pharmaceutical giants, these groups lobbied for looser opioid regulations, feigning grassroots support. This blurred the public and policymakers' understanding of the industry's true motives, shielding it from accountability. These actions not only prolonged the opioid crisis but also exacerbated the drugs' impact on the community.

Five corporations, Purdue, Janssen Pharmaceuticals, Mylan, Depomed, and Insys Therapeutics, spent nearly $9 million in payments to 14 outside groups working on chronic pain and other opioid-related issues between 2012 and 2017. In addition, physicians affiliated with these groups accepted more than $1.6 million in payments from the five manufacturers[240].

Drug companies also funded three US groups for the elderly, United Seniors Association, the Seniors Coalition, and the 60 Plus Association. The pro-industry campaigning included multi-million-dollar television advertisements. The 60 Plus Association was accused of being involved with 'astroturfing' allegedly helping to create a false grass roots campaign to defeat proposed state laws on prescription drugs.

Apart from Pfizer, which mounted a campaign in its own name, "the rest of the industry hid behind this device of using phoney seniors' organisations," according to the BMJ[241].

The scale of lobbying

Lobbying is a huge industry. A survey by Transparency International found that 2,735 companies and individuals had met with UK government ministers in just one 90-day period. In one case, former prime minister David Cameron was texting government ministers on behalf of Greensill, a financial firm that was employing him. And then Bill Crothers, a senior civil servant, was found to have a second job at Greensill.

In the USA, the lobbying industry has tripled to an annual spend of $4.9 billion since 1998, according to Statista. The biggest clients are the pharmaceuticals, insurance, and oil and gas corporations, as well as assorted business associations. It's indicative of the size and scope of the lobbyists.

I had a quick look at the job ads for lobbyists. Here's one, for the Associate Director, Public Affairs for The Integrity Council for the Voluntary Carbon Market (ICVM). This is about corporations buying 'offsets' that are used to grow trees, which mitigate the carbon that the same corporations create.

But the offsets approved by the world's leading certifier, Verra, were found to be "largely worthless and could make global heating worse", according to an investigation by the Guardian, Die Zeit and SourceMaterial, a non-profit investigative journalism organisation[242].

According to its website, ICVM is funded by various individuals and organisations. Here are a few: The Children's Investment Fund Management CIFM), which was set up by the owner of a hedge fund management firm. It focuses on 'improving the lives of children living in poverty in developing countries', which isn't quite the same as carbon offsets.

Then there's the Bezos Earth Fund, run by the world's richest man. Also The Sequoia Climate Foundation, which funds the European Climate Foundation, which also receives money from the CIFM, and from High Tide, which also funds ICVM. Someone more suspicious than me would begin to see some roundabouts going on here.

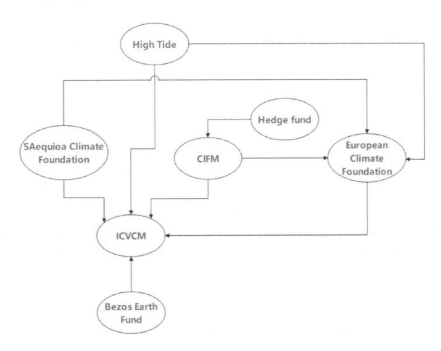

The intertwined funding of a carbon offsets organisation

'Helping' government

Another lobbyist's trick is to offer its help in producing legislation. Costa

Coffee provides us with one example. As part of its efforts to reduce carbon emissions from car use, the Scottish government had planned to restrict the building of new drive-throughs. In future, they would go ahead only in areas where they were explicitly backed by local councils.

The Costa Coffee chain (prop: Coca Cola) was unhappy with this, and argued that the legislation could hold up planning applications, as councils adapted to the national framework. It could take five years, they said.

So the company offered to 'help' the government write a 'working draft' of guidance. The government refused the company's offer, and expressed 're-gret' that it was unable to share a copy of the guidance 'for further drafting changes' because it was about to be published[243].

Framing the issue

One tactic wielded by lobbyists and PR consultants is to re-frame an issue. This lets them change how a particular issue is perceived, and thereby gain an advantage for their clients.

Over the decades, the tobacco industry has become expert at this. It's down-played smoking's severe health risks by using healthy, outdoors imagery, and euphemisms and misleading language, to sow doubt among the public. This created public uncertainty, and thus maintained the sale of their product.

Similarly, when governments have banned smoking in pubs, saying it's a public health issue, it gets re-framed by the lobbyists as 'government inter-ference in personal lifestyles'.

And now the tobacco lobby is at it again to protect their vaping revenues. They've positioned vaping as a way to wean smokers away from cigarettes. Meanwhile they're silent on the risks of inhaling tobacco, and the problem of flavoured vapes that are designed to appeal to children.

Similarly, the oil companies have sought to re-frame the climate crisis by placing the responsibility on individuals to reduce their carbon footprint, rather than the corporations that produce the oil[244].

Disseminating misinformation

Misinformation is another potent weapon, designed to obscure facts, distort science, and undermine opposing viewpoints.

The Camel cigarette poster from 1988, suggests that a young male smoker would look cool and attract women.

The oil and gas sector has regularly cast false doubt on the scientific consensus over climate change. Through the years, they've funded studies that contradicted the facts, and cherry-picked data to breed doubt and stall crucial climate policies.

Clear Energy is part of the influential right-wing website Real Clear, whom we saw earlier. Among its claims are that the UK's wind power programme is a 'scam', that 'wind-power costs are high' and 'they have been rising' (that's true, but it's due to inflation).

It says, 'official analyses produced by the Treasury and the Office for Budget

Responsibility rely on the falsehood that wind power is cheap' (false)[245]. In fact, wind power and other renewables 'are and will remain significantly cheaper than gas', says Carbon Brief[246].

A Real Clear Energy article claims net zero won't work, and wind power is a 'scam'.

Focusing on getting what they can

When the EU put forward proposals for managing AI, they ranked its various uses by the level of risk they posed.

For example, the lowest risk would be intelligent spam filters, and video games. The highest risk areas would be social scoring, facial recognition, and 'dark-pattern' AI. The latter manipulates you into taking action, such as buying a more expensive product than you intended.

And so the big tech lobbyists decided to focus on the 'High Risk' category[247], because that would be the most profitable one, and where big restrictions would be. They could afford to let the politicians require low level controls, and thus feel they'd won.

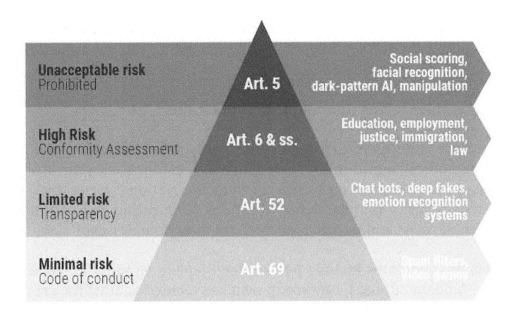

The tech firms decide which part of the regulations to challenge over the AI Act's risk-based approach.
Source: Ada Lovelace Institute

Making a contribution

Lobbyists pay contributions to the politicians, because money talks. Politicians need cash to fund campaigns, and therefore pay attention to the people who are paying them.

An elite Tory dining club, the Leader's Group, has given more than £130 million to the Conservative Party since 2010, according to openDemocracy. It has provided more than 80% of general election funds raised by the Conservatives.

The Leader's Group, which has included wealthy individuals linked to Russia, the fossil fuel industry and climate denial, is open only to those prepared to give the Conservatives at least £50,000 a year. In return, they receive regular private dinners, lunches and drinks receptions with the prime minister and other senior Tory figures, including leading cabinet ministers[248].

Embedding themselves into major organisations

Restore Trust is an astroturf organisation associated with the network of right-wing bodies housed in 55 Tutton Street, London. Each year it tries to get its supporters elected on to the board of the National Trust, the 5-million-member charity that cares for 780 miles of coastline and 500 historic properties, gardens and nature reserves, 'for everyone, for ever'.

Its favoured candidates include people like Stephen Green, the leader of a Christian fundamentalist lobby group who has lobbied against the criminalisation of marital rape[249].

Others include Philip Gibbs, a fund manager and Conservative party donor, who said the trust should be 'less political', and Andrew Gimpson, who is even worse, who described Boris Johnson as "a statesman of astonishing political gifts... impelled by a deep love of his country and a determination to serve it to the uttermost of his powers[250]

Each year, Restore Trust puts up motions at the National Trust's AGM, designed to stop the Trust from participating in Pride events, or addressing its properties' historical links to the slave trade.

But the lobbyists are often more successful. Zewditu Gebreyohanes, who has worked for the right-leaning Policy Exchange thinktank and is the director of Restore Trust (them again), got appointed as a trustee of the V&A.[251]

Acting as a double-agent

Lobbyists often juggle clashing interests, especially relating to fossil fuels.

The Guardian found over 1,500 lobbyists pledging allegiance to both fossil fuel companies and organisations that seek a green future.[252]

The lobbying firm Brown & Weinraub has twelve fossil fuel clients included tar sands oil developer Kinder Morgan, Arctic oil and gas driller Shell, the American Petroleum Institute and the Koch Companies, both of the latter two being leading funders of climate denialism.

But Brown & Weinraub also represents Syracuse University, which voted to divest from fossil fuels in 2015, as well as Stony Brook University and Pace University, which are facing pressure to divest.

It isn't a level playing field. Due to various exclusions in the law, the UK's Lobbying Act covers only 1% of lobbyists and 0.01% of civil servants[253]. But it imposes close limits on the activities of organisations like charities, and on the ways trade unions can campaign and raise funds.

Targeting key influencers

In the lobbying world, it's vital to influence key individuals who can shape public opinion and policy.

Gun control: In the USA, the gun industry targets key influencers, particularly Congress members, using lobbyists to prevent gun control legislation. Central to this effort were substantial campaign contributions to allies, securing supporters in the US Senate. Despite widespread public backing for tighter gun control, the lobbying halted reforms.

Pro-Israel lobbying: The pro-Israel lobby has had a major impact on international policy. After being nominated to serve on a human rights commission, James Cavallaro, a law professor at Wesleyan University, found his name was withdrawn after he had condemned Israel's apartheid regime.

That tweet led to the State Department withdrawing his nomination from the Inter-American Commission on Human Rights, a watchdog within the Organization for American States on which he had previously served from 2014-17. David Kaye, a former UN special rapporteur on free expression, called the withdrawal 'a huge and totally unjustified mistake.'[254]

The tech industry's influence on the UK's Digital Markets Bill

When the UK government drafted its Digital Markets Bill, the big tech firms' lobbyists sought to introduce an appeals policy that that would dilute its effectiveness, as reported by the online journal Politico.[255]

One mid-technology size firm said: "The fear is that big companies with big lawyers understand how to eke things out [during the appeals process] so that they'll keep their market advantage for years."
Consumer group Which? urged the government to stay with its proposed appeal system. "For the DMU to work effectively, the government must stick to its guns and ensure that the decisions it reaches are not tied up in an elongated appeals process," said its director of policy, Rocio Concha.

Worker safety

In Miami-Dade County, Florida, a bill aimed at shielding outdoor workers from scorching heat became a battlefield, revealing lobbyists' sway over worker safety policies. Safety measures were originally set at a 90-degree heat, but after lobbying by construction and agriculture companies, this rose to 95 degrees. This shift jeopardised workers, exposing them to heat-related risk.[256]

Promoting their own interests

Lobbyists for the oil and gas industry push for modifications to oil production, rather than phasing it out. One of their ploys is a technical solution: carbon capture. This captures carbon dioxide emissions before they reach the atmosphere. But it's expensive and unproven at scale, according to Reuters[257].

The International Energy Agency (IEA) said that the oil and gas industry is relying excessively on carbon capture to reduce emissions, and called the approach "an illusion." This sparked an angry response from OPEC which views the technology as a lifeline for its fossil fuels.

'Carbon capture' is an unproven technical solution that lets oil and gas companies continue to sell their products.

The most common form of carbon capture technology involves taking the gas from industrial chimneys. From there, the carbon can either be moved directly to permanent underground storage or used in another industrial purpose.

At the time of writing, the storage capacity for carbon capture is only 0.1% of the world's 37 billion metric tons of annual energy and industry-related carbon dioxide emissions.

What's to be done?

We need increased transparency: Stricter regulations mandating comprehensive disclosure from lobbyists and PR consultants are crucial to mitigate undue influence.

Transparency empowers citizens by revealing who shapes public policy, which enabling scrutiny of motives. Disclosure reduces the likelihood of unethical lobbying practices and increases transparency and responsibility. If lobbyists are compelled to reveal their clients, challenges, and expenditures, they'll be less inclined to participate in covert transactions.

Make the information accessible: Having readily available information is crucial in countering the influence of public and lobbyist relations professionals. Keeping comprehensive databases on lobbying activities, funds, and outcomes is an important way for governments to empower their citizens.

Educate the public: Citizens need the knowledge gathered by public awareness activities and educational initiatives to navigate the impact of lobbyists and PR consultants effectively. Knowing the tactics used by lobbyists helps the public think more critically and understand the real goals behind the messages they receive.

Set ethical guidelines: Establishing and strictly enforcing ethical criteria for lobbyists and public relations experts is crucial. Conflicts of interest and the revolving door phenomena, in which former government officials move into lobbying careers, should be strictly addressed by these rules.

Reform political campaign finance: Reforming how money is spent on political campaigns is crucial to reducing the outsized influence of corporations and the rich. The influence of large money in elections and policy making can be reduced if the government strengthens the regulations now in place.

Reforms such as contribution limits, strict transparency rules, and the promotion of public funding choices are needed to level the playing field. These reforms lessen thc chance of corruption and guarantee that voters' preferences, rather than campaign donations, shape policy outcomes.

For major issues, create binding legislation: Lobbyists and the corporations love voluntary agreements and self-regulation. But Elon Musk withdrew X, formerly Twitter, from the EU's voluntary code of practice on online disinformation. And as a libertarian who believes in free speech, he got rid of the content checkers, with the result that lies, hate speak and conspiracy theories flourish on his platform. Without legislation and penalties, governments and citizens are powerless.

Trade associations: the corporate pushers

The World Elephant Polo Association. The International Association of Youth Hypnotists. And the Association for Dressings & Sauces.

They look like names made up for a comedy TV show. But they're all quite genuine. Indeed, the dressings and sauces guys date all the way back to 1926. So they and many like them are by no means part of the 21st century zest for new fads.

Such trade associations are quite harmless. Until, that is, someone threatens their freedom of action.

Then they leap into action, protesting about the need for flexibility and the problems likely to result from legislation.

Take, for example the Land, Planning and Development Federation (LPDF). Here's what they have to say about themselves:

> "Land promoters play a crucial role in increasing the supply of housing in the UK, using their financial resources, experience and planning expertise to deliver land with planning permission, ready for developers to build out."

Sound perfect, doesn't it? But the Campaign for the Protection of Rural England (CPRE) thinks otherwise: "'Land promoters' exploit legal loopholes at the expense of communities and the countryside," says the CPRE.[258]

Note the CPRE's inverted commas above, suggesting that the main role of the LPDF members is not to promote land, but something altogether different. Profit, maybe?

It says land promoters 'persuade landowners to allow them to pursue planning permission on their land for a 20-25% share in the profits once it is sold on for development, without having to bear any risk of investing in land or building a development themselves.

'The only regard land promoters pay to planning constraints, such as protected landscapes and settlement boundaries, is in how to get around them – usually by targeting areas that are unable to demonstrate a five-year housing land supply.'

So what we have here is a trade association that benefits corporations and rich people. And it complains about 'political interference in the process at all levels,' (translation: democracy gets in our way).[259]

Where I live, Land Value Alliances (LVA), a 'land promoter', says it's been appointed (it doesn't say by whom), to put forward a plan to build 1,700 houses (or 'dwellings' as they call it) on a 325-acre 'garden village' scheme (translation: lots of identikit houses) on the edges of Frome, Somerset.

LVA is working for an unknown 'SGC landowners consortium'. Exactly who they are is unknown, but we'll assume they're farmers whom LVA has approached, and shown them how much money they could make if LVA parcelled up all their fields and put houses on them.

Also hired by the shadowy consortium is 'Grassroots Planning', a company whose name suggests community engagement and environmental protection, but which actually works for big house builders like Barratt, Bloor and by Capita, the outsourcing business.

What do trade associations do?

I've gone into some detail of how land promoters and their trade body, the LPDF work. But what about trade associations in general. Are they problematic?

A trade association will benefit corporations and the wealthy in a number of ways.

- It helps them to **avoid or weaken regulations** that would increase their costs or reduce their profits.

- It helps corporations to **obtain subsidies and other government benefits**. For instance, the agricultural industry lobbies for farm subsidies, which cost taxpayers billions each year, and largely benefits the biggest farms.

- It helps corporations to **avoid paying taxes**. For example, the pharmaceutical industry has lobbied for tax breaks on research and development, which have saved the industry substantial sums of money.

- It helps corporations **shape public opinion in their favour**. The International Air Transport Association (IATA) has long resisted restrictions and reduction in air travel as a way to reduce emissions. Instead, it suggests technological solutions (such as less thirsty engines)[260] and a reliance on offsets. IATA's focus is on continued expansion of air travel[261].

Trade associations have been criticised for lobbying on behalf of corporations to the disadvantage of wider society for a number of reasons, including:

- **Undue influence:** Trade associations have substantial money and resources, which they can use to lobby governments and policymakers on behalf of their member corporations. This gives them undue influence over public policy, and can lead to policies that benefit corporations at the expense of the public interest.

- **Lack of transparency:** Their lobbying activities are not always transparent. This makes it difficult for the public to know how trade associations are influencing public policy.

- **Misleading information:** Trade associations sometimes spread misleading information about the products and services of their member corporations.

Here are some examples of where UK and European trade associations have lobbied to hinder legislation, and thus protect its own members:

Opposed to workforce protections

The UK's Recruitment & Employment Confederation (REC) argued against measures to increase the minimum wage, arguing that it would lead to job losses. The UK government's Low Pay Commission said:

> "The Recruitment & Employment Confederation (REC) told us that lower differentials [by introducing the minimum wage] brought a risk 'that it will reduce the incentive for an individual to take on a job with added responsibilities and demands'. Whitbread told us that rising wages 'will put pressures on our plans to invest in skills development and pay progression for our employees.'"[262]

And when measures to reduce working hours were mooted, the European Automobile Manufacturers' Association (ACEA) lobbied against them, saying it would make European car manufacturers less competitive.

Anti environmental measures

The European Automobile Manufacturers' Association (ACEA) successfully lobbied to water down the EU's proposal to reduce vehicle pollution from nitrogen dioxide.

The carmakers said the proposal was "entirely disproportionate, driving high costs for industry and customers with limited environmental benefits[263]."

But the Consortium for Ultra-low Vehicle Emissions (Clove) said half the projected savings from the new Euro 7 standards on car emissions would be lost due to damage caused by excess nitrogen dioxide[264]. This gas was responsible for 49,000 premature deaths in the EU and 5,750 in the UK in just one year.

In another case - an attempt to halt measures to reduce carbon dioxide emissions from cement production - the European Cement Association (CEMBUREAU) said it would make European cement producers less competitive[265].

Anti competition

In the EU, the European Pharmaceutical Manufacturers' Association (EFPIA) has lobbied against measures to make it easier for cheaper generic drugs to enter the market, arguing that it would reduce innovation in the pharmaceutical industry.

Nathalie Moll, the EFPIA's director general, said: "Whether it is naivety, blind optimism or a more conscious decision for Europe to rely on innovation from the U.S. and Asia, everyone should be in no doubt that what we have seen as draft proposed legislation would be extremely damaging to the competitiveness of Europe's innovative pharma industry[266]." Translation: we want to keep the prices high.

Anti trade union

The Confederation of British Industry (CBI) is the main lobby group for British businesses. In the past, the CBI has called for a number of reforms to restrict trade union power. They include making it more difficult for trade unions to organise strikes[267].

Conclusion

In each case, the trade associations claimed the legislation would be too burdensome for businesses, or would make them less competitive. But legislators said the trade associations were simply trying to protect their own members' profits at the expense of consumers, workers, the environment and competition.

Trade association lobbying is a powerful tool that corporations and the wealthy use to influence government policy. It helps them to avoid or weaken regulations, obtain subsidies and other government benefits, avoid paying taxes, and shape public opinion in their favour.

And in so doing, trade association members become worthy members of the Concierge Class, helping corporations and the wealthy to make more money.

What's to be done?

Trade associations are in hock to their members, and they don't bite the hand that feeds them. So there's little hope that they'll reform.

We need to build awareness of the ways that trade associations support the aims of corporations.

Individuals in each association must recognise the injustice that selfish behaviours create, and understand how its actions might affect the workforce, the environment, and the level of competition. It takes courage.

Why politicians support the capitalists

In Chapter Three, The Enablers, we saw how, once in power, right-wing politicians support the needs of corporations and the wealthy, rather than those of weak and vulnerable people.

But outside government they act as Pushers. They do that either because they need to pander to their donors, or because they think such policies are vote winners. But mostly it's due to ideology. Let's have a look at each.

Economic ideology

Right-wing politicians generally believe in a free market economy, in which the government should play a minimal role in regulating businesses or re-distributing wealth.

They believe uncontrolled businesses are the most efficient way to create economic growth and prosperity, and that government intervention distorts the market and stifles economic activity.

These politicians believe in individual responsibility and self-reliance, and don't see that government needs to create greater equality.

Because of that, they support policies that benefit corporations, such as tax cuts, deregulation and free trade agreements. They also oppose policies that benefit weak and vulnerable people, such as welfare programmes, public services and trade unions.

Donor base

Right-wing politicians receive significant financial support from corporations and wealthy individuals. These donors are motivated by a desire to see the government implement policies that benefit their interests, such as tax cuts and deregulation.

As a result, the politicians are more likely to support policies that favour corporations and the wealthy.

Political strategy

Right-wing politicians argue that these groups are the "job creators" and "taxpayers" who drive the economy, and that policies that benefit them will ultimately benefit everyone. Conversely, they say policies that benefit the poor and vulnerable are simply handouts that create a cycle of dependency.

Not all politicians are the same, and there is a wide range of views within the right-wing spectrum. Some are more compassionate than others, and may be more willing to support policies that benefit those in need.

But in general they frequently end up as part of right-wing governments, and then implement legislation that benefits corporations and the rich. And thus they become the Enablers, we saw in Chapter Three.

What's to be done?

Politicians are driven by ideology or hope for advancement. And in the UK, many of us live in 'safe' constituencies that always return the same party, which limits the possibility of changing our MP.

So, opinion formers among the Concierge Class should push for proportional representation, which produces governments that more accurately reflect the views of the voters.

Meanwhile, we should vote tactically, to maximise the probability that a progressive candidate will win. And we can support such candidates by knocking on doors or leafleting.

Finally, we should engage with our friends and neighbours, raising local issues as examples of the problems the state is in, with the aim of building awareness.

The junk tanks

How Right-wing Think Tanks Affect Government Policy

Should we cut taxes for the wealthy, weaken employment protection, or privatise the NHS?
Right-wing think tanks are where these ideas start.

They work to advance conservative values, free-market beliefs, and minimal government involvement.

They then communicate their findings to the public and government decision-makers through publications, events and the media.

The think tanks that support free-market concepts include the Institute of Economic Affairs (IEA) and the Adam Smith Institute in the United Kingdom. These groups frequently support tax cuts as a way to boost economic expansion.

Tax cuts for corporations: The Institute of Economic Affairs (IEA) has created research that promotes business interests by arguing for lower corporate tax rates. They say it will increase investment and boost the economy.

Tax cuts for the rich: The UK's 2010–2015 coalition government lowered the highest income tax rate from 50% to 45%, citing proposals from the think tanks. The IEA has also advocated for a flat tax rate, which disproportionately favours high-income people.

Deregulation: This frequently appears in these think tanks' policy recommendations. The idea of lowering bureaucratic barriers for companies contributed to the UK's decision to leave the European Union, primarily motivated by a desire for regulatory autonomy. Think tanks like the Legatum Institute supported Brexit, arguing it would enable a more business-friendly climate.

Privatisation: This is another area of policy where the think tanks have a significant impact. In the UK, the Thatcher government sold off the railways, bus companies, docks and ports, aerospace businesses, and the water and gas and electricity utilities[268]. Many are now owned by foreign businesses.

Privatising the NHS: For years, think tanks like the Institute of Economic Affairs have pushed for giving more NHS work to private companies. This started with outsourcing and the private financing initiative (PFI). Private healthcare providers and management consultants have profited from these policies.

Trade Policies: The think tanks back free trade policies like the **Comprehensive and Progressive Agreement for Trans-Pacific Partnership (CPTPP)** and the North American Free Trade Agreement (NAFTA). Free trade agreements are supposed to encourage economic growth by giving businesses (read: multinationals, especially American ones) access to more markets.

The risk is that CTPP could let companies sue governments for supporting important state-owned businesses against dumping by foreign companies, or maintaining higher standards of animal welfare in food production. For example it could stop the EU and UK supporting small banana producers in favour of the giant multinationals like Dole, Chiquita and Del Monte.

Restrictions on trade unions: Several UK think tanks support policies that restrict trade union power. These include the following:

The Centre for Policy Studies (CPS) has been a vocal critic of trade unions. The CPS has called for a number of reforms to restrict trade union power, including:

- Making it more difficult for trade unions to organise strikes.
- Reducing the amount of money that trade unions can spend on political campaigning.
- Giving employers more power to dismiss trade unionists.

The Adam Smith Institute (ASI) believes that trade unions have too much power. The ASI has called for a number of reforms to restrict trade union power, such as:

- Making it more difficult for trade unions to collect membership fees.
- Limiting the scope of collective bargaining.
- Banning trade unions from striking in the public sector.

Adopting these policies would empower companies to lower wages, worsen employees' conditions, and reduce safety. And when an individual finds they've been bullied, underpaid or put at risk, they'll find no trade union is there to support them.

Influencing public opinion: One of the most important aspects of the job done by right-wing think tanks is influencing public opinion. These groups use a multifaceted strategy to influence public opinion in favour of laws that support their worldview of limited, pro-business government and conservatism. Here's how they do it.

Research and implied expertise: Right-wing think tanks start by analysing the topics and regulations that correspond to their ideological perspective. This is usually done by a group of academics, economists and policy analysts. The aim is to produce evidence and justifications for their policy stances. By contrast, progressive think tanks are often seen as do-gooders or idealists who don't understand the real world.

Framing the Narrative: A key to swaying public opinion is presenting the problem in a way that appeals to the target audience. They try to make their policy ideas more appealing to the general public by emphasising personal independence and individual liberty.

Media Engagement: The think tanks engage with the media to spread their research findings and policy proposals. This includes writing opinion pieces in the press, offering knowledgeable analysis, and participating in radio and television programmes.

Public Events and Seminars: Think tanks host conferences, seminars, and public events where they share their analysis and recommendations for public policy. Through these events, they can interact directly with the general public, decision-makers, and other stakeholders.

Online Presence: Right-wing think tanks are well-represented online, thanks to their websites, blogs and social media accounts. Their reports and policy briefs are then readily available to the public on their websites.

Educational Initiatives: The think tanks develop educational resources. These materials are intended for use in schools, universities, and other educational institutions to embed their beliefs in the next generation.

Lobbying and Advocacy: The think tanks typically engage in advocacy and lobbying activities to sway politicians and officials. They try to persuade decision-makers to adopt policies that comply with their suggestions by outlining their research and analysis.

Dark money

Right-wing think tanks are notoriously shy about revealing who is finding them, largely because it would reveal they're supported by corporations and the wealthy.

But voters are slowly waking up to this. They believe Britain's think tanks – that often have charitable status – are opaque and need to open up about their funding[269].

A majority (59%) of the British public believe think tanks aren't transparent, with only 19% of respondents disagreeing.

It goes for people of all ages, political leanings, voting intentions and social classes, with clear majorities for reform whichever side of the Brexit debate voters fall. The research comes amid a growing debate about the role of Britain's policy research organisations. Researchers at the Centre Think Tank found:

- 22% of UK think tanks don't reveal their total income

- Only 32% of think tanks reveal all funders who have donated more than £7,500

- Overall, right-wing organisations are less transparent than left-wing organisations – and yet have more cash.

One example is the Taxpayers' Alliance (TPA), which was given the lowest possible grade for transparency by Who Funds You, a British project that rates the transparency of funding sources.

According to Wikipedia[270], the Midlands Industrial Council, which has donated £1.5m to the Conservatives since 2003, has given around £80,000 on behalf of 32 owners of private companies. And David Alberto, who owns the mezzanine materials company Avanta, has donated a suite in Westminster worth £100,000 a year, because he opposes the level of tax on businesses.

Guardian columnist Owen Jones criticised the TPA, saying, "The TaxPayers' Alliance is a right-wing organization, funded by conservative businesspeople and staffed with free-market ideologues. And yet it presents itself as though it were simply the voice of the taxpayer. After all, 'alliance' itself implies some sort of broad coalition. From its early days, the Alliance's pronouncements were invoked by news outlets more or less as the impartial mouthpiece of the hardworking taxpayer."

What's to be done?

The government needs to introduce legislation that will reform lobbying and ensure transparency of funding.

Economists are more political than you'd think

I was sitting in an economics lecture at the London Business School, many years ago, and the professor was going on about the primacy of markets, the need to reduce government spending, and the benefits of low tax. To my ears it sounded a bit polemic.

In the coffee break after the lecture, I decided to challenge him. "I suppose it depends on whether you come from the left or the right?" I said, staring at my shoes.

He fixed me with a stony stare. "Economists don't do politics," he said. And he walked away.

Well, that put me in my place. But it made me wonder whether economists really lacked political opinions?

Had I been a bit more worldly wise, I might have realised that many of the best-known economists hold right-wing views, and therefore support corporations and the wealthy.

A paper from Columbia University shows that economists are biased. It found that "macroeconomists and financial economists are more right-leaning on average …. and economists at business schools, no matter their specialty, lean conservative."[271]

Based at Cardiff University, Patrick Minford defended Mrs. Thatcher's policies, and supported subsequent Conservative government views on inflation and unemployment. He's a strong supporter of Brexit, and supported the poll tax whereby everyone one, rich or poor, paid the same amount local tax.

Or take the economist James Forder, Academic and Research Director at the IEA.

A follower of Milton Friedman, he says we should accept the importance of price, rather than trying to regulate markets with licensing rules and obligations and prohibitions put on public bodies[272].

James Forder: Opposed to regulation.

In other words, let's not regulate.

Economists believe in a single explanation of complex phenomena. Everything can be reduced to an equation:

the supply-and-demand curve, or the Phillips curve, which links inflation and unemployment.

Economists say there are laws of economics that hold true wherever they're applied. Reduce the price of something, and sales will go up. People make rational choices about their finances. And governments shouldn't spend more than they're currently earning. That's what they're taught in economics school.

But economists don't understand that the world is a messy place. Human beings aren't always logical. We have neuroses, we're petty, and we continually make mistakes.

And we rarely have full understanding about the choices we're asked to make.

In short, economists are right leaning, with little understanding of the real world. And business school academics promote policies that benefit the rich.

None of this would matter if they were simply pontificating at their students from their podiums. What matters is that they influence the media and, through them, the government. It emboldens the politicians to introduce policies that favour the rich.

Like the UK's Office for Budget Responsibility (OBR), the US Congressional Budget Office (CBO) comments on US government budgets. Most of the 230 staff are economists. So it's a double whammy: the CBO is staffed by economists, and they listen to right-wing academics. So they're hardly likely to support a leftist or progressive perspective. Not only that but Doug Elmendorf, its former Director, admits that the CBO's forecasts are based largely on 'judgement calls'[273].

Another paper examined whether a higher top rate of tax would make rich people evade tax? In other words, would it reduce the amount of money the government gets from rich people? It's known as income elasticity. The paper sought the views of left- and right-leaning economists. Surprise, surprise! The most right-wing economists said the optimal top rate of tax should be 58%, while the most left-wing said the optimal rate would be 84%.

So it all depends on which economist you listen to.[274] If the government heeds the right-wing economists, there will see no point in putting up taxes on rich people.

And that effect is boosted by the media's preference for promoting the views of right-wing economists, which means government officials and MPs see more right-of-centre views.

What the right-wing economists believe

Right-wing economists think markets send out signals that accurately tell people how much anything is worth.[275]

They believe this information is readily available, free, and always sufficient for anyone to make all the decisions they need to make. The market needs to be kept pure and uncluttered by government interference so that it sends out the right data.

That means there should be minimal government action and tax should be kept low, because both interfere with the purity of the market.

The right-wing economists believe that markets work fast, so we can all respond immediately. And we have no other priorities or distractions in life.

The trouble with this position is that it conflicts with reality. It ignores the fact that companies combine to fix prices, that monopolies restrict choice, and that corporate marketing sends out mendacious messages that people believe.

It also ignores the fact that, if allowed, many businesses will reduce wages, introduce unsafe processes and ingredients, and deceive their customers.

Businesses that haven't adopted unethical practices will either be forced to do the same, or go bust.

The economists have models, filled with algebra, that support for their views. But the models only work in a perfect world, filled with people who have complete knowledge of the market, whose only role is that of a consumer, and who owe no allegiance to family and friends.

Thus their inevitable solution is to recommend low tax, small government, and light regulation. Right-wing economists are thus a gift to the wealthy because they endorse and validate their selfish needs, often with fancy algebra that people don't understand.

Talking of algebra, here's one of Patrick Minford's: $P=P^* + \epsilon$

Here, P is the 'equilibrium price' for a product. It's the price a product sells at when supply and demand match.

Then there's P*. That's the price you expect to see if your theory works.

P* is P plus ϵ, the epsilon being 'a small error', caused in this case by information you hadn't, ahem, foreseen at the time you formed your expectations.
In other words, the equation says: "You expect the price to be what it should be".

Or to put it another way: "The world will be what I think it should be. And if I'm wrong it's because something happened I didn't expect".

Anyone can conjure up an equation like that. I labour this point only to demonstrate that we don't need to be over-awed by economists' apparent expertise.

Their motivation

Note, however, that unlike most of the Pushers, right-wing economists don't seek to gain advantage from their work. It's an important distinction.

No, they spread their views for reasons of simple, unalloyed belief. Trained to believe the words of their teachers, they believe in the absolute truth of their algebra and graphs.

And in so doing they delight corporations and the wealthy, who clap their hands and say, "We agree! Interfere less, and we'll make ~~more profit~~ the world a better place."

What's to be done?

We should recognise that economists have political opinions, which are mostly right of centre.

Hence, we should recognise they're merely another section of the Concierge Class, advocating policies that support the corporations.

Pleading poverty: museums and galleries

It's 10.15am on an autumn Tuesday morning in Vienna. It's a quiet time for Leopold Museum as visitors are drifting in.

Suddenly, two protesters from Letzte Generation (the Last Generation) pour what looks like petrol over Kilmt's painting, *Death and Life.*

Visitors are horrified, believing the painting is damaged.

The museum later said the painting wasn't harmed, though there was the damage to the glass and security framing.

And the reason for the stunt? The Leopold Gallery gets sponsorship from the Austrian oil and gas company OMV, but the protesters were making a more general point about the impact of oil and gas companies on the climate. And because of the horror it aroused, the activists got the publicity they wanted for their cause.

Corporations and wealthy individuals and corporations are often major donors to museums and galleries. And there are several reasons why museums and galleries are taking these controversial donations:

Protesters smear a Gustav Klimt painting.
Source: Letzte Generation

- It's difficult for them to get sufficient government funding to meet all of its needs.

- Wealthy donors can provide massive financial support, which allows the institutions to expand their collections, host more exhibitions and reach new audiences.

- Rich people sometimes OM have personal ties to a particular museum or gallery, or may be interested in supporting a specific cultural event.

But there are also risks associated with taking funding from the rich. Taking funding from the wealthy can create a conflict of interest for the institution. For example, if it receives funding from an energy company, it's less likely to host exhibitions on climate change or some other environmental issue.

It's lending its prestige, and providing favourable publicity that the donor gets from being seen as a philanthropist. And it's helping to change public opinion.

But visitors can be dismayed by the choice of donor, which in turn damages the institution's reputation.

There are many examples of controversies over museums and galleries taking funding from corporations and the wealthy:

- **The Sackler family**, which owns Purdue Pharma, the manufacturer of OxyContin, has been widely criticised for causing the opioid epidemic. And the family were accused of using their philanthropy to whitewash their reputation.

- **The Science Museum** in London was criticised over a sponsorship deal with Shell for an exhibition exploring technologies to remove carbon dioxide from the atmosphere. Critics say the exhibition served to muddy the waters over Shell's role in damaging the climate.

- **BP**, the oil and gas company, used to fund the Tate Modern art gallery until protests obliged the gallery to end its sponsorship deal. Activists and artists argued the Tate was implicitly endorsing BP's impact on the environment.

- **Leonard Blavatnik**, a Ukrainian born multimillionaire has handed out money to public institutions, in many cases getting a building named after him. Blavatnik made the largest ever donation to Harvard's medical school – a huge $200 million. Oxford University accepted more than $100 million. And the National Portrait Gallery got £10m.

When Blavatnik gave $12 million to the USA's Council on Foreign Relations, 55 international relations scholars wrote: "It is our considered view that Blavatnik uses his 'philanthropy' – funds obtained by and with the consent of the Kremlin, at the expense of the state budget and the Russian people – at leading western academic and cultural institutions to advance his access to political circles,"

So it's obvious that these institutions are accepting money from unsavoury individuals and organisations.

It's also clear that much of the money is dirty. How can one individual have hundreds of millions of dollars in their bank account? Where did the money come from? And who has been harmed in the reaping of those profits? All too often it's either the planet, or the hapless citizens of Russia or some other kleptocracy.

Leonard Blavatnik made his money in the privatisation of state-owned assets, following the collapse of the Soviet Union.

And rather than putting their ill-gotten gains into humanitarian causes, the donors get the prestige and satisfaction of seeing their name on the gallery, and get to attend black tie events there.

The directors and senior staff of the galleries and museums know this. And they decide to take the money, brazen it out, and yield to criticisms only under duress.

They'd love the controversies to go away, knowing the population has a short attention span. But with donors' names on the plaques and the exhibition credits, it's hard to make them disappear.

They'd also like to see themselves as uninvolved in politics, being merely managers and custodians. Unfortunately, taking money from plutocrats and oil companies is a highly visible activity. And the act of receiving the money is itself a political decision.

"Museums cannot be activists," said Nicholas Cullinan, the director of the National Portrait Gallery, while also saying the museum had "red lines" over who it would accept money from - this after being obliged to give up its relationship with BP.

We may feel some empathy for the institutions. But in many cases the donations are designed to extend the organisation's buildings or create a new exhibition: they aren't essential to its future.

In summary, the institutions are supporting the corporations and the rich. By taking the money and putting the rich person's name on their latest extension, the gallery is burnishing the donor's image, and easing their way into high society. And all this at the expense of the planet and its people.

What's to be done?

Members of the Concierge Class involved in museums and galleries mustn't allow themselves to be ensnared by corporations and the rich, despite the offer of huge sums of money.

They should understand why the wealthy want to engage with them, and that it comes with a reputational price tag.

How the clerics side with the rich

'What's religion got to do with the Concierge Class?', you might ask.

Plenty, is the answer.

The clerics are in a position of power. They preach at their congregations from the pulpit, minbar or amud. They support reactionary ideas, as we shall see. And they do the work of a higher power, as they see it. That makes them part of the Concierge Class.

Let's have a look at the harm caused by the clerics and their followers, and see if there are any solutions.

- **They contain hateful content**: Christian teaching tells us that God damned the human race and cursed His entire creation because of the acts of two people. He drowned pregnant women and innocent children and animals at the time of the flood. And he killed Egyptian babies at the time of the Passover. He sanctions slavery (Leviticus 25:44-46); he ordered religious persecution (Deuteronomy 13:12-16); and he caused cannibalism (Jeremiah 19:9).

- **They justify discrimination:** Some religious texts have been used to justify discrimination based on gender, sexuality, or other factors, or even harmful actions like violence against specific groups. These practices are morally reprehensible and contradict the principles of fairness and equality.

- **They're exclusionary**: Each religion believes that the others are wrong. They create otherness, creating 'in' and 'out' groups in the community. Catholics believe you can't get to heaven if you haven't confessed your sins. Hindus have killed Moslems in India. Jews spit on Christians in Israel[276], and the murderous wars in Yugoslavia were marked by religious affiliation[277]. Religious belief is largely, if not entirely, why we've had so many wars down the centuries.

- **They restrict individual freedoms:** Many religions impose restrictions on personal choices and behaviours, such as diet, sexual conduct or dress code. They can be oppressive and infringe basic human rights. How can it be right to deny your child a blood transfusion?[278]

- **They promote harmful social norms:** Religious teachings on gender roles, sexuality, or other social issues are mostly outdated or harmful in contemporary society. For example, teachings that view women as subordinate to men, or condemn homosexuality as sinful, perpetuate inequalities. They hinder social progress and justice.

- **They teach children much of what they do is sinful**. Sinful thoughts, sinful glances, sinful views. Sinful acts. The churches teach that the only way a child can be absolved of its of their guilt is through the church and its precepts

- **They conflict with scientific advances:** Religious doctrines often clash with scientific findings or discoveries, leading to tension and challenges in reconciling faith and reason. For example, the theory of evolution contradicts creationist stories found in most religious texts. Clinging to outdated beliefs in the face of scientific evidence hinders progress.

- **They value God over democracy**: In their world view, the spiritual trumps the secular. Jehovah's Witnesses, the Christadelphians, the Amish, the Hutterites and the Exclusive Brethren forbid voting. This means they exclude their followers from contributing to the real world.

- **The churches support conservative values**: According to Nurit Novis-Deutsch of the University of Haifa, "Studies consistently find that religious people tend to be more conservative politically and support existing social arrangements rather than new ones. In one large-scale study of the extent to which religiosity accounted for ideological orientations, religiosity was consistently related to right and conservative ideologies in 15 of 16 countries, across religions[279]."

  The paper continues: "The conservative world view holds a darker view of human nature, considering people to be selfish and weak, and maintaining that society needs to rely on experience, institutional authority, traditions and rules in order to maintain social order. Reliance on reason, ideology, abstract values and utopian visions are considered to have dangerous consequences. Concrete, specific and time-honored political arrangements are preferred; duties are emphasized over rights."

- **The churches have long been allied to the establishment**: Being part of the establishment, the religious hierarchy has always been close to the monarchy and the powerful.

  The Catholic Church opposed land reform in Latin America; and its opposition benefited wealthy landowners, who were able to keep their land and maintain their wealth.

When a new king ascends the throne, the crown will be placed on his head by an archbishop: it illustrates the nature of their mutual need.

King Charles is crowned by the bishops. It implies the clerics are in charge of the state.

In short, they hold people back from viewing the world objectively, and free from dogma. They contribute to a medieval world view that supports conservative values.

But in the UK, only 5% of the population attend a Christian church. And it's declining all the time.

So you could argue that religion isn't important. You could also point out that some clerics stand up for the poor and dispossessed, and that's true.

So why do we care? Well, let's look at the schools.

The religious schools

Religious schools make up a substantial minority of state-funded schools in England. Nearly a third of schools (31%) are run by a religious order[280].

And as we've seen, only 5% of the population are actively involved in religion.

Thus the number of religious schools is out of all proportion to the population's church attendance. So there's a strong case for converting them to secular schools.

But it's more than just numbers. It's really about values and pedagogy. Bound by adherence to the church's dogma, Catholic priests will, if pressed, talk about sin: the wrongfulness of gay sex, and time-honoured the sin of abortion. Using contraception is 'intrinsically evil'[281]. They believe in a man with a beard, who lives in the sky, is actually three people, and performed miracles for bronze-age tribes people in Palestine. God is apparently benign, yet condemns us all for the curiosity of one person, a fault he blames on a woman. And so on, and so on.

As I've said, religion is exclusionary. For each sect, theirs is the one true path to salvation. Hence the bitter strife we see around the world. Separate schools based on religion have fostered the troubles in Northern Ireland,

So, no matter how well-intentioned they are, religious schools serve to widen differences rather than bring people together. Granted, these days the religious schools have classes that teach about other religions, but that doesn't free the school from its underlying beliefs.

Moreover, the clerics are unsuitable as teachers. A study of 63,235 people, published by the US National Library of Medicine[282] shows that religionists make poor academics:

> "Put simply, religious individuals are less likely to engage logical processes and be less efficient at detecting reasoning conflicts; therefore, they are more likely to take intuitive answers at face value and this impairs performance on intelligence tests."

It therefore implies they're unsuited to managing schools.

It isn't hard to abolish religion from schools. Schools in France are secular, and have been since the first secularisation law of 1882.

What's to be done?

Overall, the clerics are clearly members of the Concierge Class. They have an influence in many ways similar to the monarchy. They tell people that they're subject to a higher power, they aren't free agents, and they should be obedient.

Accordingly, we should make our schools secular, removing them from the control of the religious orders.

We also need to disestablish the Church of England, and remove the Bishops from the House of lords.

When science allies with the corporations

Over 1,000 scientists have signed the 'Dublin Declaration', in support of meat production and consumption. Most of signatories appear to be researchers in animal, agricultural and food sciences. So they should know.

The Dublin Declaration says the arguments against meat eating are 'reductionist' and based on zealotry. Livestock are precious to society, it says, and calls for a "balanced view of the future of animal agriculture".

But hang on a minute. Who exactly are these scientists?

According to Unearthed, Greenpeace UK's journalism project, the signatories and the document's promoters have major links to the livestock industry and its consultants.[283]

Well, there's a surprise.

The six-member organising committee that developed the declaration includes Prof Dr Peer Ederer, Prof Dr Frederic Leroy, and Collette Kaster.

- Ederer runs the Global Food and Agribusiness Network (GFAN), a company that provides research and advice to clients in the meat and livestock sector. He said recently on social media that veganism was an "eating disorder requiring psychological treatment".
- Leroy is a food scientist at Vrije Universiteit Brussels and president of the Belgian Association of Meat Science and Technology. He's called plant-based meat alternatives "dietary comedy[284]".

- And Kaster is the chief executive of the American Meat Science Association.

The declaration's website is hosted by a meat industry research project called the International Meat Research G3 Foundation, which is registered to the same address as the Polish Beef Association (PBA).

Prof. Peter Smith of the University of Aberdeen, UK, a lead author on eight reports by the authoritative Intergovernmental Panel on Climate Change, said: The Dublin Declaration reads more like livestock industry propaganda than science".

And Prof. Jennifer Jacquet of the University of Miami, US, said: "The Dublin Declaration is another instance of the livestock industry taking a page out of the fossil fuel playbook to fight action on climate change. It tries to leverage the academic profession and its institutions to downplay the role of livestock in climate change."

It's a ploy that's been used for decades. Here are the main reasons why it happens:

Conflicts of interest: When scientists have financial or other ties to corporations, they're more likely to produce research that's favourable to those corporations, even if it is not accurate or complete. A 1954 study funded by the tobacco industry found that there was no "significant increase" in the risk of lung cancer among smokers[285].

But we now know that smoking is the leading preventable cause of death in the world. Expect to see more research in the coming years by scientists employed by the vaping industry that 'prove' the value of vaping.

Research bias: Scientists may also be biased in their research, even if they don't have any direct financial ties to corporations. For example, scientists who are funded by corporations may be more likely to choose research topics that are favourable to those corporations.

Those who are employed by pharmaceutical companies can exaggerate the benefits of their drugs by carefully selecting the research questions and methods to produce the result that sits them best. The pharmaceutical company Merck was forced to withdraw its drug Vioxx from the market after it was linked to an increased risk of heart attacks and strokes. Merck had previously funded scientists to produce research that downplayed the risks of Vioxx[286].

Misleading or fraudulent research: In some cases, scientists have published misleading or fraudulent research in order to support the aims of corporations. ExxonMobil has funded scientists to produce research that contradicted the scientific consensus on climate change[287]. And Volkswagen has funded scientists to produce research that downplayed the emissions of its diesel vehicles[288].

The depressing story of SSRIs

SSRI antidepressants are widely prescribed by psychiatrists in treating depression. According to a BBC Panorama programme, 83 million such drugs were dispensed in 2021. 23% of British women are taking antidepressants. And more than two million people have been taking antidepressants for over 5 years.

But Prof David Healy of Bangor University is an outspoken critic of them.

Specifically, he says they're addictive, they stop working over time, they cause suicide, and drug manufacturers have suppressed negative research findings[289].

Papers are still appearing in the Lancet and other medical journals, promoting the effectiveness of SSRIs, despite growing evidence to the contrary.

Healy, who has been vilified for his statements, isn't opposed to SSRIs, but merely that their hazards should be recognised[290].

Ever controversial, Healy has said that 50 per cent of literature on drugs is written by anonymous scribes with scientific backgrounds, who are paid to produce reports for publication. And he's been criticised for portraying psychiatrists as greedy and duped.

What needs to happen

David Healy

Scientists must refuse to support unethical corporations, despite the lure of money and fame. They should ensure they're aware of the role that corporations lay in promoting their products.

They must not allow themselves to be used by corporations to produce misleading statistics.

And they must always place the needs of patients and ethics first.

The gilded cage

Imagine you're a science academic, teaching in the area of solvents.

Part of your work involves attending conferences to keep up to date on scientific developments. During coffee breaks and over lunch, you chat to people, including scientists who work in industry. You listen to their concerns, and hear about the many challenges they face.

You even get an invitation to visit a new state-of-the art plant in Germany, where they're making headway in developing new processes. It gives you important insights into the future.

And that gives you an idea for a scientific paper which might be accepted by a prestigious journal. So you sit down to write. But you need some background data, and so you call up your friend in Germany. She's delighted to help.

And the good thing is, it's all above board. The company isn't paying you. You're a free agent.

Or are you? Is this the slippery slope of 'capture', the thin end of the wedge?

Members of the Concierge Class sometimes get captured, and hardly notice their gilded cage.

Capture and co-option are two related concepts that describe how corporations and wealthy individuals influence the behaviour of regulators, trade bodies, politicians and scientists to serve their own interests, rather than the public good.

Capture is when an organisation or individual becomes unduly influenced by a particular industry or special interest group, and begins to adopt their viewpoint. They may even start to act as their publicist, without necessarily realising what has happened. This can happen through a variety of means, such as lobbying, campaign contributions, and revolving doors between the public and private sectors. We'll talk more about this later in the book.

Co-option is similar, but involves corporations and wealthy individuals winning over the same bodies and individuals by giving them a role in the design or implementation of a programme. It's not a genuine form of participation, however, because they don't want the advice of the co-opted, merely their endorsement. They can do this by giving them a seat at meetings, funding research, providing speaking engagements, or offering consulting opportunities.

Imagine, for example, that an oil company offers to discuss green issues with government, NGOs or the public. It adopts a placatory tone, but does it intend to make any major change? The invitees must therefore decide whether and how to engage with the corporation. Should they accept the invitation and push for change? If they engage with the corporation, will they end up co-opted? Or should they reject the invitation, boycott the programme, and lose influence?

Critics even argue that the Concierge Class try to elevate members of historically oppressed communities (black and LGBTQ for example) into their groups, in the name of 'diversity'. This represents another version of co-option, where the elite becomes more demographically diverse, but the same old structures remain, and the poor are kept in their place.

Regulatory capture

If a regulatory agency is captured by the industry it's supposed to regulate, it's less likely to enforce regulations or may even weaken them altogether. This can lead to harm to the public, such as environmental pollution or unsafe products.

The Deepwater Horizon was a BP rig looking for oil 4 miles (66km) off the Gulf of Mexico, when it exploded, killing 11 crew members and igniting a fireball. It blazed unstoppably for two days before sinking, with oil gushing from the seabed, and was the largest marine oil spill in history.

The Deepwater Horizon on fire.

An investigation found that the regulator, the Minerals Management System (MMS), was dependent on the oil industry's expertise[291]. While drilling leases doubled between 1982 and 2007, MMS staffing resources decreased by 36 percent[292].

It was thus reliant on the industry's judgement of suitable safeguards that should be incorporated into regulations. Critics said the oil industry's deep pockets gave it leverage over MMS decisions. None of BP's engineers or executives have ever faced criminal charges.

Trade body capture

If a trade body is captured or controlled by its industry or professional members, it may start lobbying for policies that benefit them, even if the policies harm the public. For example, The National Farmers' Union (NFU) has been criticised for its close ties to the government and for its lobbying on behalf of large-scale intensive farming practices. This has led to accusations that the NFU's interests are not aligned with those of small-scale farmers or consumers[293].

Critics have also accused the British Property Federation (BPF) of lobbying for policies that benefit property developers, at the expense of tenants and local communities. It has opposed measures to increase affordable housing provision and has lobbied against taxes on property speculation and other policies that would benefit the public but harm the profits of its members[294][295].

Political capture

The UK's conservative party is heavily reliant on housing developers, major landowners, and those with large property portfolios, according to a report by Transparency International UK. The party received over 80% of its political donations from individuals and companies related to substantial property interests between 2010 and 2020[296]. No other political party had such as high ratio of donations from this industry.

Similarly, the US political system is widely seen as being captured by money. In the 2020 election cycle, corporations and wealthy individuals spent over $14 billion on campaign contributions and lobbying. This gave them a significant level of influence over politicians, who are heavily reliant on their financial support to promote their policies to voters.

Scientific co-option

Capture and co-option have a negative impact on scientific research. If corporations are able to co-opt scientists, they can manipulate the design of the research, or amend the findings to support their own interests.

Breakfast cereal companies have been accused of funding research that exaggerates the health benefits of their products. A study funded by Kellogg's claimed that eating breakfast cereal was associated with better academic performance. However, this study was criticised for its lack of control for other factors that could have influenced academic performance, such as socioeconomic status[297].

What's to be done?

Anyone who works with for-profit businesses needs to be alert to the possibility of being coerced, captured or co-opted by them.

We need to ask ourselves: who funds the organisation? What are its motives? How does it stand to benefit? Who will lose out?

The sweet taste of money

Food scientists have long been criticised for their role in creating ultra-processed foods.

Their work puts profits ahead of public health: they create foods that are addictive and designed to appeal to our unhealthy cravings. So let's have a quick look at this special branch of the Concierge Class.

Food scientists create junk food, including white bread, breakfast cereals, crisps, ice cream, biscuits and cakes, and sweets.

And the dangerous foods they produce involve processed meats: salami, sausages, hot dogs and bacon which cause bowel cancer, according to a study published in the International Journal of Epidemiology[298]. It examined whether people who eat an average of 76 grams of processed and red meat a day – approximately 3 slices of ham – are at increased risk of bowel cancer. This is similar to the average amount of such meats that people in the UK eat each day.

The main finding from the study was that eating even moderate amounts of processed meat increases bowel cancer risk.

Ultra-processed foods (UPFs) are thus a major contributor to the current public health crisis; and food scientists are at the heart of the concierge class problem.

UPFs are those that have undergone a significant degree of processing, often with added sugars, fats, salt, and preservatives. These foods are typically high in calories, low in nutrients, and contribute to a variety of health problems, including obesity, heart disease, type 2 diabetes, and some types of cancer.

This cheese burger contains 62 ingredients, including 12 E numbers.

Ultra-processed foods are also often environmentally unsustainable. Producing ultra-processed foods often requires a lot of energy and resources, and it can lead to pollution.

Among the major food ingredient companies that employ food scientists are the following:

- **Cargill** has come under criticism for numerous issues, including slave labour, pollution, rainforest deforestation, and mercury poisoning[299].

- **Archer Daniels Midland** was fined for allowing money laundering[300]. The FCA fined it £6.5 million ($7.9 million) for multiple shortcomings between 2014 and 2016. The company got a third of its profit from "high-risk clients" during the period and had dozens of customers who were based in jurisdictions notorious for their money-laundering risks and who were "politically exposed persons," the regulator said. Its failings continued even after 'clear warnings,' said the regulator.

- **Ingredion** is an 'ingredients solutions' company. It makes sweeteners, starches, nutrition ingredients and biomaterials (whatever they are). Sweeteners such as syrups, maltodextrins, dextrose and polyols make up 35% of its sales.

You'll also find food scientists researching and developing new food products in:

- **Research institutions:** Food scientists also work for research institutions, such as universities and private research companies.

- **Consultancy firms:** Food scientists also work for consultancy firms that develop products for food companies

Note, however, that not all UPFs are the same. A study of 260,000 people in seven European countries found there was a link to cancer for animal-based UPFs and artificially and sugar-sweetened beverages. But ultra-processed breads and cereals or plant-based alternatives were not associated with risk[301].

What's to be done?

In this era of 'fake news' and 'junk science', scientists have a responsibility to limit their work only on ethical tasks, of which UPFs and related ingredients are not a part. It isn't a sufficient argument to say that others will take your place; that's the argument for selling cocaine to children.

Note also that anyone who works in the junk food business has a degree of culpability. This includes the directors, marketers, sales people, and those in finance.

But enough of science. Let's look at something more entertaining: the world of sport.

How corruption became a fixture in sport

You've got a ticket to watch Manchester City play Man United. It's 3-0 to Man City. Sergio Agüero, City's top scorer, is on top form. What a great match. The crowd is excited.

But wait a minute. What's the shirt that Agüero is wearing? It's got 'Etihad' in big letters on it.

Etihad is owned by the United Arab Emirates. So is Manchester City football club itself.

Sergio Agüero, associated with Etihad.

The UAE doesn't have democratically elected institutions, and its citizens can't change their government or form political parties. Homosexuality is illegal, and women can't marry without the permission of a legal guardian. Academics and activists who criticise the regime face imprisonment.

Apfa, the Association of Professional Flight Attendants, has campaigned against Etihad and other United Arab Emirates airlines, saying they're "well-known in our industry for their discriminatory labour practices and deplorable treatment of female employees".

The Wall Street Journal reported that Etihad 'may fire women if they become pregnant' and that it forces flight attendants to live in 'confinement' in secure compounds'[302].

Apfa has also criticised Oscar-winning actor Afa Nicole Kidman for starring in Etihad's ads, noting that Kidman is a United Nations women's goodwill ambassador.

As you'll know, this is all about sportswashing, spending huge sums of money on buying clubs and sponsoring teams and players.

"The UAE's enormous investment in Manchester City is one of football's most brazen attempts to 'sportswash' a country's deeply tarnished image," said Amnesty International.

When the British academic Matthew Hedges was sentenced to life imprisonment in the UAE for spying[303], his trial had lasted just five minutes and no lawyer was present. But on social media, voices among the Manchester City fans were loud in support of the UAE.

Sportswashing isn't exclusive to the UAE. Almost every elite team and venue is sponsored by some corporation or plutocrat. But the fans only want to talk about the sport, and rejoice that the money has paid for top players, whether or not they come from 11,782 km away, as in the case of Sergio Agüero.

When the wealthy buy and sell clubs, they become ever more distant from the local community. And the advertising and the merchandise serves to promote the corporations and benefit the owners. Sport has become a rich men's playground.

The multi-millionaire Hollywood actors Ryan Reynolds and Rob McElhenney paid £2m for Wrexham football club, and have since paid more for players. Their first year's wage bill was £2.3 million, and has risen substantially since then. The Hollywood duo is thought to have spent around £10 million so far.

But for the club it's a Faustian pact. The owners need the club to win.

"We're heavily invested in building this club, the stadium itself, and if we don't get promoted this year, the club is completely, totally, and wholly unsustainable," Reynolds says at the start of the Season 2 of 'Welcome to

Wrexham' that aired on Disney+.

McElhenney had a similar view: "If Wrexham isn't sustainable, then they've failed on their promise to the community and the team will be fucked."

That raises the question of what he means by 'sustainable'. It probably translates as: 'If Wrexham isn't making me enough money'.

Reynolds and McElhenney, proud purchasers of a football club.

We could ask what 'promise' the footballers ever made to 'the community', except to try their hardest?

And what does, 'The team will be fucked' mean? Does the implied threat mean the owners will sell up?[304]

In the same tone, McElhenney tells the unpaid Wrexham women's team: "You're all very important to us, and we want to continue to support you. And if you keep winning, it makes it a lot easier," before adding they should score more goals next time.

The club is now thought to worth £8 million. So if the owners sold it, they'd make four times what they bought it for less than three years ago. And the owners got £9m from the two Disney+ TV series[305], as well as income from other sources.

Are the owners moving on to pastures new? The duo has invested in the Alpine Formula One motor racing team, suggesting their ties to Wrexham may only be skin deep, that they may be getting bored, or that the whole thing was only about a multi-millionaire' investment.

The Wrexham squad gets paid almost double that of their League Two competitors, which is an essential point. The media positions Wrexham as plucky underdogs with a fairytale story. But what really happened was that two very rich men bought a very poor team in a poor league and spent more than anyone else to buy players way above Wrexham's level. In other words they bought success. And that means other teams are disadvantaged.

Conclusion

Here's what Fruh, Archer and Wojtowicz write in an article called 'Sportswashing: Complicity and Corruption' in the 'Sport, Ethics and Philosophy' journal[306]:

> The distinctive wrongs of sportswashing are twofold: first, it makes participants in sport (athletes, coaches, journalists, fans) complicit in the sportswasher's wrongdoing, which extends a moral challenge to millions of people involved with sport.

> Second, sportswashing corrupts valuable heritage associated with sporting traditions and institutions. Finally, we examine how sportswashing ought to be resisted.

> The appropriate forms of resistance will depend upon different roles people fill, such as athlete, coach, journalist, fan. The basic dichotomy of resistance strategies is to either exit the condition of complicity, for example by refusing to participate in the sporting event, or to modify one's engagement with the goal of transformation in mind.

> We recognize this is difficult and potentially burdensome:

sports are an important part of many of our lives; our approach attempts to respect this.

In other words, many people are complicit. Going back to Manchester City, we can point the finger at the sporting bodies that regulate football, the club directors who sold out to the UAE, the players, their manager and the trainers who went to work for the UAE, and the fans who support the UAE. To which we can add the journalists who present Wrexham as a fairy story and ignore the underlying unpalatable truth.

Too many people are knowingly failing to face the facts: that rich people and autocratic states buy their way into sport, corrupt a noble tradition, and present themselves as good people.

As the paper says, we all have a responsibility to abandon our state of complicity. It means either refusing to participate in the sport or changing the way we engage with it.

Footballers can tackle hunger

In sport, as in other fields, there are exceptions. Here's one of them:

Footballer Marcus Rashford has been praised for his actions as a political activist and philanthropist to drive societal change.

Marcus Rashford

He's campaigned against racism, homelessness and child hunger in the UK. Rashford is from a working-class family; his mother is a single parent who often had to work multiple jobs to feed their family, sometimes skipping meals herself to ensure Rashford and his siblings ate.

During the UK Covid lockdown, Rashford worked with the poverty and food waste charity FareShare to deliver meals to those in the Greater Manchester area who were no longer receiving their free school meals, as well as to children who attended community centres and school breakfast clubs. This raised over £20 million to provide food for children nationwide who, if still at school, would be receiving free school meals. The charity provided four million meals across the country.

Rashford also wrote an open letter to the UK government calling on them to end UK child poverty. The government subsequently changed its policy regarding free school meals for children during the summer holidays, with Rashford's campaign credited as a major turning point in the government's decision. Rashford's actions were described as a "political masterclass" by The Guardian[307].

Sport: what needs to happen?

Sports fans need to develop an awareness of the reality behind sportswashing and sponsorship.

The club owners should refuse to take corrupt money. And as the authors of the journal article said, participants at all levels should either refuse to participate in the sporting event, or modify their engagement with the aim of transforming the club or sport.

What's next?

This ends our look at The Pushers, those who publicise and praise corporations and the wealthy.

We'll move on to examine the Suppliers, which includes anyone who provides goods and services to business and the rich. As we'll see, some are more culpable than others.

5. The Suppliers

How architects and developers make sky high profits

If you're walking down Fenchurch Street in London, you'll see an ugly 37-storey building looming over you. It gets wider as it rises, which allows for bigger floors at the lucrative upper levels, so the owners can make more money. This is 20 Fenchurch Street, the so-called Walkie Talkie.

Hold on to your hat as you walk down the street, lest you get blown away by its downdraft. It's been known to whisk away restaurant food trolleys, and nearly knock people off their feet.

When first opened, its concave design focused sunlight onto the street below, melting cars and scorching pedestrians. So the owners had to install screens on the upper floors.

'Thuggish': 20 Fenchurch Street.

The building is plonked "way outside the city's planned cluster of high-rise towers, on a site never intended for a tall building," said the Guardian. "It looms thuggishly over its low-rise neighbours like a broad-shouldered banker in a cheap pinstriped suit," the newspaper went on.

It's just one example of how architects bow to the god of profit, meeting the desires of the developers of build ever taller buildings; because more floors mean more profit. And the result is a sprawl of identikit buildings across the cities of the world.

These tall buildings have a number of negative impacts on ordinary people, blocking sunlight, casting shadows and creating wind tunnels. They're usually out of keeping with the local area, expensive to maintain and energy-intensive.

They even get built in World Heritage sites, like The Liverpool Museum. Described by its owners as 'magnificent', this was called "a giant shed" by some critics, and 'a godawful mess' by the Guardian, which said it 'fails to complement the city's proud past'.

Some buildings are unsafe. This can happen for a number of reasons, such as cost-cutting, poor planning, or a lack of expertise. Grenfell Tower in London was a residential high-rise that was clad in flammable materials. This made the building vulnerable to fire; and a major blaze in 2017 killed 72 people.

Why do architects do this?

There are a number of reasons why architects may choose to support corporations and the wealthy, sometimes to the disadvantage of ordinary people. Some of these reasons include:

- **A genuine interest in creating new forms of buildings**. We can't blame architects for wanting to move architecture forward. Otherwise, we'd all still be living in huts made of wattle and daub. There is a place for inspirational new buildings.

- **Financial gain:** Architects can earn a lot of money by working for wealthy clients and corporations. It's especially tempting for young architects who are struggling to pay off their student loans.

- **Recognition and prestige:** Architects often gain recognition and prestige by working on high-profile projects for wealthy clients and corporations. This can lead to more work and higher fees in the future.

- **Lack of awareness:** Some architects are simply not aware of the negative impact their work will have on ordinary people. They may be more focused on the financial, creative and professional benefits of working for corporations and the rich.

- **Personal taste:** Architects often design buildings that reflect their personal post-modernist tastes, rather than designing buildings that blend in with their surroundings. This can create a sense of alienation and displacement for ordinary people who live in the area. The modernist architecture of the Pruitt-Igoe housing complex in St. Louis, Missouri was widely criticised for its negative impact on the community. The complex was eventually demolished in the 1970s.

As well as the architects, the problem also lies with the planning authorities that permit such buildings, or don't have the knowledge or critical skills to see the reality behind the shiny brochures. There's a difficult line to tread between rejecting buildings for their modernity, and accepting those are simply unsuitable.

And let's bear in mind that architects are also the same profession responsible for fine buildings that people love.

The developers

Few buildings in the UK are 'listed' as buildings of important merit. And of those, only 5% get Grade II listing, characterised as 'Particularly important buildings of more than special interest'.

One of those is the cathedral-like Liverpool Street railway station, completed in 1875 and built of wrought iron and glass. In 1975 British Rail wanted to demolish it, but the outcry prevented it.

Busier than ever, the building now suffers from overcrowding. So Network Rail, the railway company, wants to demolish it again. And to pay for that, it needs to put a multi-storey tower on top of it.

Their plan, they say, is the only way to significantly improve the experience of using the terminus.

Liverpool Street Station as it currently is.

John Darlington, director of projects at the World Monuments Fund Britain, likens to "putting two massive sumo wrestlers on top of this historic building."

Connor McNeill, conservation advisor for the Victorian Society blames the railway for overcrowding at Liverpool Street. "These stations are overcrowded because the trains don't run on time," he says. "However much money you spend on a station it only takes one or two trains to be cancelled for passenger numbers to get to dangerous levels."

But hey, there will be a public swimming pool! The developers say they'll include a pool which can be used by local schools, by people working in the offices below, and by the public, with pricing that's in line with council-run lidos nearby.

But others have reservations about its viability. "Coordinating children to swim outdoors - in the rain too, whilst 16 floors up, in the middle of the City of London is a pipe dream," said one critic. "I'd rather see the cost of building this pool, and it will be huge, is put into a proper lido in a community that needs it," they said.

The Guardian's Rowan Moore says the plans would alleviate some but not all of the station's bottlenecks, and they don't prove that the same could be achieved by less drastic means. "The developers claim their improvements will cost the vast sum of £450m, but refuse to show the workings behind the figure due to "commercial confidentiality", he said.

"This reticence", he went on, "is consistent with a tendency towards obfuscation that has accompanied the proposals ever since they were unveiled. Given the scale and impact of this orgy of construction and disruption, the burden of proof is surely on them to demonstrate its necessity, which they still haven't done."

Rupert Wheeler, chair of the neighbouring Spitalfields Society was appalled by the scale of the Liverpool Street plan. "It is just enormous. That is fundamentally what is wrong with it in terms of urban scale," he said. Pointing out that all the natural light would be lost, he said: "As an architect, if someone has asked me to come up with a design which expresses pure and uninhibited greed, I would probably have come up with a scheme like this one."

I've spent time discussing this one building because it exemplifies the way property owners and developers work.

Imagine you own an asset, in this case a railway station that serves the needs of commuters. And so you say to yourself, "We could make a lot more money out of this. Those old Victorians didn't really think this through. They could have got rid of the glass vaulted arches, and put 20 stories on top of it."

Sellar, the developers, have form on this. They wanted to build a 72-storey pole of luxury flats in Paddington, an area of mostly two-storey houses[308]. They were forced to withdraw it under a welter of criticism.

But developers have a simple strategy which they use over and over again. They put forward an outrageous proposal. And then, in the face of criticism, they make it slightly smaller. It appeases the planners and critics, and makes them think they've won. And the developers build what they originally had in mind.

So here are worthy members of the Concierge Class - all those who work for developers and architects, helping to maximise the companies' profits and those of their corporate clients.

The housing problem

But the problem is much wider than just the vast city buildings. It's also about housing.

Britain has a severe lack of housing. In particular, it lacks *affordable* housing. The most recently available data shows social housing represents only 13% of all housing starts, for reasons we'll see in a moment. So, construction of housing is largely in the hands of developers. They like to build detached or semi-detached houses that will appeal to private buyers. This uses up a lot of scarce land, and is expensive to build compared to more dense types of property development.

Young people with limited savings, along with those on low incomes, are unable to afford such houses. So they have to rent; and there's a severe lack of housing to rent. People end up living with their parents, and can't take up jobs in the many parts of the country where housing is expensive.

Developers are sometimes accused of sitting on their land banks, unwilling to build too many houses in case the prices were to fall. Local planning departments are also blamed for being too cautious about giving content for housing.

But the biggest problem lies first in the sell-off of council homes, which started back in 1980. And some of these problems can't be blamed on the developers. They merely take advantage of a nasty situation.

What's to be done?

There are a number of ways we can deal with the problem of architects supporting corporations to the disadvantage of ordinary people. Some possible solutions include:

- **Educate them:** Architects need to be trained to understand the ethical implications of their work. They need to be aware of the potential negative impacts of their designs on a community. And this requires their lecturers to be socially aware.

- **Educate the planners**: Local authority planning departments should be helped to understand what their area needs.

- **Hold architects accountable:** Architects should be held accountable for the safety and sustainability of their designs. They should also be held accountable for the impact of their work on communities.

The problem of tall, dense commercial buildings relates specifically to corporations and the wealthy. The government needs to legislate so that the needs of city dwellers are properly included in the decision-making process, rather than just the developers. And it needs to give planning departments the powers and requirements to create a city meant for people.

For housing, government legislation needs to enforce the percentage of any housing development that's genuinely affordable or for social rent. Legislation should prevent the sale of social housing, a problem that created the current housing crisis. Housing associations must become more accountable to the people they serve.

Finally, rented housing must be made secure and not subject to undue price hikes.

Cleaning up in the housing market

People tend to grumble about estate agents. Their fees are too high, there's a lack of transparency about the buying and selling process, and they sometimes misrepresent the properties they're selling.
To a large extent, the problem is less about the estate agents than the greed of the buyers, and the need for a better sense of reality among both buyers and sellers.

But these are just ordinary complaints. What we're concerned with here is whether estate agents – and the solicitors and others involved in housing - support the rich.

At one level, of course they do. The wealthy like expensive houses. And who wouldn't? If I were truly affluent, I might want an eight-bed house in the country with a swimming pool and a paddock to exercise my children's ponies.

For the avoidance of doubt, I have several children, but none of them have ponies.

And estate agents' only have one task: to sell whatever houses they're offered. It takes as much time to sell a flat for £100,000 as it does to flog a £5 million house. So, for the estate agent it's an easy decision. At 1%, you make £1,000 on the cheap one and £50,000 on the other.

But more to the point is whether they - and the solicitors and conveyancers who do the legal work - are complicit in crime?

Money Laundering

Houses are a great way to launder dirty money. Let's say you're an official in one of the 'Stans', and you've received £1m in return for selling off a government business cheaply. The money is now in your Swiss bank account. So you buy a house in the UK for £1 million, and sell it a year later for about the same amount. The cash in your UK bank account is now totally clean, assuming no one asks too many questions.

But the trouble is you have to buy and sell it through a UK-based solicitor. And they're required to check where the money came from.

Cigar-smoking, Leeds-based Mansoor Hussain led an opulent lifestyle that included executive planes, super yachts, high-performance cars, and VIP events with celebrities. He posed for photos with Beyoncé, Meghan Markle and Simon Cowell.

But the National Crime Agency (NCA) reckoned he laundered money for gangsters, including a drug-dealing killer.

Unable to pin any crime on him, they resorted to an Unexplained Money Order, which obliged him to open his books and demonstrate the sources of his money.

Eventually he agreed to surrender property valued at £10 million. This comprised 45 houses, offices and apartments. The brand name 'PoundWorld', which Hussain had acquired following the collapse of the original chain, was also included in the settlement.

Hussain had pretended to be a respectable businessman for more than 20 years, as he expanded his property portfolio in West Yorkshire, Cheshire and London.

Mansoor Hussain with Beyoncé.

The court was told that Hussain was a professional money-launderer whom criminals regarded as a 'clean skin' - a businessman free of convictions.

The NCA said the money for his property purchases must have come from Hussain's criminal associates, because they could find no legitimate source for his wealth. He'd paid virtually no income tax in some years, and many of his 77 companies were dormant.

Subsequently, the NCA said one of his closest associates was Bradford gangster Mohammed Khan, known on the street as "Meggy". He was jailed for life for murder - and investigators had long considered him one of the most significant organised crime bosses in northern England, involved in drug and firearms trafficking operations.

Hussain frequently drove Khan to and from his court appearances.

We don't know what steps Hussain's estate agents and solicitors took to check his bona fides. But who knows, maybe the police are even now knocking on their doors?

How to launder money

There are two main ways to launder money through property:

- **Use a shell company.** Shell companies are ones that exist only on paper and have no real business activity. You can use them to launder money by buying and selling properties without revealing the true identity of the buyer or seller.

- **Find a solicitor and estate agent who won't ask questions.** Estate agents may be reluctant to report suspicious activity to the authorities for fear of losing business.

Here are some examples the UK's property market being used to launder money:

- The UK's National Crime Agency (NCA) has estimated that £4.4 billion of dirty money is laundered through housing each year.

- In 2019, the NCA seized a £50 million mansion in London that was linked to a Kazakh oligarch.

- The NCA also arrested a man who was alleged to have laundered £100 million through the purchase and sale of properties in the UK. He was accused of using the proceeds of crime to purchase luxury properties and cars. And it arrested a group of people who were alleged to have laundered £150 million through the purchase and sale of properties in London. The group was accused of using a complex network of shell companies to conceal the source of the funds.

- The US Department of Justice charged a Chinese businessman with money laundering for buying a £20 million mansion in Beverly Hills with the proceeds of corruption.

- HMRC fined Countrywide Estate Agents £215,000 for failing to comply with anti-money laundering regulations. The company was found to have failed to conduct due diligence on customers and to report suspicious transactions309. With 600 branches and 74,000 properties on its books, the fine won't have troubled the firm.

- HMRC also fined 68 other estate agents a total of £519,000 for breaching anti-money laundering regulations. But at only £7,600 per estate agent, it doesn't seem a big deterrent.

Estate agents and conveyancers are required by law to verify the identity of their clients, report suspicious transactions to HMRC. But the lure of money will encourage some to ignore the law. That makes it easier for criminals to launder money through housing.

So, despite these measures, the problem of money laundering in the property market persists.

And it's the estate agents and legal practitioners, those members of the Concierge Class, who are helping criminals and plutocrats to clean their dirty money. And meanwhile the UK victims suffered at the hands of criminals, while foreign states lose out to crony capitalism.

What's to be done?

Once again, the wealthy can't operate without help. They need someone in the middle to make their transactions work. In this case, it's criminally-minded estate agents and solicitors.

All who support sellers and buyers need to be aware of their ethical responsibilities.

And the police need to be better funded in order for them to catch the crooks who make the wealthy even richer.

Private schools: how to buy privilege

"Send your child to a private school, and buy them privilege" is the slogan their promoters don't use. But that's essentially what private schools do.

The schools perpetuate inequality, as they're accessible only to families who can afford the high fees. By attending such schools, the children of the wealthy benefit from the advantages they offer, such as smaller class sizes, more resources, and a wider range of extracurricular activities.

This leads to a self-perpetuating cycle of inequality, as rich people's children are more likely to have successful careers and pass on their privilege to their children[310]. Here's how they gain an advantage over everyone else:

1. On a like-for-like basis, the pupils get better grades. A study by the Sutton Trust found that private school pupils are more likely to achieve higher grades than state school pupils, even when accounting for their prior attainment. This suggests that private schools provide a significant academic advantage to their pupils.[311]

2. They're more likely to attend university - and a more respected one. A study by the Institute of Fiscal Studies found that private school pupils are more likely to go on to university and to secure high-paying jobs than state school pupils.[312]

As a corollary, children of similar ability who are taught in the state sector are much less likely to go to higher-ranking universities. This tells us that private schools offer their pupils a significant career advantage.

3. They have access to better teachers. A study by the National Audit Office found that private schools are more likely to employ experienced and qualified teachers than state schools. This is probably due to the fact that private schools have more resources to recruit and retain high-quality staff, and such schools offer an easier environment in which to teach.

Harm is done to state education

By this we mean to the 93% of children who go to state schools.

1. Private schools drain talent and resources away from state schools.

When bright pupils and committed parents choose to send their children to private schools, it weakens state schools and makes it more difficult for them to provide a high-quality education for all pupils.

This leads to larger class sizes, fewer resources, a narrower range of extracurricular activities, a less diverse student body, and lower morale among staff and pupils. This is particularly concerning in the context of the UK's already underfunded state education system.

2. Private schools get unfair tax advantages, which could pay for improved state education

The schools don't have to pay VAT or business rates. Removing those unfair tax breaks, and allowing for the need for extra places in state schools, would boost the public finances by £1.3–1.5 billion per year in the medium to long run, says the IFS. This would pay for a 2% increase in state school spending each year[313].

The schools get tax exemptions by claiming to be charities. But they aren't. To qualify as a charity, a school must demonstrate that it benefits the public. In 2011, the high court ruled that this means "in all cases, there must be more than minimal or token benefit for the poor". The schools boast about how they support poor families. But as data from the Independent Schools Council, (ISC) shows[314], they give out much more money in *non*-means-tested grants than in means-tested ones (£710m compared with £496m a year).

In other words, the schools don't ask about family income when handing out most of their grants, meaning they're liable to go to the rich.

3. Parents whose children attend those schools avoid paying tax on the fees, which again deprives the state of much-needed income.

The rich avoid paying tax on school fees, by putting their money into a trust for the benefit of their children[315].

4. The government pays private schools to educate the children of the military.

Another factor is the hidden government subsidy given to private schools: it pays them to educate the children of the military, even though there are 40 state boarding schools.

In the most recent annual data, the UK government paid £81.5 million to private schools to educate 7,800 children of military parents.[316] For example, Millfield School receives around £745,000 a year. That money could go into the state boarding sector.

But it's a personal choice?

Some people believe that sending your child to a private school is a personal choice, like buying a washing machine.

To limit or deny them that opportunity would be an unfair restriction on their freedom, they say.

But a washing machine is a relatively low-cost purchase, and doesn't limit others from making that same choice.

Isaiah Berlin distinguished between two basic concepts of freedom, namely *freedom from* or negative freedom, and *freedom to* or positive freedom. 'Freedom from' is the absence of obstacles or constraints to your own action.

Millfield School gets £745,000 a year from the government.

By contrast, 'freedom to' gives you access to a range of desirable opportunities, regardless of whether you take advantage of them or not. Private education provides the child with an unfair advantage in life that's denied to other children.

In summary, *freedom to pay* for your child's education reduces the *freedom from inequality* that state-educated children suffer from.

The Concierge Class in private education

The Concierge Class is alive and well in private education. You might have some sympathy for the teachers who prefer teaching obedient, motivated children, rather than having to work in overcrowded classrooms, and teach malnourished kids from impoverished families.

But as in other sectors of the concierge class, those who teach in private schools don't see themselves as supporting the rich, or contributing to inequality. They don't see the big picture, looking no further than their next classroom deadline.

As we'll see later in the next chapter, my Culpability Index indicates the extent to which any member of the concierge class contributes to the undermining of democracy. The teachers and administrators in private schools score four on the index, the highest possible marks.

What's to be done?

The government should take four steps to reduce the inequality caused by the private schools:

1. Remove the schools' charitable status.

2. Make the private schools pay VAT and business rates.

3. Stop the rich from saving money on school fees by abusing the trust system.

4. Stop funding places in the private schools for the military.

Doing this would reduce the massive hidden benefits flowing unfairly to the rich. It would reduce the number of children being privately educated, and make it less mainstream. It would also allow the government to put more money into state education.

Universities should be pressured to prioritise children from the state sector, whose grades will reflect the lack of privilege that private education bestows.

As members of the Concierge Class, teachers should reflect on their responsibility to society, and not work in private schools because of the harm it does.

Algorithms that make you angry

As you walk down the high street, a camera on a lamp post is sending information about your face to an algorithm.
Conservatives say it's designed to catch criminals. Human rights groups see it as an invasion of privacy. Others point out the risks: a study by the US federal government showed African American and Asian faces were up to 100 times more likely to be misidentified than white faces, and the highest false-positive rate was among Native Americans[317].

Meanwhile, a corporation is making money from this. The global facial recognition market has reached sales of $6 billion, and is scheduled to attain $18 billion soon. Companies are selling facial recognition algorithms designed for use on mobile devices. Others are developing the hardware. They're being put into technologies such as augmented reality, virtual reality and artificial intelligence.

And talking of mobile devices, do you scroll through your phone, flicking past one image after another, in the hunt for entertainment? The companies' algorithms are monitoring you, modifying your behaviour, keeping you on their site for as long as they can, and learning about you, so they can sell your presence to advertisers.

When you've used X (Twitter), are you feeling more angry, more hostile to people you disagree with? That's the findings of a study by computer scientists at Cornell University and University of California, Berkeley. The researchers found that tweets being shown to people on their news feeds now promote "emotional content"[318].

The result made Twitter users react more emotionally than they would have done in the past. Supporters say that 'engaging in discussions is part of human nature'. And it's true that populist newspapers have long sought to wind people up with news that will spread fear and anger. But computer technology does it so much better, because it knows you personally.

And who is responsible for all this? The IT coders and developers support corporations in a number of ways, and not just for social media companies:

- **Designing addictive or manipulative software:** Developers create software that is designed to keep users engaged for long periods of time, even if it's detrimental to their well-being. As mentioned above, social media platforms employ algorithms that promote engagement by showing content likely to elicit strong emotions, such as anger or fear. This can lead to excessive screen time, reduced attention spans, and increased susceptibility to misinformation.

- **Showing clickbait content:** Facebook and Twitter's algorithms favour content that gets people to click on it, regardless of its quality or accuracy. To make that happen, it's designed to be sensational and manipulative. Clickbait content is usually misleading and sometimes harmful, and it contributes to the spread of misinformation. One example is 'bait and switch', where the product or price is less attractive than what you were promised.

- **Creating 'dark pattern' coding:** This is knowingly deceptive code or copy that deceives you into taking certain actions, such as buying a higher priced product than you had intended. Alternatively, there are 'roach motels' which are easy to enter, but difficult to get out of. For example, the website may fail to remind you that your subscription is about to fall due, or it may require you to phone the company if you want to cancel[319].

- **A negative impact on children:** Facebook and X (Twitter) are particularly harmful to children, who are more susceptible to the effects of social media addiction and manipulation. Children who spend a lot of time on social media are more likely to experience cyber-bullying, depression and anxiety.

- **Privacy violations and data breaches:** Some developers are involved in designing systems that collect and store vast amounts of personal data without adequate safeguards. This data can be used for targeted advertising, surveillance, or other purposes without users' full knowledge or consent. Data breaches can also expose sensitive personal information, leading to identity theft, financial fraud, and reputational damage.

- **Facilitating harmful or illegal activities:** Some developers work for companies that engage in unethical practices, such as online gambling, or are employed by fossil fuel businesses.

- **Creating echo chambers and filter bubbles:** social media and search engines create echo chambers where users are exposed only to information that confirms their existing beliefs. This leads to polarisation, social division and a decline in critical thinking skills. But the corporations make more profit.

In still worse cases, developers write code for criminal gangs that steal people's data, or hold sites to ransom. Or they may work for rogue states that spread misinformation.

For example, the German foreign ministry discovered that in just one month X, formerly Twitter, had allowed more than 1m German-language posts from an estimated 50,000 fake accounts, amounting to a rate of two every second. They were aimed at undermining the government's support for Ukraine[320]. Disinformation on this scale could have damaging effects on any country's elections.

What's to be done?

As with other members of the Concierge Class, most coders don't think about the ethical implications of their work. And there are big gradations in how culpable they are, depending on the impact of their clients' business on society.

The average developer is a small cog in the wheel, usually working on one small part of the system, and may be unable to see what it adds up to.

So although each individual needs to understand the role they're playing, the harm it can do, and the way it supports corporations, the focus of action must be by governments on the five tech giants, known as MAAMA: Microsoft, Apple, Alphabet (Google), Meta (Facebook), and Amazon, their suppliers and X (Twitter).

After a very slow start, the EU, US and other governments have started to push back against the giants' monopoly positions, their anti-competition issues (known as anti-trust in the US); and problems relating to privacy and the use of users' data.

Slave labour and the recruitment agents

Recruitment agencies play a vital role in the modern workforce, connecting employers with candidates.

And many of these agencies are quite mundane. If you're an engineer, you can check what jobs a specialist recruitment like Hays or Nolan has on its website. Or you go to one of the aggregators, like Indeed or Monster Jobs.

But there's also a dark side to recruitment. It's particularly prevalent in low-paid jobs, in agriculture and domestic service, and in developing countries.

Low-wage migrant labourers, for example, had to pay millions of dollars to recruiters in order to secure jobs in Qatar, the previous World Cup's host country[321].

Bangladeshi men who went to Qatar paid over $1.5 billion (£1.14 billion) between 2011 and 2020. And from 2015 to 2019, Nepali men spent up to $400 million to get there.

On average, the workers from Bangladesh paid fees of $3,000. As they earned as little as $275 a month, many of them had to work for at least a year, just to cover their hiring costs.

In order to pay their fees, such workers often have to take out high-interest loans or sell land, which makes them susceptible to debt bondage, a type of slavery in which they can't quit their jobs until the obligation is paid off.

As if the exorbitant fees weren't problem enough, the recruiters have been accused of misleading workers about the terms and conditions of their employment. Some confiscate workers' passports, making it difficult for them to leave the country or change jobs. And they place workers in jobs with long hours, low wages and dangerous working conditions.

Of the three million people living in Qatar, just 10%, or 380,000 are Qatari citizens. The remaining 90% are non-citizens, primarily migrant workers.

But it's not just in far-away lands that recruiters abuse low-wage workers.

Amazon and other warehouse staff recruiters

According to the Bureau of Investigative Journalism, temp agencies Adecco and PMP Recruitment have left Amazon workers out of pocket, with wages going missing or arriving late.[322]

Amazon says it pays for 20 hours minimum work for all staff, including workers hired by agencies. But the Bureau found agency workers saying shifts were regularly cancelled at the last minute and they were offered much less than 20 hours work a week.

In the three months leading up to Christmas, Amazon recruited nearly 10,000 workers. And thousands of the job adverts placed with Adecco were found to be on effectively zero-hour contracts. Those employed by PMP Recruitment were on "minimum-hours contracts" which only guarantee a certain number of hours per year. PMP denied that.

On the Reeds job site, the Bureau found that adverts for Amazon jobs posted by the two agencies represented more than half of all the warehouse jobs adverts across the UK.

PMP Recruitment and Adecco have been accused of poor working conditions in the past. TrustPilot, the consumer review website, gives PMP 1.2 stars out of five. 95% of the 208 reviews by former staff rate the company as 'bad'. Adecco isn't far behind, with 89% of reviewers also rating it as 'bad'.

Former staff list a litany of complaints about the agencies, from unreliable working hours, under or late payments, to shifts being cancelled at short notice and not receiving compensation.

Gangmasters in the agricultural industry

Gangmasters, the intermediaries between farmers and agricultural workers, have been criticised for a range of issues, including:

- **Paying workers below the minimum wage**, failing to provide them with proper rest breaks and overtime pay, and housing them in cramped and unsanitary conditions.

- **They exploit migrant workers** who are often more vulnerable to exploitation due to language barriers and lack of familiarity with UK laws. These workers may be subjected to long hours, dangerous working conditions and debt bondage.

- **Human trafficking:** Some gangmasters have been linked to human trafficking, forcing workers into servitude and subjecting them to physical and psychological abuse.

These criticisms have been made by a range of sources, including government reports, trade unions, and non-governmental organisations. A report by the UK's Gangmasters Licensing Authority (GLA) found that 25% of gangmasters inspected were found to be breaching minimum wage regulations[323].

60% of farmers were concerned about the exploitation of migrant workers in their supply chains, according to the National Farmers' Union. And a report by the Anti-Slavery International found that there were an estimated 13,000 victims of modern slavery in the UK, with agriculture being one of the sectors most at risk[324].

Domestic staff recruiters

The media regularly carries articles about the growing demand for butlers, with almost all saying that demand outstrips supply. Specialist butler schools have sprung up, teaching people how to lay out the cutlery, or how to open the front door to guests (hint: walk backwards, keeping your feet at 90 degrees to the door).

But that's just for the few. Domestic staff are especially vulnerable to modern slavery because they often work in isolation and are dependent on their employers for food, shelter, and immigration status.

There have been a number of high-profile cases of domestic workers being exploited by wealthy employers and the recruiters. A wealthy Saudi couple in the UK were convicted of enslaving two Indonesian women who worked as domestic workers in their home. The women were forced to work long hours without pay and were subjected to physical and psychological abuse[325].

The problem of modern slavery

The most recent global slavery index estimates that 40 million women, men and children are living in modern slavery. 25 million of them are in forced labour and 15 million are living in forced marriages. One in four victims of modern slavery are children[326].

But the true number is likely to be much higher, as many victims are hidden in plain sight.

Modern slavery is found in all sectors of the economy, but it's prevalent in agriculture, construction, manufacturing and domestic work. It's also common in supply chains, where workers can be exploited by subcontractors.

The victims of modern slavery are often people who are vulnerable and marginalised, such as migrants, refugees and internally displaced people. They may also be people with disabilities, women or children. Traffickers and exploitative employers target these groups because they're less able to defend themselves or escape from exploitation.

The traffickers use a variety of methods to lure their victims. They may promise them good jobs, education or marriage. Once the victims are trapped, traffickers use threats of violence, deportation or financial ruin to control them. Traffickers may also confiscate their victims' passports and other identity documents, making it difficult for them to escape.

Modern slavery in China

The Global Slavery Index (GSI) estimates that 5.8 million people are living in modern slavery in China.

It says the Chinese Communist Party 'uses forced labour as a means of racial and religious discrimination, political coercion and education, and as punishment for holding views ideologically opposed to the state.'

It continues: "Chinese slave labour involves mass surveillance, political indoctrination, forced separation of families, forced sterilisation, torture, sexual violence, and arbitrary detention in so-called "re-education camps" within the Uyghur Region."[327]

Products made by slave labour

Annually, G20 countries import more than $460 billion worth of products at risk of being produced with forced labour, estimates the Global Slavery Index.

Electronics are the highest value at-risk import for the majority of G20 countries, worth an estimated US$244 billion. This is followed by garments and palm oil. Solar panels are the fourth highest value at-risk product, reflecting the high global demand for renewable energy products.

If you've ever been attracted to cheap products shown in Temu ads on your phone, you aren't alone. The company has than 80,000 suppliers and is one of the most downloaded apps in Apple's app store.

"Consumers should know there is an extremely high risk that Temu's supply chains are contaminated with forced labor," said the US House Select Committee on the Chinese Community Party in its report.

The scale of Temu is rivalled only by the fast-fashion retailer Shein, the world's largest online-only retailer. Shein has also been accused of using slave labour.

Hotel slavery

Living in the Philippines, Mrs. Agaton's husband was incapacitated after a stroke and the youngest of their three children had special needs. So she applied to work in the United States through a labour recruitment agency in Manila. By the time she arrived in Portland, Oregon in 2008 with a dozen other Filipino workers, she owed $3,000 for her visa, airfare and interest on money she'd borrowed from a lending agency recommended by the recruiter.

According to the New York Times[328], the contract specified 40 hours per week at $8.50 an hour as a housekeeper, but none of the hotels she worked at in Arizona, Michigan and Louisiana gave her those wages, and they seldom gave her that many hours. "The agency tricked us," she said. "I was treated as a slave."

Deductions, the cost of a bus pass and an inflated amount for rent were withheld from her pay check, Ms. Agaton said. She working only three to four hours a day, only three days a week.

Who from the Concierge Class are involved?

The abusive recruitment and slave labour market has its own hierarchy. At the top are a few senior managers who market their services and liaise with employers. The orders are then fed down to local recruiters in the towns and villages. These make grandiose promises, far away from the eyes of the world, and are themselves paid on piecework, that is, by the number of people they recruit.

Huge numbers of people benefit from modern slavery. They include:

- Factory managers where goods are produced by forced labour

- Drivers who transport the products of forced labour, or who transport people into slave labour

- Recruiters who advertise the jobs

- The managers in hotels and nail bars who set the victims to work

- The tyrannous governments who use slave labour as a means of coercion and punishment.

- And finally we consumers, who buy such products and services

The question remains, who is more culpable? Taking just the labour recruitment chain, recruiters on the ground are unlikely to get paid much, and their work is precarious. They may be driven by the same desperate need as the workers themselves. The recruitment managers in China, Bangladesh and Nepal, however, know much more about the ultimate working conditions.

And the people at the top of the pile, those who give the orders in Qatar, the UK and the West are the most culpable of all.

What's to be done?

We all need to arm ourselves with knowledge about the signs of modern slavery, and report it.

And while there is much greater awareness now on the part of governments about modern slavery, they need to resource the police to break up the distribution chains and arrest those engaged in the trade.
Social services need to be properly funded to support the victims.

We're headed back to the Edwardian era

It's Monday morning, 6.45am. Down at the at the main entrance to the West India Docks Gate No.1, a crowd of 1,500 men is waiting in the rain to see if they can get a day's work.

They're herded into a shed, hemmed in with iron railings from end to end. On the other side of the railings, a foreman walks up and down 'with the air of a dealer in a cattle market, picking and choosing from a crowd of men, who, in their eagerness to obtain employment, trample each other under foot, and where like beasts they fight for the chances of a day's work.'[329]

That's what it was like, working in the docks in 1889. And it caused huge poverty and resentment.

According to Mick Lemmerman, a historian of the Isle of Dogs, "The 'call-on' system relied on there being more dockers than there was work, so that the dock companies always had enough labour for the peaks, and did not have to pay wages when there were less ships to be handled.

"This kept wages low (in the 19th century, dockers earned less than half that of agricultural labourers), encouraged cronyism and corruption, and it meant that many dockers frequently went without work. There was acute poverty among dockers' families[330]."

30,000 dockers went on strike, and eventually brought about an overhaul of employment on the docks. That lasted 100 years until 1989, by which time containerisation and lack of investment by the port owners had dramatically reduced the number of ships calling at the port.

Waiting for the call-on at the docks. The posts mark the entrance.

But for all the advances of the 20th and 21st century, history often repeats itself.

And this time, the call-on system has become 'platform capitalism'.

Instead of waiting on the dock side, contractors around the world log on to the gig economy platforms, like Upwork, Freelancer and Fiverr. There are 12 million contractors on Upwork, waiting to be called forward. The majority are from the United States (8 million), followed by India (2.3 million), the United Kingdom (500,000), and Canada (400,000).

But freelancers in India, Pakistan, and the Philippines almost certainly get more work than their numbers would indicate because their rates are considerably lower.

Post a job for a graphic designer, and 30 qualified people will apply in the next 25 minutes.

And I've a confession: I've used the Upwork platform a lot. My history shows I've posted 1,149 jobs, hired for 87% of them, employed people for 4,388 hours of work, and paid over £247,000 on the work. Mind you, that's over 21 years.

Over that time I've seen the hourly rate come down and down. For example, if you seek a UK-based Linux system administrator, they might quote you £60 an hour. But on Upwork you can hire one in India for as little as £20 an hour.

Writers' fees have halved, which in real terms is a much greater drop if you allow for inflation. And with the arrival of generative AI, which can create new content by scraping and then synthesising work previously done by others, prices have plummeted in some categories of work.

The Fourth Industrial Revolution, when telecommunication and digital technology emerged, has brought about a massive change in the design of work.

The mobile phone arrived in 1973, followed by the Osborne laptop, in 1981. Phones and laptops allowed workers to operate beyond the office.

And then the internet was introduced in 1991. Back then, the 1G (first generation) internet allowed for mobile phone calls and text messaging and worked at 64 kb a second. 5G runs at 10 gigabytes a second, an increase of 15,625,000%.

You could argue that the revolution has benefited people in the developing world, those who need to work from home or do extra work on the side. But it's also led to an increase in the precariat.

It's not just small businesses like mine that use these sites. On the Tongal platform, global corporations including Disney, Nickelodeon, PayPal, Warner Bros, Lego, Paramount, National Geographic, 20th Century Fox, and Mattel are using self-employed contractors to bid for ad-hoc work.

The life of the gig worker

In gig work, there are few employers and many gig-seekers. This puts power in the hands of company owners, and makes use of excess labour.

According to a survey by the International Labour Organization (ILO), "Most workers on online web-based platforms (86%) and delivery platforms (69%) expressed the desire to do more work. However, they are unable to get extra gigs because of excess labour supply and scarcity of tasks[331]."

The report also notes: "Over 60% [of gig workers] on online web-based platforms are highly educated. Contrary to expectations, so are over 20% of app-based taxi drivers and delivery workers. This may reflect employment contexts, such as a lack of local employment opportunities that correspond to workers' skill levels."

As the report says, platform work provides flexible work schedules, freedom to choose tasks, and the choice to work anytime anywhere make platforms popular. But it also presents challenging working conditions. They include low earnings and income volatility, unfair termination of workers' accounts, and limited access to work and social protection.

The platforms' algorithms "shape work processes and performance in ways that limit platform workers' autonomy. To make a decent living, they end up working long hours, which has an impact on work–life balance and can lead to stress."

The delivery drivers

There are countless 'self-employed' drivers working for Evri, Yodel and Deliveroo.

Although Amazon drivers are classified as self-employed, they use a van with an Amazon logo, and are given specific routes. The company has a huge workforce, to whom they don't guarantee any work[332].

Their criticisms include the lack of available shifts, the high cost of van hire, and the speed at which drivers have to work. They often need to urinate into a bottle in order to avoid delays[333], and their employer is a contractor, NGC, not Amazon. The van they have to rent is owned by yet another company (also owned by NGC).

To drive for Domino's the pizza business, you have to use your own car, which means less cost for the company, and more depreciation for your vehicle. Uber Eats is the same.

An advertisement for Domino's drivers. But bring your own car.

It can be hard to get a shift as many riders are competing for the same delivery. You may just sit around in your car for hours on end with no work[334].

Unfortunately, there are too many workers applying for what looks like easy work, and the employers know that. The companies are in control, and if the gig worker doesn't like it, their only option is to resign. Another worker will be waiting to take the job.

So, who are the Concierge Class in this field of work?

Mariano Zukerfeld[335] of Buenos Aires University distinguishes several types of worker, as shown in the table below. The ones we've been looking at are shown as gig workers. These are the ones who work *through* the platform. In other words, they bid for work through it.

But there is another group, he points out, who labour *'behind the platform'*, such as Amazon warehouse workers.

And moving up the ladder, there are there the hardware and software developers.

To which, for the purposes of this book, we would add the platforms' directors and managers.

As with other areas of activity, it's the people in managerial positions who are the most culpable, while the gig workers and the lower ranking employees are the victims or the drudge workers, due to their precarious work.

What's to be done?

Many countries are now working on solutions, including in Denmark, Brazil, and France. But they aren't the norm.

And regulating digital labour platforms is difficult, as it involves companies across the world.

Type of Work and Labour	Sub-type of Workers	Goods and Services Produced	Examples
Behind the Platform	Services Workers	Services	Warehouse and delivery workers of Amazon
	Industrial Workers	Physical Goods	Hardware builders in Amazon
	Informational Workers	Informational Goods	Software developers in Amazon
Through the Platform	Self-employed Owners	Physical Goods and Related Services	Airbnb hosts, Amazon sellers
		Informational Goods	Authors sharing music through Spotify App developers for Play Store or App Store
	Gig Labour	Services	Delivery workers of Deliveroo Uber drivers TaskRabbit cleaning workers
		Informational Goods	Software developers, writers, audiovisual content producers, and microtaskers on Upwork, and Freelancer Crowdworkers on Amazon Mechanical Turk
	Prosumers	Informational Goods	Content creators for Facebook or YouTube Data producers for all platforms
		Audience Labour	Audiences paying attention to ads on Facebook or YouTube

Source: Mariano Zukerfeld

Each government needs to bring pressure to the platforms, as has happened with Uber. And we need inter-governmental dialogue and coordination.

What's next?

In this chapter, we've looked at a range of Suppliers whose work benefits corporations and the wealthy. In many cases, the companies use gig labour, relying on an excess of labour; and in some cases it descends into indentured and slave labour.

Coming up next: what's to be done? I summarise the problems, and see what solutions we can introduce.

6. Conclusions

So many problems. Food banks. Precarious housing. A decline in real wages. Discontent. Strikes. And meanwhile the wealthy are quaffing champagne on their yachts. It feels like the 1920s.

How will it end? The decade that followed the 1920s was one of bank crashes, unemployment, fascism and a world war.

For that reason alone, it's important to achieve social and economic change.

Let's see how it might turn out, and why the Concierge Class need to get engaged.

Why the Concierge Class needs to change

Most members of the Concierge Class assume life will continue as before. They anticipate occasional changes of government, from right or centre-right to centre-left. But they don't imagine those changes will greatly affect them.

That's probably true. Governments rarely support any legislation that would seriously harm the interests of the affluent.

Those most likely to vote are the middle class and the elderly. And so a radical leftist government is much less likely than a harsh right-wing one.

But the past is not a useful predictor of the future.

You could have been walking the streets of San Francisco on 17th April 1906, not knowing that 80% of the city would be destroyed the following day by an earthquake. No one could have forecast that a virus that emerged in Wuhan in November 2019 would kill 6.9 million people around the world. And who could have foreseen that the assassination of the heir to the Austro-Hungarian empire would lead to World War 1?

Political changes happen when we least expect it. In retrospect, the collapse of the USSR and the abandonment of apartheid rule in South Africa look obvious. But at the time they weren't.

So it's unwise - and probably wrong - to assume that the current situation will continue forever.

The ripple effect tells us that small movements can gain a wider momentum, in the same way that the butterfly effect can have unexpected impacts. And an inflection point happens when a key event changes the trajectory. All of these ideas tell us that the past is no guide to the future.

The effects of inequality

If the country continues to disadvantage ordinary people, the already wide disparity between rich and poor will increase. And that poses a risk for the Concierge Class and everyone else.

Until recently, centre-left parties assumed that the very rich could be tolerated as long as everybody's standard of living was rising. But that view is being questioned. Wages have fallen behind living costs, the gap between rich and poor has become extreme, and government services have declined.

And with living standards falling in the West, the average person no longer sees any advantage in supporting the status quo. Anger is growing.

Increased inequality plus a decline in living standards creates resentment. Anger is growing. In its extreme, that leads to revolution, as the figure below shows.

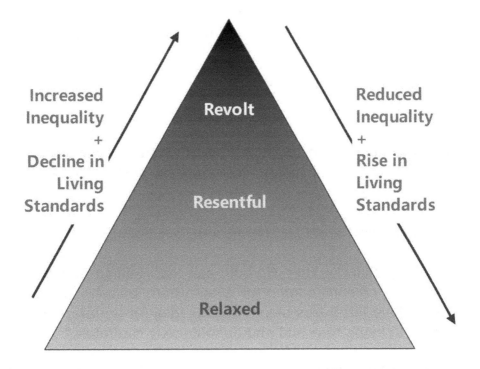

Growing inequality, allied to a fall in living standards, causes anger. The reverse is also true.

Revolutions that lead to a participative and equal society are vanishingly rare. As the Arab Spring showed, they mostly end up with authoritarian rule.

But even the carefree Concierge Class wouldn't like the disruption to their comfortable lives that revolution would bring.

Such events are caused by precarity, poverty, globalisation, alienation, and a loss of confidence in democracy. They're enhanced by conspiracy theories and disinformation on social media, including replacement theory and hostility to immigration, all of which are likely to play a greater part in future elections.

But the corollary also applies. Reduce inequality, and people's anger subsides.

The worst-case scenario

If we don't do something to fix the glaring inequities in this economy, the pitchforks are going to come for us. No society can sustain this kind of rising inequality.

You might think I wrote that last paragraph. But I didn't.

It was written by Nick Hanauer. He built and then sold an Internet advertising company to Microsoft in 2007 for $6.4 billion, in cash. Then he was the first person to lend Jeff Bezos money for his idea for an internet bookshop. And he admits to being "a proud and unapologetic capitalist."

Talking to his fellow plutocrats, he says: "There is no example in human history where wealth accumulated like this and the pitchforks didn't eventually come out. You show me a highly unequal society, and I will show you a police state. Or an uprising. There are no counterexamples. None. It's not *if*, it's *when*[336]."

The most ironic thing about rising inequality, he says, is how completely unnecessary and self-defeating it is:

> "If we do something about it, if we adjust our policies in the way that, say, Franklin D. Roosevelt did during the Great Depression— so that we help the 99 percent and pre-empt the revolutionaries and crazies, the ones with the pitchforks—that will be the best thing possible for us rich folks, too. It's not just that we'll escape with our lives; it's that we'll most certainly get even richer."

He goes on to demonstrate how Henry Ford paid his workers more money so they could buy his cars. And how Seattle has flourished by paying people a handsome minimum wage, something Hanauer pushed for.

The pitchfork crazies won't absolve the Concierge Class. On 9th November 1938 the maddened mobs smashed the windows of bourgeois Jewish bakers and jewellers, because they saw them, wrongly, as the cause of their problems.

So it's up to the Concierge Class to fix the problem. They have the power to make changes.

Can the Concierge Class be persuaded?

Within the Concierge Class, there are two types, as we shall see. Each has a different outlook on life, and any attempt to convert them must take that into account.

They are: the *Ideologue* and the *Apparatchik*.
Idealogues have a vision. They believe people should be self-reliant, that state intervention distorts the market, and government gets in the way of business. These neoconservatives believe in a small state and a laissez-faire

economy - until the banks or their own businesses need government support or a grant, in which case they're first in line for state help.

The ideologues see chaos and drift, and believe that the antidote is rule by a strong man or woman. They believe duty is more important than civil rights, and that stability is essential.

Many countries are ruled by authoritarian leaders. In America, Republicans have been rehabilitating General Franco, the Spanish dictator of the late 1930s. In the Middle East and North Africa, many countries are ruled by strong men: Tunisia, Libya, Egypt, Yemen, Syria and Bahrain.
Democracy is vulnerable to the arguments of the ideologues. It can be easily swept away, especially when the alternative is 'strong leadership'. Democracy's failings are obvious, while its strengths are obscure.

The ideological members of the Concierge Class are few in number. But they're highly influential. And they're found, as we've seen, among economists, think tanks, right-wing politicians, and some journalists and editors.

The apparatchik by contrast is someone who is simply obeys orders, and doesn't think about the implications of their actions. They're more common in education, the civil service and not-for-profit organisations, and in the lower ranks of the Concierge Class, because they do what they're told.

They aren't especially influential in persuading the wider public, but as Pushers (Chapter 4), they work hard to promote their clients' needs.

Below is a figure that distinguishes between the different characteristics of the ideologue and the apparatchik.

	Ideologues	Apparatchiks
Driven by	Ideology	Loyalty to the boss and the profession
Level of political engagement	High engagement	Low engagement
Social class	Upper and middle classes	Middle class
Age	Young and middle age	Middle age
Values	Personal freedom	Hard work
Political opinion	Far right	Centre right
Political party	Conservative	Conservative or Liberal Democrat

Can we change their values?

Apparatchiks: At home and at leisure, the apparatchik can be influenced by those they encounter. But since they're likely to converse only with other members of their class, at the golf club, or after work in the pub, they rarely meet people with a different opinion.

At work, however, the apparatchik is affected by their boss. If the boss were to raise ethical issues, or reflect on the impact of their actions on weaker members of society, the apparatchik is more likely to adopt those same values.

Equally, if enough colleagues raise the issue of precarity, the apparatchiks will push for change. We've seen that people can change their mind. For example, the percentage of British people saying global climate change is a major threat to the country rose from 48% to 75% in the nine years to 2022[337].

Ideologues: By contrast, an ideologue will counter any such comments at work with an opposing argument.

The ideologue is less likely to be swayed by conversation. To foster any kind of community spirit, we'd have to go back to the ideologue's childhood.

If schools actively promote the value of kindness, showing bullying to be cruel and wrong, young apparatchiks might be encouraged to lead a better life, one that's more communitarian. But it places a big responsibility on the part of already burdened teachers and school managers.

And it's by no means bound to work for all people. There are many examples of right-wing ideologues who are raised by centrist or left-wing parents, despite, or perhaps because of, their parents' attitude to the world.

But the school is a laboratory for every type of young person and all kinds of interactions, whereas parents can only pontificate to their individual child. The teacher can intervene and bring warring parties together. It can be a form of restorative justice, where an offender gets to understand the impact of their actions on the victim.

Nevertheless, all is not lost for the ideologues. In the UK, there is only a 16-point difference between left and right who believe 'climate change poses a major threat to the country' (84% to 68%). It indicates that even right-wing people can change their position on major issues.

Moving from III to AAA

The challenge is to move members of the Concierge Class from the three 'Is' to the three 'As'.

The three 'Is' stand for Ignorant, Individualist and Integrated. Such people are *Ignorant* of the impact of what they're doing. They see themselves as *Individuals*, disengaged from the community and far removed from the cares of ordinary people. And they're *Integrated* into the capitalist system, with many believing themselves to be part of the elite.

Note, too, that 'I' is a powerful, selfish word. It's the opposite of 'We', a word about community and camaraderie.

We need to help them move to the three 'As'. That's Awareness, Agency and Action.

Awareness involves waking up to the implications of their work. *Agency* means having the ability or willingness to create change. And *Action* is about taking practical steps to reduce the power of corporations and the wealthy.

Who is the most culpable?

The role each member of the Concierge Class plays affects their degree of responsibility. Some are small cogs in the wheel, while others play a major role in supporting the rich.

So we need a Culpability Index, one that lets us assess the gravity of any individual's behaviour. It will also let us see the extent to which we ourselves are guilty.

So here it is.

The Culpability Index is based on four criteria:

1. **Impact on the client and on society**: How much does the organisation's work benefit the client, financially or politically? How does its work affect society?

2. **Awareness**: Does the individual realise the impact of the work they do? As in criminal justice, ignorance isn't a defence. But the lower you are in an organisation, the less likely you are to know what's going on. And the higher you are on the ladder, the more responsibility you need to take for your actions.

3. **Personal Benefit**: How much money or other advantage does the individual gain from supporting the wealthy individual or the corporation? Or are they simply a victim of circumstances?

4. **Agency**: How much scope does the individual have to change what they're doing? How high up the ladder are they? How easy is it for them to turn down the client or boss?

Let's test the index by seeing how different professionals score. I've chosen a set of people who support the corporations or the rich, in one way or another. There's a tax haven lawyer, a gun trade association, a politician who bends legislation to suit their wealthy friends, the director of a museum that takes funding from an oligarch, a yacht sales person, and a domestic cleaner.

As a table below shows, a **lawyer** who's setting up a tax avoidance programme scores four out of four on the Culpability Index. They know what the outcome of their work is - it lets someone avoid paying the tax that's designed to improve society.

The work they do will cause a major loss of government income, and hence reduced welfare or healthcare. They personally benefit because they're well paid for what they do. And they're capable of rejecting the client's request - if they had the moral courage to do so. They score Four out of Four.

The director of a **gun trade association** knows that lobbying for reduced gun control will kill people. The lobbying benefits the association's members ideologically and economically. The director gets no advantage other than a salary. But they have agency, in that they could agree to tighter controls. So they score a Four.

Weapon manufacture is of course an extreme example, and culpability depends on the nature of each industry. Many trade associations are relatively harmless, but all of them are likely to oppose any legislation that would make life harder for them; and that usually works against the public interest.

The **politician** doesn't gain any major personal benefit, simply fitting in with an ideology and supporting their friends. There may be instances where they're taking a backhander or some other benefit, but the average politician is driven by beliefs rather than personal gain. So the politician scores a Three. Voting to pass legislation that benefits corporations and the rich would increase their score to a Four.

The museum director is aware of the donor's background, but the donation doesn't give the individual a major benefit other than an income. The museum gains an advantage, in the form of a large sum of money, but if the donor is a member of the kleptocracy the whitewashing will help to keep them in power. The director also has the power to reject the donation. As a result they score a Three.

The **yacht salesperson** doesn't undermine democracy by selling the plutocrat a yacht. They aren't really aware of the nature of their client - or more likely the client's representative who's come to buy the yacht. The sales person simply sees them as yet another good prospect. The salesman gains a personal benefit from the commission they make on the sale of the £5 million yacht. And they have the ability to reject a client on the basis of their criminality or wrongful doing. They score a Two.

And finally **the cleaner** who polishes the rich person's staircase has no real awareness of who the client is. Their work doesn't benefit the client, except in terms of the cleanliness of the house. The cleaner gains very little personal benefit, in terms of financial reward. And it's hard for them to turn down a reliable client, given the precarious nature of unemployment. As a result, they score zero in the Culpability Index.

	Impact on the client and society	Awareness	Personal Benefit	Agency	Culpability score
Tax haven lawyer	Y	Y	Y	Y	4
Gun trade association	Y	Y	Y	Y	4
Politician	Y	Y	N	Y	3
Museum director	Y	Y	N	Y	3
Yacht sales person	N	N	Y	Y	2
Cleaner	N	N	N	N	0

The Culpability Index

An Ethical Assessment

We've discussed the role played by the Concierge Class in general.

But what about you, the reader? Are you working for an organisation that deals with corporations and the wealthy?

And if so, does that make you a member of the Concierge Class? Moreover, does your private life support corporations and the rich?

The flow chart below sets out the thought process you could ask yourself.

To aid understanding, here's a questionnaire that expands on the flow chart.

1. About the organisation you work for

- Does the organisation you work for benefit corporations and the wealthy, either occasionally or frequently?
- If Yes, follow both lines.
- If No, your organisation doesn't promote inequality. Continue down the flow chart.

2. The work you do

Here are a set of questions to help you think about the work you do.

- Who has asked you to act? Was it your own decision or that of a superior?
- Who benefits from your act?
- Who will be affected?
- What is the impact of your actions on society?
- What alternative actions exist? Are there more just solutions?
- What would the reverse of your act be?
- What is the most beneficial outcome for society?

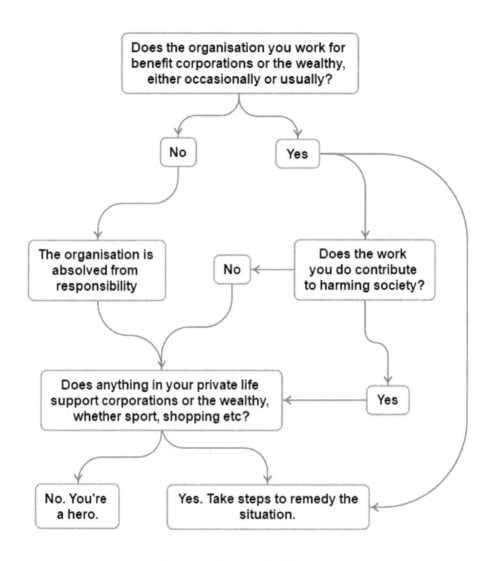

Personal culpability chart

Steps you can take

So much for the theory. What practical steps can you take to make a difference?

Change comes about through various means. In the very distant past, it was armed barons countering the divine right of kings. In recent centuries, mass demonstrations have fought for democracy and justice, as well as better wages and conditions.

More recently, we've seen people on the streets, such as the 1% Occupy movement, and Black Lives Matter. We've also witnessed people supporting the Gilets Jaune, Brexit and Trumpism.

But these aren't necessarily the kinds of actions that the individual middle-aged, middle-class, politically non-committed members of the Concierge Class are likely to take.

Moreover, mass movements that involve major demonstrations are relatively rare, and they're hard to sustain.

Sometimes it's just an idea whose time has come, like #MeToo or #BlackLivesMatter. It not the catchy hashtag in itself, but rather that some ideas are just waiting to be put into action.

Given the eye-watering levels of inequality, the failure of privatised industries like water and the Post Office, and the insecurity of much housing and many jobs, change needs to happen. As Sam Cooke said, change is gonna come.

Getting started

Tyrone Silcott was a financial advisor, showing affluent people how to make more money.

But he made the decision to retrain after 9/11. "I was sat at home, watching people who had gone to work that day throw themselves out the window, and thought: 'What do I really want to do?' It wasn't helping wealthy people squeeze out a bit more."

Tyrone Silcott

Silcott took a law degree, followed by training for the bar. Now he prosecutes in rape cases. Many lawyers don't want to do that: the work is complex, time-consuming and often poorly paid. It also occupies a lower status within the criminal justice system. Criminal barristers prefer the relative predictability of murder or organised crime. "But this is an area where I feel I can make a difference," he told the Guardian.

We don't all have to make a dramatic change in our lives. But here is how to start:

1. **Be aware of inequality**. Political awareness is something many members of the Concierge Class lack, whether through lack of curiosity, or having absorbed the narrative that's pumped out by the popular press and the other foot soldiers of the rich and powerful. You were already past that stage when you got this book.

2. **Recognise the extent to which you're contributing to the problem**. Are you a member of the Concierge Class, as indicated by the Personal Culpability flowchart above? Do you help the corporations become even richer and more powerful? I suspect you've already sought to minimise

your support. And it's impossible to completely avoid culpability. I make this book available on Amazon: I accept the hypocrisy that implies.

3. **Take action**. This can take whatever form you feel matches your skills, interests and experience. Appendix 2 has a list of possible actions.

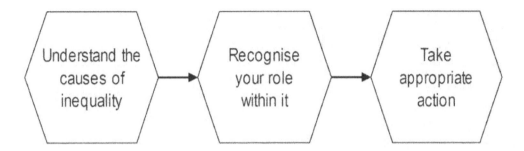

The three steps to making change

The Ethical Blueprint

Here's a blueprint that might provide you with a structure for dealing with issues at work and home.

It covers your relations with the law, your boss, colleagues, and subordinates; and most of all, yourself.

1. Dealing with the law
Obey the law, both the spirit and the rule.

2. Dealing with society
Be fair to all.

3. Dealing with your boss
Challenge unethical instructions
Raise ethical issues
Don't buy into group think.

4. Dealing with your colleagues
Tell the truth

5. Dealing with your subordinates
Don't ask subordinates to act unethically.
Engage in dialogue.
Tell the truth

6. Dealing with yourself
Be honest with yourself.
Develop a critical awareness.
Question your assumptions.
Think for yourself.

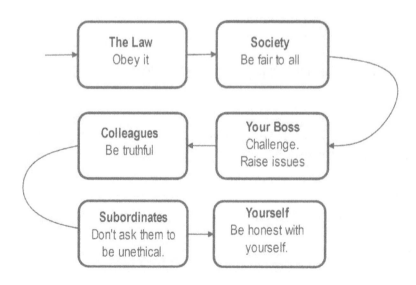

The Ethical Blueprint

What did you think of the book?

Thank you for reading The Concierge Class.

If you found the book useful, please leave a quick review wherever you got it. Reviews spread the word, and help other readers find the book.

Here's a link: https://mybook.to/ConciergeClass

And I'd welcome any thoughts or suggestions your might have about the book. You can contact me at KitSadgrove@gmail.com.

With best wishes

Kit

Appendices

Appendix 1: The problems and their solutions

This appendix contains 17 political and social problems, each one of which has been facilitated by the Concierge Class. It's a summary of the problems we've looked at in this book.

To each of them I've ascribed the causes, followed by their solutions.

Problem	Cause	Solution
Widening gap between rich and poor	Failure to tax the rich. Existence of tax havens. Presence of tax loopholes. Failure to adequately prosecute white-collar crime.	Remove UK tax havens' status. Tax corporations' profits at the point of sale. Increase corporation tax. Tax land and unearned wealth. Tax capital gains the same as income tax. Remove tax loopholes. Prosecute corporate crime.
Precarious jobs Stagnating incomes	Failure to legislate for fair employment conditions.	Legislate to reduce job precarity, especially 'gig' workers. Incentivise reshoring
Threat of job losses from AI, robotics and automation	Technological advances.	Introduce a universal basic income.

Falling standards and rising prices of utilities	Foreign and private ownership of utilities.	Take utilities into public ownership.
Offshoring of jobs	Lack of trade barriers	Impose suitable trade barriers. Incentivise reshoring.
Increasing monopolies and corporate rent taking	Globalisation Growth of the digital economy Platform businesses	Break up monopolies. Limit the scope of platform businesses Restrict takeovers.
Precarious and expensive housing	Lack of regulated social housing.	Build affordable council houses Remove the 'Right to Buy'. Legislate to ensure security and affordability of private renting. Set rent caps
Oppressive police powers.	Anti-union and anti-protest legislation.	Amend trade union and protest legislation
Climate change	Lack of energy tax. Inadequate investment in green energy and property insulation.	Tax fossil fuel tax in a way that doesn't unfairly affect the poor. Invest in green energy and insulation.
Economic instability	Lack of control over the banks. Excessive financialisation.	Overhaul the Bank of England. Regulate the stock markets. Further regulate the financial sector. Find ways to stimulate growth in the productive economy that works for all, not just the 1%.

Mainstream media bias	Lack of even-handedness regulations.	Introduce better regulation of the media.
Disinformation in social media	Fake stories posted by authoritarian and right-wing individuals, governments and plutocrats.	Impose financial penalties on social media for disinformation.
Undue influence of lobbyists	Corporate funding of lobbyists.	Ensure transparency of funding. Impose contribution limits on politicians and parties.
Crime	Lack of police funding. Attitudes of police managers and officers. Political interference in policing.	Increase police funding. Focus on serious crime. Change policing tactics.
Justice	Undue emphasis on petty crime. Failure to prosecute corporate crime.	Overhaul the justice system. Legalise soft drugs. Allocate resources and energy to corporate crime
Loss of trust in politics Lack of political representation for smaller parties	'First past the post' electoral system. Unrepresentative upper chamber in parliament. Abuse of the honours' system.	Introduce proportional representation. Amend parliament's second chamber. Amend the honours' system. Introduce the principles of subsidiarity into the UK's decision making.

Lack of political awareness	Biased mainstream media. Loss of journalism due to the internet.	Hold media and social media to account for disinformation. Ensure online media pay to use content provided by the traditional media. Amend school curricula. Make schools secular.
Inequality of opportunity	Lack of social mobility. Private schools.	Introduce wealth and inheritance tax. Remove private schools' tax and other advantages. Abolish the monarchy.

Appendix 2: Methods of non-violent protest and persuasion

Below is a list adapted from one compiled by the Commons Library at https://commonslibrary.org

There's an updated spreadsheet with tabs, here: bit.ly/CivilResistance

Treat this list as a set of ideas. Find an action that reflects your current concerns.

Methods of Nonviolent Protest and Persuasion

Group participation and development
Join a political, trade union, of social action group
Set up a new social action group
Stand for election
Join the organising or steering committee.

Workplace action
Challenge your manager
Widen the discussion in meetings
Join a trade union
Set up a trade union branch
Set up a competing progressive business or institution

Professional action
Join a professional association and lobby for change

Digital action
Post on social media

Create a hashtag
Create digital maps
Use QR Codes to spread information
Share digital files
Non-violent media hijack
Create a livestreaming event
Set up a flash mob

Make statements

Make public speeches
Write letters of opposition or support
Issue a declaration by your organisation
Create a petition

Communicate with a wider audience

Create a slogan or symbol
Design and distribute banners or posters, leaflets and books
Write articles in and letters to the print and online media
Do interviews on radio, TV and podcasts

Undertake Group Acts and Representations

Organise a deputation
Create mock awards
Lobby as a group
Picket buildings or events
Display flags
Wear symbols
Deliver symbolic objects
Light candles
Display portraits
Create signs and names

Put pressures on individuals

Barrack officials

Hold a vigil

Drama and Music
Put on plays and musical events
Carry out pranks

Processions
Hold a march, parade, pilgrimage or motorcade

Public Assembly
Hold a meeting of protest or support
Organise a teach-in

Withdrawal and Renunciation
Hold a walk-out
Turn your back
Leave your job

Actions by Consumers
Boycott goods

Action by management
Refuse to buy from suppliers
Refuse to let or sell property
Refuse to sell to specific countries or customers

Strikes
Protest strike
Lightning or quickie strike
Slowdown work
Work-to-rule
Go off work due to sickness

Non-cooperation with government

Boycott a legislative body, government department or agency
Withdraw from educational institutions

Non-compliance
Reluctant and slow compliance
Disguised disobedience
Refusal of an assemblage or meeting to disperse
Hold a sit-down or sit-in
Non-cooperation with conscription and deportation
Disobey 'illegitimate' laws
Nonviolent interjection, obstruction or occupation
Seek imprisonment
Blocking of lines of command and information
Stall and obstruct new instructions
Administrative or judicial non-cooperation
Mutiny
Overload administrative systems
Refuse to help enforcement agents
Be a whistle blower.

Non-violent physical action
Monkey-wrenching, eco-sabotage

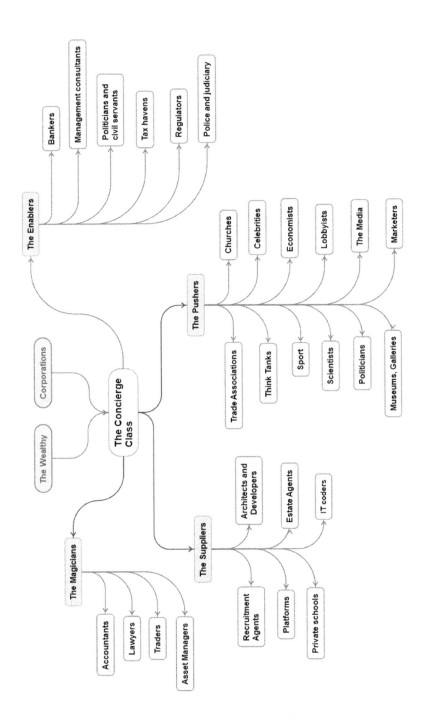

Index

Abramovich, Roman, 83

Accelerated depreciation, 63, 68

Adobe, 46

Advertising Standards Authority, 76, 165, 196

Airlines, 47, 197

Alexander Lebedev, 190

Algorithms, 64, 97, 193, 280, 281, 295

Alibaba, 158

Amazon, 6, 25, 31, 50, 53, 68, 80, 114, 157, 158, 186, 283, 285, 295, 296, 315

American Accounting Association, 73

Amnesty International, 257

Anti Money Laundering, 115

Antidepressants, 247

Apparatchiks, 305

Apple, 53, 64, 283, 289

Architects, 263, 264, 265, 268, 269

Aristocracy, 39, 43, 44, 90

Asset management companies, 101

Astroturf, 204

Azima, Farhad, 85

Bain, 157, 159, 160

Balance sheet, 59, 69, 70, 92

Bangladesh, 19, 126, 284, 290

Bank of England, 132, 145, 146, 147, 153, 319

Banking, 47, 125

Barclays Bank, 47, 97, 108, 110, 113, 114, 115, 116, 133

Barings Bank, 96

Barriers to entry, 47

BBC, 191, 247

Belton, Catherine, 82

Bermuda, 64, 68, 138

Bill Gates, 25, 28

BlackRock, 94, 101, 102, 133

Blackstone, 68

Brexit, 124, 125, 134, 191, 226, 229, 231, 313

British Amrican Tobacco, 118, 204

Bureau of Investigative Journalism, 85, 285

Buybacks, 93, 94

Campaign for the Protection of Rural England, 217

Capture, 164, 249, 252

Carbon capture, 215

Carried interest, 68, 74

Carter Ruck, 82

Catholic Church, 242, 244

Cayman Islands, 64, 138, 139

Central banks, 147, 148, 150, 151, 152

Channel 4, 187, 191

Chevron, 79

China, 49, 53, 54, 67, 126, 157, 288, 290

Climate change, 37, 319

Competition and Markets Authority, 49

Conflicts of interest, 216, 246

Consumer Choice Center, 204

Co-option, 249, 250, 252

Coral, 76

Corporation tax, 50, 136, 137, 318

Covington, 75, 77

CPS, 173, 182, 183, 227
CPTPP, 226
Credit Suisse, 110, 111, 112, 119
Culpability Index, 5, 6, 135, 279, 307, 308, 310
Daily Mail, 186, 187, 189
Daily Telegraph, 186, 187, 189, 191
Dark money, 229
Dark pattern coding, 281
David Cameron, 132, 206
Deferred Prosecution Agreement, 76
Deloitte, 43, 60, 133, 143, 156
democracy, 0, 5, 14, 24, 41, 42, 131, 145, 171, 186, 203, 218, 242, 279, 302, 309, 313
Democracy, 304
Department for Education, 103
Department of Transport, 164
Deregulation, 123, 124, 125, 169, 188, 223, 224, 226
Deutsche Bank, 110, 170
Developers, 193, 217, 252, 263, 264, 266, 267, 268, 269, 270, 281, 282, 296
Die Zeit, 207
DLA Piper, 80
Domino's, 295
Donors Trust, 194
Dyson, 31
Ehrenreich, Barbara, 15, 16, 19
Elon Musk, 25, 33, 34, 53, 193, 216
Enablers, 7, 8, 12, 105, 106, 107, 184, 223, 224
Eni, 170
Environment Agency, 164
ESG, 18
Esquire magazine, 107

Estate agents, 10, 108, 270, 271, 272, 274
Ethical Blueprint, 315, 317
Ethnic minorities, 136, 180, 181, 184, 192
Etihad, 256
EU, 13, 31, 48, 113, 124, 138, 195, 210, 216, 221, 227, 283
EU Commission, 48
Extinction Rebellion, 88
Exxon, 79
Facebook, 25, 195, 201, 204, 281, 282, 283
Fidelity Investments, 94
Financial Conduct Authority, 113, 117, 133, 163
Financial Reporting Council, 60
Financial Times, 82
Financialisation, 51
Food and Agricultural Organization, 114
Françoise Bettencourt Meyers, 29
Free trade, 50, 121, 126, 136, 223, 226
Freshfields, 79
Front groups, 204
G4S, 51, 157
Gangmasters, 286
Gannett, 186, 189
GDP, 115, 121, 175
George Monbiot, 5
George Soros, 28
Gig work, 294
GlaxoSmithKline, 199
Global Disinformation Index, 194
GMB, 147
Goldman Sachs, 158

Goodwill, 69

Google, 6, 46, 53, 64, 68, 77, 115, 195, 283

Grant Thornton, 60

Greenpeace, 245

Greensill Capital, 131, 206

Grenfell Tower, 264

Guardian, The, 116, 174, 186, 191, 207, 213, 230, 261, 263, 264, 267, 314

Gun control, 213

Hanauer, Nick, 302, 303

Harbottle and Lewis, 82

HarperCollins, 83

Harvard Business Review, 61

Health and Safety Executive, 164

Herbalife, 66, 67

HMRC, 133, 171, 173, 274

House of Commons, 43

Housing, affordable, 252, 268

Howard Schultz, 28

HSBC, 47, 93, 97, 109, 114, 116

ICIJ, 170

Idealogues, 303

IKEA, 53, 64

Inequality, 5, 13, 17, 24, 35, 42, 44, 52, 121, 136, 143, 152, 169, 275, 278, 279, 300, 301, 302, 303, 311, 313, 314

Inflation, 148

Institute for Policy Studies, 36, 37

Institute of Chartered Accountants in England and Wales, 72

Institute of Economic Affairs, 225, 226

Institute of Race Relations, 178

International Energy Agency, 215

International Labour Organisation, 113

Investment banks, 111, 113, 114

IPO, 158

IPPR, 136

Ireland, 41, 64, 112, 244

IT, 19, 39, 63, 156, 182, 193, 281

ITV, 191

James Dyson, 30

Jeff Bezos, 25, 28, 186, 302

Jonathan Harmsworth, 186, 189

JPMorgan, 96

Judges, 175

Kaplan Hecker & Fink, 81

Kardashians, 201, 202

Kellogg's, 252

KKR, 68

KPMG, 60, 143

Ladbrokes, 76, 190

Land, Planning and Development Federation, 217

Lawyers Are Responsible, 88

LGBTQ, 250

Libor, 97

Liverpool Street railway station, 266, 267

Lloyds Bank, 47, 114, 116, 125

Lobbying, 77, 112, 206, 213, 228

Lobbyists, 9, 54, 168, 191, 203, 204, 206, 208, 210, 213, 214, 215, 216, 320

London Stock Exchange, 91, 97

L'Oréal, 29

Lucozade, 196, 197, 199

Luxembourg, 7, 31, 52, 59

Magicians, 6, 7, 12, 55, 59, 105

Management consultants, 154, 160,

161, 162, 226

Manchester City FC, 256, 257, 260

Marcus Rashford, 260

Mark Zuckerberg, 25, 28, 193

Marketing, 54, 195, 196, 199, 200,
203, 233

Markets, 45, 46, 47, 49, 90, 91, 96,
98, 99, 111, 123, 124, 150, 157, 158,
163, 167, 188, 226, 230, 231, 233,
319

McKinsey, 157, 159, 161

Metro, The, 189

Metropolitan Police, 176, 178

Michael Rapino, 25

Microsoft, 25, 46, 51, 65, 283, 302

Midlands Industrial Council, 230

Migrant labourers, 284

Milton Friedman, 231

Ministry of Justice, 157, 181

Mirror, The, 189, 190

Modern slavery, 286, 287, 288, 290,
291

Monaco, 7, 32

Monarchy, 40, 41, 42, 43, 44, 242,
245, 321

Money laundering, 35, 76, 84, 109,
115, 119, 143, 254, 271, 274

Morgan Stanley, 158

Murphy, Richard, 145

National Crime Agency, 271, 272, 273

NatWest, 108, 114, 148

News Corp, 186, 189

NHS, 118, 126, 155, 156, 162, 225, 226

Novartis, 170

OECD, 121, 122

Oligopolies, 47, 48

Opioid crisis, 204, 205

Orphan drugs, 68

Outsourcing, 19, 156

Panama Papers, 109, 110, 140, 141

Pandora Papers, 143

Patrick Minford, 231, 234

philanthropy, 9, 32, 237, 238

Piketty, Thomas, 20

Platform capitalism, 292

Platforms, 11, 19, 48, 186, 281, 293,
294, 295, 296, 297

Police, 12, 25, 52, 71, 75, 128, 169,
170, 176, 177, 178, 179, 180, 182,
183, 184, 273, 275, 291, 302, 319,
320

PPE Medpro, 131

PR, 204, 208, 215, 216

Precarity, 299, 318, 319

Prison, 170, 179

Private equity, 102

Private schools, 13, 191, 275, 278

Privatisation, 125, 155, 156, 188, 226

Privilege seeking, 51

Professional Managerial Class, 16

Proportional representation, 134, 135

Public opinion, 5, 8, 24, 188, 213,
219, 222, 227, 228, 237

Purdue, 205, 237

Pushers, 7, 8, 9, 12, 122, 184, 185,
203, 223, 235, 261, 304

PWC, 60, 61

Qatar, 284, 290

QE, 151, 152, 154

Quantitative easing, 151

Real Clear, 193, 209

Recruitment agencies, 283

Regulators, 55, 89, 99, 106, 107, 119,
163, 164, 165, 168, 200, 249

Regulatory capture, 250
Religion, 193, 240, 241, 243, 244
Rent seeking, 49, 51
Research bias, 247
Retail banks, 108, 125, 148
Revolving door, 131, 132, 133, 216
Right to buy, 129
Rise of the Meritocracy, 21
Rosneft, 83
Rothchild, 141
Royal Bank of Scotland, 47, 110, 125, 171
Royal Mail, 124, 126, 156
Royalty, 39, 40, 53
Rupert Murdoch, 185, 186, 189
Ryanair, 47, 197
Sam Bank-Friedman, 34
Samsung, 53
Santander, 114
Schillings, 82
Schools, 102, 190, 228, 231, 243, 244, 245, 267, 275, 276, 277, 279, 280, 287, 306, 321
Science, 179, 209, 245, 246, 249, 255, 334
Scientists, 4, 10, 16, 245, 246, 247, 249, 252, 253, 254, 255, 281
SEC, 67, 75
Secondary capital raisings, 91
Securitisation, 52, 163
Self-regulation, 168
Serco, 157
Shell, 79, 93, 138, 196, 199, 213, 237, 273
Shell companies, 31, 71, 84, 138, 139, 140, 141, 273
Silicon Valley Bank, 111

Slapps, 82, 89
Slave labour, 254, 288, 289, 290, 298
Social media, 193
Société Générale, 96
Software, 33, 45, 51, 65, 79, 164, 186, 281, 296
Sport, 255, 256, 257, 259, 260, 261
Sportswashing, 257, 259
SSRIs, 247, 248
Starbucks, 28, 63, 64, 94
State Street, 101
Stevenson, Gary, 89, 95
Stock market, 59, 90, 91, 93, 94, 95, 97, 98, 104, 105, 108, 152
Stock-based compensation, 99
Stop and search, 176, 180, 182, 184
Strikes, 126, 127, 128, 187, 292, 299, 324
Subsidies, 51, 219, 222
Sun, The, 188, 189
Supermarkets, 46
Suppliers, 7, 10, 12, 46, 193, 261, 263, 297
Switzerland, 112, 119, 138, 139, 141
Tariffs, 50, 51, 55, 126
Tax cuts, 187, 225, 226
Tax evasion, 109, 119, 145, 170, 173
Tax havens, 8, 31, 65, 68, 71, 73, 74, 98, 106, 109, 138, 139, 143, 144, 145, 318
Taxpayers' Alliance, 229
Teachers, 7, 12, 19, 52, 75, 235, 244, 276, 279, 280, 306
Ted Baker, 70
Telecommunications, 47
Temu, 289
Thames Water, 100

Thatcher, Margaret, 129, 226, 231
Think tanks, 4, 9, 55, 185, 203, 225, 226, 227, 228, 229, 304
Thomas Cook, 60, 61, 69
Tobacco, 118, 200, 203, 204, 208, 209, 247
Tony Blair, 133, 143, 157
Trade associations, 4, 9, 163, 217, 219, 220, 222, 309
Trade unions, 21, 121, 127, 155, 187, 188, 213, 222, 223, 227, 286
Trafficking, 110, 272, 286
Transparency, 83, 173, 206, 215, 252
Transparency International, 83, 173, 206, 252
TV, 165, 186, 191, 192, 198, 201, 217, 258, 323
Twitter, 34, 88, 195, 203, 204, 216, 281, 282, 283
Uber, 53, 80, 81, 82, 295, 297
UBS, 29, 97, 109, 112, 171
Ultra-processed foods, 254
Unemployment, 149
United Arab Emirates, 185, 186, 256
Upwork, 50, 293
Vanguard, 26, 94, 101, 103
Vaping, 10, 203, 205, 209, 247
Volkswagen, 79, 164, 247
Wages, 19, 54, 93, 94, 136, 146, 147, 149, 188, 220, 227, 234, 284, 285, 289, 291, 299, 313
Walmart, 65
White-collar crime, 171, 174, 175, 176, 182, 183, 192, 318
Wrexham FC, 257, 258, 259, 260
Zero-hours, 136, 188

References

1 https://www.monbiot.com/2023/09/20/unspeakable/

2 https://www.dissentmagazine.org/online_articles/on-the-origins-of-the-professional-managerial-class-an-interview-with-barbara-ehrenreich/

3 https://democracyproject.nz/2022/09/08/bryce-edwards-how-politics-got-captured-by-the-middle-class-and-why-its-a-problem/

4 https://www.bigissue.com/news/social-justice/uk-poverty-the-facts-figures-effects-solutions-cost-living-crisis/

5 https://www.finance-watch.org/esg-ratings-must-disaggregate-esg-parameters-to-repair-sustainable-investors-trust/

6 https://web.archive.org/web/20180702060908/https://blogs.lse.ac.uk/politicsandpolicy/money-makes-people-right-wing-and-inegalitarian/

7 https://www.forbes.com/sites/gigizamora/2023/10/03/the-2023-forbes-400-self-made-score-from-silver-spooners-to-bootstrappers/?sh=78c0dce332c5

8 https://www.ubs.com/global/en/family-office-uhnw/reports/billionaire-ambitions-client-report-2023.html

9 https://moneyweek.com/who-is-the-richest-woman-in-the-world

10 https://www.apa.org/news/press/releases/2019/05/social-class-exaggerated-belief

11 https://www.independent.co.uk/business/james-dyson-work-from-home-rights-b2241381.html

12 https://www.amnesty.org/en/location/asia-and-the-pacific/south-east-asia-and-the-pacific/singapore/report-singapore/

13 https://www.cnbc.com/2019/10/15/this-economist-says-the-perfect-tax-rate-for-the-rich-is-75percent.html

14 [https://www.probonoeconomics.com/news/charity-donations-from-uks-richest-down-20-despite-higher-earnings].

15 https://www.pnas.org/doi/pdf/10.1073/pnas.1118373109

16 https://www.sciencedirect.com/science/article/abs/pii/S2352250X17300441?via%3Dihub

17 https://www.npr.org/2022/11/18/1137492483/ftx-investors-worry-they-lost-everything-and-wonder-if-theres-anything-they-can-

18

19 https://nypost.com/2023/11/25/news/king-charles-secretly-profits-off-assets-of-dead-brits-report/

[20] https://www.theguardian.com/uk-news/2021/feb/07/revealed-queen-lobbied-for-change-in-law-to-hide-her-private-wealth

[21] https://www.thehumanfront.com/to-use-a-personal-title-is-to-accept-inequality-part-iii-the-ruling-upper-class/

[22] https://socialistworker.co.uk/background-check/who-owns-britain-how-the-rich-kept-hold-of-land/

[23] https://www2.deloitte.com/uk/en/pages/about-deloitte-uk/articles/social-mobility.html

[24] https://www.telegraph.co.uk/news/society/11383148/Why-the-aristocracy-always-win.html

[25] https://brittontime.com/2022/09/02/8-inheritance-tax-loopholes-for-2022-23/

[26] https://www.studysmarter.co.uk/explanations/microeconomics/microeconomics-examples/uk-supermarket-oligopoly/)

[27] https://www.gov.uk/government/publications/energy-bills-support

[28] https://www.investopedia.com/terms/o/oligopoly.asp

[29] https://www.ukessays.com/essays/economics/advantages-and-disadvantages-of-the-oligopoly-market-system-economics-essay.php

[30] http://colbournecollege.weebly.com/uploads/2/3/7/9/23793496/unit_1_the_uk_aviation_industry_score_sheet_lo_1___2.pdf

[31] https://www.cnbc.com/2017/06/27/the-largest-fines-dished-out-by-the-eu-commission-facebook-google.html

[32] https://www.ft.com/content/809007e6-274f-11de-9b77-00144feabdc0

[33] https://www.gov.uk/government/case-studies/furniture-parts-cartel-case-study

[34] https://www.gov.uk/government/news/construction-firms-fined-nearly-60-million-for-breaking-competition-law-by-bid-rigging

[35] https://www.theguardian.com/business/2020/jul/14/accountancy-watchdog-attacks-poor-work-from-biggest-firms

[36] https://hbr.org/2002/11/why-good-accountants-do-bad-audits

[37] https://www.callaccountant.co.uk/blog/how-did-starbucks-manage-with-paying-zero-uk-corporation-tax-to-hmrc/

[38] https://www.reuters.com/article/idUSKCN0T51ZS/

[39] https://unctad.org/system/files/official-document/diaepcbinf2015d5_en.pdf

[40] https://www.bbc.co.uk/news/uk-politics-23019514

[41] https://itep.org/offshoreshellgames2017/

[42] https://www.hsgac.senate.gov/subcommittees/investigations/media/levin-mccain-statement-on-ireland-tax-avoidance-and-apple

[43] https://www.theguardian.com/business/2021/feb/21/ikea-faces-1bn-bill-for-alleged-franchise-tax-evasion

[44] https://oxfamilibrary.openrepository.com/bitstream/handle/10546/620548/cr-prescription-for-poverty-180918-summ-en.pdf

45 https://www.bloomberg.com/news/articles/2015-06-04/microsoft-s-puerto-rico-tax-dodge-left-trail-very-hard-to-stifle

46 https://goodjobsfirst.org/shifting-burden-vital-public-services-walmarts-tax-avoidance-schemes/

47 https://itep.org/35-years-of-tax-avoidance-by-wealthy/

48 https://en.wikipedia.org/wiki/Barry_Minkow

49 https://en.wikipedia.org/wiki/Hollywood_accounting

50 https://factsaboutherbalife.com/the-facts/the-herbalife-pyramid-scheme/

51 https://ourfinancialsecurity.org/2021/10/close-the-carried-interest-loophole-that-is-a-tax-dodge-for-super-rich-private-equity-executives

52 https://www.menendez.senate.gov/newsroom/press/menendez-reintroduces-bill-to-end-taxpayer-funded-subsides-for-big-oil-companies

53 https://www.gao.gov/products/gao-19-83

54 https://itep.org/notadime/

55 https://www.investopedia.com/terms/d/depreciation.asp

56 https://www.irs.gov/publications/p946#en_US_2021_publink1000107195

57 https://www.newyorker.com/news/our-columnists/donald-trumps-business-failures-were-very-real

58 https://www.nytimes.com/interactive/2020/09/27/us/donald-trump-taxes.html

59 https://www.opendemocracy.net/en/oureconomy/thomas-cook-tale-two-moral-hazards/

60 https://www.theguardian.com/business/2020/jan/22/ted-baker-balance-sheet-error-worse-than-feared-as-woes-deepen

61 https://www.expressnews.com/news/local/article/ex-accountant-for-cartel-tells-of-money-laundering-4446636.php

62 https://narcos.fandom.com/wiki/Guillermo_Pallomari

63 https://www.icaew.com/insights/viewpoints-on-the-news/2022/aug-2022/eth-ics-essentials-sectorspecific-advice-for-accountants

64 https://publications.aaahq.org/api/article-abstract/18/1/53/6415/Making-Tax-Havens-Work-The-Necessity-of-Tax?redirectedFrom=fulltext

65 https://www.gov.uk/government/publications/named-tax-avoidance-schemes-promoters-enablers-and-suppliers/current-list-of-named-tax-avoidance-schemes-promoters-enablers-and-suppliers

66 https://www.gov.uk/government/publications/named-tax-avoidance-schemes-promoters-enablers-and-suppliers/current-list-of-named-tax-avoidance-schemes-promoters-enablers-and-suppliers

67 https://www.nytimes.com/2015/06/06/business/dealbook/how-a-carried-inter-est-tax-could-raise-180-billion.html

68 https://www.gov.uk/government/publications/use-of-marketed-tax-avoidance-schemes-in-the-uk/use-of-marketed-tax-avoidance-schemes-in-the-uk

69 https://www.cov.com/en/news-and-insights/news/2023/10/national-law-

journal-names-covington-white-collar-litigation-department-of-the-year

[70] https://www.jdsupra.com/legalnews/false-claims-act-supreme-court-news-1014458/

[71] https://www.bbc.co.uk/news/business-67629280

[72] https://en.wikipedia.org/wiki/Ladbrokes_Coral

[73] https://www.jdsupra.com/legalnews/false-claims-act-supreme-court-news-1014458/

[74] https://arstechnica.com/information-technology/2014/01/silicon-valley-attempts-to-slow-new-global-tax-avoidance-reform-proposals/

[75] https://www.bostonreview.net/articles/susanna-bohme-dole-banana-workers-pesticide-nicaragua/

[76] https://corporatewatch.org/wreckers-of-the-earth-company-directory-2021/

[77] https://www.supremecourt.uk/cases/docs/uksc-2018-0068-judgment.pdf

[78] https://www.freshfields.de/49bd71/globalassets/imported/ims/release-attachments/en_deals_vw_settlement_usa.pdf

[79] https://www.bbc.co.uk/news/business-41053740

[80] https://www.bbc.co.uk/news/business-41053740

[81] https://www.reuters.com/business/finance/prosecutors-charge-winterkorn-with-giving-false-testimony-german-parliament-bild-2021-06-09/

[82] https://www.dlapiper.com/en/capabilities/practice-area/intellectual-property/patent-litigation

[83] https://www.juve-patent.com/cases/hogan-lovells-prevails-for-eli-lilly-before-dutch-court-of-appeal/

[84] https://www.vox.com/2019/4/3/18293950/why-is-insulin-so-expensive

[85] https://www.law.com/international-edition/2021/02/19/uk-supreme-court-rules-uber-drivers-are-workers-handing-company-major-defeat/

[86] https://www.huffingtonpost.co.uk/entry/amazon-anti-union-consultant_n_63dad3c8e4b07c0c7e077a50

[87] https://www.reuters.com/legal/litigation/uber-loses-appeal-block-92-million-mass-arbitration-fees-2022-04-18/

[88] https://www.dailymail.co.uk/news/article-11671541/MP-accuses-London-law-firms-helping-organised-crime-authoritarian-states-silence-critics.html

[89] https://www.legalfutures.co.uk/latest-news/dozens-of-law-firms-enabling-corruption-report-finds

[90] https://www.thebureauinvestigates.com/stories/2023-01-15/hacked-evidence-and-stolen-data-swamp-english-courts

[91] https://www.pirical.com/blog/heres-the-uk-legal-market-in-numbers-infographic

[92] https://pbi.trust.org/analysis/?year=2020

[93] https://www.thomsonreuters.com/en-us/posts/wp-content/uploads/sites/20/2022/01/Lawyers-Tax-Professionals-Survey-2022.pdf

94 https://www.rollonfriday.com/news-content/top-lawyers-refuse-prosecute-climate-protestors

95 https://rooseveltinstitute.org/wp-content/uploads/2020/07/RI_Stock-Buybacks-key-example-of-extractive-corporate-power-Fact-Sheet-201910.pdf

96 https://www.ons.gov.uk/economy/investmentspensionsandtrusts/bulletins/ownershipofukquotedshares/2022

97 https://www.quantifiedstrategies.com/what-percentage-of-trading-is-algorithmic/

98 https://www.ig.com/uk/trading-strategies/what-are-the-average-returns-of-the-ftse-100--230511

99 https://www.ons.gov.uk/economy/investmentspensionsandtrusts/bulletins/ownershipofukquotedshares/2020

100 https://hbr.org/2014/09/profits-without-prosperity

101 https://www.theguardian.com/environment/2022/nov/30/more-than-70-percent-english-water-industry-foreign-ownership
It also owns 9% of Lloyds Bank.

102 https://www.theia.org/sites/default/files/2022-09/Investment%20Management%20Survey%202021-22%20full%20report.pdf

103 https://www.theguardian.com/society/2022/apr/18/english-councils-pay-1m-per-child-for-places-in-private-childrens-homes

104 https://www.theguardian.com/society/2023/dec/23/england-childrens-care-homes-backed-by-private-equity-firms-double-over-five-years

105 https://www.bmj.com/content/339/bmj.b2732.long

106 https://www.huduser.gov/portal/periodicals/em/winter23/highlight1.html

107 https://www.economicliberties.us/our-work/new-money-trust/#

108 https://www.investopedia.com/terms/c/closed-endinvestment.asp

109 https://www.theia.org/sites/default/files/2022-09/Investment%20Management%20Survey%202021-22%20full%20report.pdf

110 https://weownit.org.uk/public-ownership/water

111 https://www.businessinsider.com/us-economy-recession-richcession-wealthy-spending-luxury-savings-pandemic-2023-7?r=US&IR=T

112 https://www.icij.org/investigations/panama-papers/explore-panama-papers-key-figures/

113 https://www.economicsobservatory.com/why-did-credit-suisse-fail-and-what-does-it-mean-for-banking-regulation

114 https://time.com/6264787/credit-suisse-svb-recession/

115 https://www.theguardian.com/news/datablog/2011/nov/12/bank-bailouts-uk-credit-crunch

116 https://www.ilo.org/wcmsp5/groups/public/---ed_emp/documents/publication/wcms_858641.pdf

117 https://palestinecampaign.org/campaigns/stop-arming-israel-3/

[118] https://www.ft.com/content/10c3e16b-d1c7-4f76-a2f8-b92d54b1e2a7

[119] https://www.ran.org/issue/whos-funding-forest-destruction/

[120] https://feedbackglobal.org/research/bankrolling-the-butchers/

[121] https://www.fstech.co.uk/fst/Are_UK_Banks_Failing_In_The_Fight_Against_Money_Laundering.php

[122] https://www.theguardian.com/money/2023/dec/09/charities-barclays-frozen-bank-accounts

[123] https://www.nomisweb.co.uk/query/select/getdatasetbytheme.asp?theme=49

[124] https://www.ukfinance.org.uk/system/files/2023-09/UK%20Finance%20Payment%20Markets%20Report%202023%20Summary.pdf

[125] https://www.accesstocash.org.uk/

[126] https://www.fca.org.uk/financial-lives/financial-lives-2022-survey

[127] https://www.fsb.org.uk/resources-page/locked-out.html

[128] https://publications.parliament.uk/pa/cm201719/cmselect/cmscotaf/1996/199606.htm#_idTextAnchor017

[129] https://www.nhs.uk/common-health-questions/lifestyle/what-are-the-health-risks-of-smoking/

[130] https://en.wikipedia.org/wiki/List_of_recessions_in_the_United_Kingdom

[131] https://www.economicsobservatory.com/why-did-credit-suisse-fail-and-what-does-it-mean-for-banking-regulation

[132] https://cpag.org.uk/child-poverty/child-poverty-facts-and-figures

[133] https://cpag.org.uk/child-poverty/child-poverty-facts-and-figures

[134] https://blogs.lse.ac.uk/politicsandpolicy/the-sunak-government-should-understand-tax-cuts-will-not-create-economic-growth/

[135] eprints.lse.ac.uk/107919/1/Hope_economic_consequences_of_major_tax_cuts_published.pdf

[136] J Browne and A Hood, *Living standards, poverty and inequality in the UK: 2015-16 to 2020-21*, Institute for Fiscal Studies, 2016

[137] https://www.centreforcities.org/reader/improving-urban-bus-services/deregulation-makes-improving-bus-services-harder-for-mayors/

[138] https://governmentbusiness.co.uk/news/25102019/bus-funding-cut-40-cent-last-decade

[139] https://en.wikipedia.org/wiki/2008_United_Kingdom_bank_rescue_package

[140]

[141]

[142] https://weownit.org.uk/blog/biggest-ever-poll-shows-huge-support-nationalisation

[143] https://www.globalrightsindex.org/en/2023/violations/right-to-strike

[144] https://tribunemag.co.uk/2022/06/trade-union-laws-rmt-strike-industrial-relations-legislation

[145] https://www.nerinstitute.net/blog/trade-unions-collective-bargaining-and-

economic-performance

[146] https://www.ier.org.uk/resources/trade-union-act-2016-what-says-what-it-means/

[147] https://www.rcn.org.uk/magazines/Action/2023/Jul/Anti-strike-act

[148] https://neweconomics.org/2022/05/the-damaging-legacy-of-right-to-buy

[149] https://www.gov.uk/government/news/time-to-invest-in-our-water-security

[150] https://www.ft.com/content/ee03d551-8eee-4136-9eeb-7c8b51169a99

[151] https://positivemoney.org/wp-content/uploads/2022/06/Positive-Money-The-Power-of-Big-Finance-Report-June-2022.pdf

[152] https://www.newstatesman.com/politics/uk-politics/2021/04/first-past-post-elections-proportional-representation

[153] https://www.ippr.org/blog/cutting-corporation-tax-not-magic-bullet-for-increasing-investment

[154] https://www.taxjustice.net/2014/02/18/cayman-islands-hide-32-trillion-haven-map/

[155] https://gfintegrity.org/wp-content/uploads/2015/09/Ford-Book-Final.pdf

[156] https://www.oecd.org/ctp/harmful-tax-practices-2017-9789264283954-en.htm

[157] https://schjodt.com/news/marshall-islands-and-british-virgin-islands-on-the-eu-blacklist-of-tax-havens

[158] https://www.lseg.com/content/dam/ftse-russell/en_us/documents/policy-documents/low-taxation-jurisdictions.pdf

[159] https://www.icij.org/investigations/panama-papers/

[160] https://kpmg.com/ky/en/home/industries/banking.html

[161] https://bbcincorp.com/offshore/articles/how-to-open-a-bank-account-in-cayman-islands

[162] https://www.funds-europe.com/fund-centres-offshore-wars

[163] https://www.swissinfo.ch/eng/business/switzerland-clings-on-as-world-s-top-offshore-wealth-centre/48621870

[164] https://www.publiceye.ch/en/media-corner/press-releases/detail/offshore-in-switzerland-welcome-to-shell-companies-paradise

[165] https://www.investopedia.com/ask/answers/060716/why-singapore-considered-tax-haven.asp

[166] https://www.icij.org/investigations/panama-papers/

[167] https://www.icij.org/investigations/panama-papers/20160403-panama-papers-global-overview/

[168] https://www.icij.org/investigations/panama-papers/five-years-later-panama-papers-still-having-a-big-impact/

[169] https://en.wikipedia.org/wiki/List_of_people_named_in_the_Panama_Papers

[170] https://www.ifcreview.com/news/2022/january/netherlands-senate-approves-purchase-of-rembrandt-amid-tax-haven-controversy/

[171] https://www.icij.org/investigations/panama-papers/five-years-later-panama-

papers-still-having-a-big-impact/

[172] https://www.nytimes.com/2021/06/12/us/Sheldon-adelson-taxes-offshore-trusts.html

[173] https://billmoyers.com/2013/12/18/how-billionaires-like-sheldon-adelson-exploit-an-accidental-tax-loophole/

[174] https://www.theguardian.com/business/2012/jul/21/offshore-wealth-global-economy-tax-havens

[175] https://www.nytimes.com/2021/09/02/business/renaissance-irs-robert-mercer-james-simons.html

[176] https://cthi.taxjustice.net/en/how-index-works/faq

[177] https://www.bbc.co.uk/news/world-58780465

[178] https://www.taxresearch.org.uk/Blog/2022/02/14/the-operations-of-the-big-4-accountants-within-tax-havens-are-a-threat-to-democracy-so-why-wont-they-close-them-down/

[179] https://www.bbc.co.uk/news/business-65308769

[180] https://www.bbc.co.uk/news/business-65397276

[181] https://positivemoney.org/2019/09/bank-of-england-confirms-positive-money-analysis-of-house-prices/

[182] https://committees.parliament.uk/writtenevidence/37938/pdf/

[183] https://weownit.org.uk/company/deloitte

[184] https://www.lawgazette.co.uk/law/bar-serco-and-g4s-from-moj-contracts-demands-khan/5037305.article

[185] https://www.lawgazette.co.uk/law/bar-serco-and-g4s-from-moj-contracts-demands-khan/5037305.article

[186] https://www.google.com/search?client=firefox-b-e&q=In+India%2C+Amazon+India+decided+to+shut+down+its+food+delivery+and+edtech+businesses+

[187] https://insights.issgovernance.com/posts/kraft-heinz-agrees-to-450-million-settlement-over-destructive-cost-cuts-following-merger/

[188] https://www.acg.edu/news-events/news/updated-mckinsey-report-on-greek-economy/

[189] https://medium.com/centre-for-public-impact/a-manifesto-for-better-government-8121132f45ef

[190] https://www.unitetheunion.org/media/1108/unite-diversification-revisited.pdf

[191] https://www.unitetheunion.org/media/1108/unite-diversification-revisited.pdf

[192] https://www.red-gate.com/simple-talk/wp-content/uploads/imported/682-ROffElctronicCopy.pdf

[193] https://www.bristol.ac.uk/policybristol/policy-briefings/external-management-nhs/

[194] https://prospect.org.uk/health-and-safety-executive/

[195] https://www.independent.co.uk/climate-change/news/water-pollution-sewage-environment-agency-funding-b2154848.html

[196] https://labourlist.org/2022/08/truss-235m-environment-agency-cut-doubled-sewage-discharge-labour-says/

[197] https://www.theguardian.com/business/2015/oct/04/vw-scandal-emissions-test-body-conflict-of-interest-accusation

[198] https://www.regulation.org.uk/ob-regulators_behaviour.html

[199] https://marketinglaw.osborneclarke.com/advertising-regulation/is-asa-losing-the-plot-as-six-of-ten-most-complained-about-ads-in-2013-are-exonerated/

[200] https://www.nutraingredients.com/Article/2023/09/13/not-fit-for-purpose-legal-expert-argues-asa-is-failing-the-industry

[201] https://www.thedrum.com/news/2021/11/24/asa-refutes-bias-claims-activists-criticize-handling-land-rover-complaints

[202] https://www.icij.org/investigations/ericsson-list/as-us-style-corporate-leniency-deals-for-bribery-and-corruption-go-global-repeat-offenders-are-on-the-rise/

[203] https://www.thebureauinvestigates.com/stories/2023-09-30/just-11-wealthy-people-prosecuted-for-tax-fraud-last-year

[204] https://www.thisismoney.co.uk/money/markets/article-12710041/Former-RBS-boss-Fred-Shred-Goodwin-enjoying-500k-gold-plated-pension.html

[205] https://thepresidentialhustle.com/fred-goodwin-net-worth-life-quotes-2018/

[206] https://www.bevanbrittan.com/insights/articles/2022/fines-and-prison-sentences-for-health-and-safety-manslaughter-offences-on-the-rise/

[207] https://www.transparency.org.uk/toward-transparency-britains-offshore-financial-centres

[208] https://www.taxwatchuk.org/tax_crime_vs_benefits_crime/

[209] https://www.theguardian.com/uk-news/2023/nov/21/uk-millionaires-tax-wealth-treasury-jeremy-hunt-patriotic-millionaires-uk

[210] https://yougov.co.uk/politics/articles/45044-three-quarters-britons-support-wealth-taxes-millio

[211] https://patrioticmillionaires.uk/latest-news/report-out-of-touch-when-it-comes-to-taxing-extreme-wealth-the-house-of-commons-flags-behind-even-the-richest-in-the-country

[212] https://medcraveonline.com/FRCIJ/white-collar-crime-recidivism-deterrence-and-social-impact.html

[213] https://medcraveonline.com/FRCIJ/white-collar-crime-recidivism-deterrence-and-social-impact.html

[214] https://www.ojp.gov/ncjrs/virtual-library/abstracts/white-collar-vs-street-crime-sentencing-disparity-how-judges-see

[215] https://drive.google.com/file/d/1KROqxMDFNhUb6X98c062p6obLFAELTNI/view

[216] https://www.thetimes.co.uk/article/bianca-williams-met-police-culture-war-rwt0r309s

[217] https://www.dailymail.co.uk/news/article-12677007/just-giving-page-raises-

money-met-officers-sacked-stop-search-bianca-williams-partner-ricardo-dos-santos.html

[218] https://www.theguardian.com/uk-news/2023/nov/19/police-county-lines-strategy-cruelly-targets-black-youth-in-uk

[219] https://greenworld.org.uk/article/changing-attitudes-police-climate-protest

[220] https://www.brightblue.org.uk/the-sad-irony-of-prisons-in-the-uk/

[221] https://assets.publishing.service.gov.uk/media/5d1c732ee5274a08cdbe45c4/impact-short-custodial-sentences.pdf

[222] https://prisonreformtrust.org.uk/project/prison-the-facts/

[223] https://assets.publishing.service.gov.uk/media/5a814a3d40f0b62305b8e241/associations-between-ethnic-background-being-sentenced-to-prison-in-the-crown-court-in-england-and-wales-2015.pdf

[224] https://en.wikipedia.org/wiki/Evening_Standard

[225] https://en.wikipedia.org/wiki/Gazprom

[226] https://www.suttontrust.com/wp-content/uploads/2020/01/Leading-People_Feb16.pdf

[227] https://www.isdglobal.org/explainers/anti-vaccine-conspiracies/

[228] https://www.sourcewatch.org/index.php?title=DonorsTrust

[229] https://pressgazette.co.uk/news/uk-government-sets-out-plans-to-force-big-tech-to-pay-for-news/

[230] https://www.independent.co.uk/news/uk/shell-advertising-standards-authority-people-bristol-youtube-b2352737.html

[231] https://www.marketingweek.com/lucozade-sport-ad-banned-for-claiming-it-fuels-and-hydrates-better-than-water/

[232] https://thenextweb.com/news/cereal-offenders-weetabix-forced-to-remove-weetakid-app-for-making-kids-feel-inferior

[233] https://www.hsph.harvard.edu/news/features/advertisings-toxic-effect-on-eating-and-body-image/

[234] https://www.jpost.com/health-and-sci-tech/health/stars-of-hollywoods-golden-era-were-paid-to-promote-smoking

[235] https://news.liverpool.ac.uk/2013/03/08/celebrity-endorsement-encourages-children-to-eat-junk-food/

[236] https://www.smh.com.au/lifestyle/health-and-wellness/how-many-times-have-the-kardashians-tried-to-sell-us-dodgy-health-products-20220919-p5bj8o.html

[237] https://www.smh.com.au/business/markets/kim-kardashian-launches-her-own-investing-firm-20220908-p5bgbr.html

[238] https://www.theguardian.com/society/2023/jun/18/lobbyists-with-links-to-big-tobacco-fund-pro-vaping-facebook-campaigns

[239] https://tobaccotactics.org/article/consumer-choice-center/

[240] https://www.hsgac.senate.gov/library/files/fueling-an-epidemic-exposing-the-financial-ties-between-opioid-manufacturers-and-third-party-advocacy-groups/

[241] https://www.ncbi.nlm.nih.gov/pmc/articles/PMC1125226/
[242] https://www.commondreams.org/news/carbon-offset-deforestation
[243] https://theferret.scot/costa-lobbyists-tried-write-rules-on-drive-throughs/
[244] https://energy.economictimes.indiatimes.com/news/oil-and-gas/how-oil-companies-put-the-responsibility-for-climate-change-on-consumers/104368169
[245] https://www.realclearenergy.org/articles/2023/12/20/britains_net_zero_disaster_and_the_wind_power_scam_1000250.html
[246] https://www.carbonbrief.org/analysis-uk-renewables-still-cheaper-than-gas-despite-auction-setback-for-offshore-wind/
[247] https://corporateeurope.org/sites/default/files/2023-03/The%20Lobbying%20Ghost%20in%20the%20Machine.pdf
[248] https://www.opendemocracy.net/en/dark-money-investigations/revealed-the-elite-dining-club-behind-130m-donations-to-the-tories/
249 https://en.wikipedia.org/wiki/Christian_Voice_(UK)
250 https://www.theguardian.com/books/2022/sep/28/boris-johnson-by-andrew-gimson-review-a-fawning-defence
251 https://www.theguardian.com/culture/2022/aug/31/government-appoints-anti-woke-activist-as-va-trustee
[252] https://www.theguardian.com/us-news/2023/jul/05/double-agent-fossil-fuel-lobbyists
[253] https://theconversation.com/uk-lobbying-rules-explained-why-no-one-seems-to-be-in-legal-trouble-159741
[254] https://truthout.org/articles/pro-israel-lobby-doesnt-deserve-exemption-from-criticism-of-money-in-politics/
[255] https://www.politico.eu/article/the-fight-over-the-uks-landmark-competition-bill-heats-up/
[256] https://www.miamiherald.com/news/local/environment/climate-change/article279745304.html
[257] https://www.reuters.com/business/environment/why-carbon-capture-is-no-easy-solution-climate-change-2023-11-22/
[258] https://www.cpre.org.uk/wp-content/uploads/2019/11/LandZpromotersZbriefingZ2018.pdf
[259] https://committees.parliament.uk/writtenevidence/39499/pdf/
[260] https://www.iata.org/en/programs/environment/flynetzero/#tab-1
[261] https://www.iata.org/contentassets/1d7b998cda0a46a1ab31d4ee3cce5eaf/chart-forecasted-evolution-of-air-transport-pax-traffic.pdf
[262] https://assets.publishing.service.gov.uk/media/63c7ed5bd3bf7f6bece2bfed/Low_Pay_Commission_Report_2022.pdf
[263] https://www.theguardian.com/environment/2023/nov/07/eu-poised-to-water-down-new-car-pollution-rules-after-industry-lobbying

264 https://retrofit4emissions.eu/

265 https://cembureau.eu/media/3mzpw1xv/17542-cembureau-position-paper-carbon-border-mechanisms-2020-april.pdf

266 https://www.politico.eu/article/european-union-big-pharma-medicines-pharmaceutical-industry-drugs/

267

268 http://www.telegraph.co.uk/finance/comment/alistair-osborne/9980292/Margaret-Thatcher-one-policy-that-led-to-more-than-50-companies-being-sold-or-privatised.html

269 https://bylinetimes.com/2023/11/03/time-to-tackle-dark-money-in-politics-as-voters-demand-transparency-over-britains-opaque-think-tanks/

270 https://en.wikipedia.org/wiki/TaxPayers%27_Alliance

271 https://fivethirtyeight.com/features/economists-arent-as-nonpartisan-as-we-think/

272 https://web.archive.org/web/20220501192705/https://iea.org.uk/James-Forder/

273 https://www.vox.com/policy-and-politics/2017/3/13/14860856/congressional-budget-office-cbo-explained

274 https://papers.ssrn.com/sol3/papers.cfm?abstract_id=2535453

275 https://www.taxresearch.org.uk/Blog/2021/09/27/the-differences-between-right-wing-centre-ground-and-non-market-believing-economists/

276 https://www.adl.org/resources/press-release/adl-urges-israeli-chief-rabbinate-denounce-ultra-orthodox-practice-spitting

277 https://en.wikipedia.org/wiki/Sectarian_violence_among_Christians#Yugoslav_wars

278 https://www.sciencedirect.com/science/article/abs/pii/027795369090048W

279 https://link.springer.com/chapter/10.1007/978-3-030-94691-3_11

280 https://ffteducationdatalab.org.uk/2022/07/faith-schools-and-academisation/

281 https://en.wikipedia.org/wiki/Christian_views_on_birth_control

282 https://www.ncbi.nlm.nih.gov/pmc/articles/PMC5742220/

283 https://amp.theguardian.com/environment/2023/oct/27/revealed-industry-figures-declaration-scientists-backing-meat-eating

284 https://twitter.com/fleroy1974/status/1676901464545935362

285 https://www.ncbi.nlm.nih.gov/pmc/articles/PMC5342645/

286 https://www.ucsusa.org/resources/merck-manipulated-science-about-drug-vioxx

287 https://www.science.org/doi/10.1126/science.abk0063

288 https://www.nytimes.com/2018/01/25/world/europe/volkswagen-diesel-emissions-monkeys.html

289 https://www.scientificamerican.com/article/many-antidepressant-studies-found-tainted-by-pharma-company-influence/

290 https://davidhealy.org/shock-mutilate-and-poison-the-medical-mission/
291 https://www.biologicaldiversity.org/news/media-archive/a2010/MMSRelation-shipBigOil_WaPo_8-24-10.pdf
292 https://jelr.law.lsu.edu/2014/11/19/changing-direction-how-regulatory-agen-cies-have-responded-to-the-deepwater-horizon-oil-spill-part-i-of-ii/
293 https://www.ethicalconsumer.org/food-drink/national-farmers-union
294 https://www.theconstructionindex.co.uk/news/view/developers-oppose-new-planning-levy-system
295 https://www.theconstructionindex.co.uk/news/view/developers-oppose-new-planning-levy-system
296 https://www.transparency.org.uk/house-of-cards-UK-housing-policy-influence-Conservative-party-donations-lobbying-press-release
297
298 https://news.cancerresearchuk.org/2021/03/17/bacon-salami-and-sausages-how-does-processed-meat-cause-cancer-and-how-much-matters/
299 https://en.wikipedia.org/wiki/Criticisms_of_Cargill
300 https://www.bloomberg.com/news/articles/2023-10-02/fca-fines-archer-dan-iels-midland-unit-for-shoddy-crime-controls?leadSource=uverify%20wall
301 https://www.thelancet.com/journals/lanepe/article/PIIS2666-7762(23)00190-4/fulltext
302 https://www.huffingtonpost.co.uk/2015/04/07/nicole-kidman-etihad-airways-un-women-goodwill_n_7016742.html
303 https://www.theguardian.com/world/2018/nov/21/british-academic-matthew-hedges-accused-of-spying-jailed-for-life-in-uae
304 https://www.theringer.com/tv/2023/9/12/23868855/welcome-to-wrexham-season-2-ryan-reynolds-rob-mcelhenney
305 https://uk.news.yahoo.com/welcome-wrexham-much-ryan-reynolds-165119199.html?guccounter=1
306 https://www.tandfonline.com/doi/full/10.1080/17511321.2022.2107697
307 https://en.wikipedia.org/wiki/Marcus_Rashford
308 https://www.theguardian.com/commentisfree/2017/feb/07/urban-heritage-conservation-areas-sajid-javid-paddington-cube
309 https://www.gov.uk/government/news/estate-agents-targeted-in-money-laun-dering-crackdown
310 https://www.suttontrust.com/our-research/elitist-britain-2019/
311 https://www.suttontrust.com/wp-content/uploads/2019/12/PotentialForSuc-cess.pdf
312 https://www.ifs.org.uk/uploads/publications/wps/WP201430.pdf
313 https://ifs.org.uk/news/removing-tax-exemptions-private-schools-likely-have-little-effect-numbers-private-sector
314 ISC Annual Census. https://www.isc.co.uk/research/annual-census/

315 https://www.walji.uk.com/can-i-put-private-school-fees-through-my-business and https://www.keystonetrust.co.uk/private-education-school-fees/

316 https://questions-statements.parliament.uk/written-questions/detail/2021-06-28/23128

317 https://www.washingtonpost.com/technology/2019/12/19/federal-study-confirms-racial-bias-many-facial-recognition-systems-casts-doubt-their-expanding-use/

318 https://www.standard.co.uk/news/tech/elon-musk-twitter-algorithm-cyberbullying-discrimination-cornell-uc-berkeley-b1084490.html

319 https://en.wikipedia.org/wiki/Dark_pattern

320 https://www.theguardian.com/world/2024/jan/26/germany-unearths-pro-russia-disinformation-campaign-on-x

321 https://www.theguardian.com/global-development/2022/mar/31/migrant-workers-in-qatar-forced-to-pay-billions-in-recruitment-fees-world-cup

322 https://thebristolcable.org/2021/02/amazon-agency-avonmouth-bristol-warehouse-workers-allege-underpayment-and-zero-hour-contracts-adecco-pmp-recruitment/

323 https://www.gla.gov.uk/media/8946/glaa-annual-report-and-accounts-2021-22-web-version.pdf

324 https://www.antislavery.org/wp-content/uploads/2017/02/UK-slavery-fact-sheet-2016.pdf

325 https://www.standard.co.uk/news/world/saudi-diplomat-made-two-women-work-like-slaves-in-london-home-8936743.html

326 https://www.weforum.org/agenda/2021/01/how-to-stop-modern-slavery/

327 https://www.walkfree.org/global-slavery-index/country-studies/china/

328 https://www.nytimes.com/2017/04/10/travel/new-report-human-trafficking-exploitation-of-hotel-industry-workers.html

329 Dock, Wharf, Riverside, and General Workers' Union. A brief history of the Dockers' Union. Commemorating the 1889 Dockers' Strike. By Ben Tillett (1910). Ben Tillett

330 https://islandhistory.wordpress.com/2014/01/08/the-call-on/

331 https://www.ilo.org/digitalguides/en-gb/story/world-employment-social-outlook-2021#introduction

332 https://www.theguardian.com/commentisfree/2021/feb/04/self-employed-amazon-driver-company-delivered

333 https://www.vice.com/en/article/z3mge3/selling-bottles-of-amazon-drivers-pee

334 https://uk.indeed.com/cmp/Uber-Drivers/reviews?fjobtitle=Delivery+Driver

335 https://www.jstor.org/stable/48691516?seq=7

336 https://www.politico.com/magazine/story/2014/06/the-pitchforks-are-coming-for-us-plutocrats-108014/

[337] https://www.pewresearch.org/global/2022/08/31/climate-change-remains-top-global-threat-across-19-country-survey/